Y0-BSS-187

The State of Working Canada, 2000

Falling Behind

Andrew Jackson,
David Robinson
with Bob Baldwin
and Cindy Wiggins

Canadian
Centre
for Policy
Alternatives

Copyright © 2000 Canadian Centre for Policy Alternatives

All rights reserved. No part of this book may be reproduced or transmitted in any form or by any means, electronic or mechanical, including photocopying, or by any information storage or retrieval system, without permission in writing from the publisher.

Canadian Cataloguing in Publication Data

Jackson, Andrew
    Falling behind : the state of working Canada, 2000

A joint project of the Canadian Centre for Policy Alternatives and the Canadian Labour Congress

ISBN 0-88627-216-5

1. Labour--Canada--Statistics. 2. Canada--Economic conditions--1991- --Statistics. 3. Canada--Economic policy--1991 --Statistics. I. Robinson, David II. Baldwin, Bob III. Wiggins, Cindy IV. Canadian Centre for Policy Alternatives V. Canadian Labour Congress VI. Title.

HC115.J28 2000   338.971'009'049   C00-900263-4

Printed and bound in Canada

Published by

Canadian Centre for Policy Alternatives
410-75 Albert St
Ottawa ON K1P 5E7
Tel 613-563-1341   Fax 613-233-1458
www.policyalternatives.ca
ccpa@policyalternatives.ca

Falling Behind
The State of Working Canada, 2000

TABLE OF CONTENTS

Introduction and Acknowledgements   1

Preface, by Ken Georgetti   5

CHAPTER 1: **The Declining Economic and Social Well-Being of Canadian Working People**   **9**

Income: The Composition of Income   10
The Level of Overall Income   12
Why Did Canada Do So Badly in the 1990s?   16
Earnings from Employment   18
Security of Employment and Income   21
Poverty and Inequality   26
The Tax/Transfer System and Low Incomes   32
Canada in an International Context   38
Conclusion   44

Tables
1.1   The Composition of Household Income by Income Group (Families and Individuals Combined)   11
1.2   The Distribution of Income Among Families by Major Source   12
1.3   The Growth and Stagnation of the Income of Canadians   13
1.4   Real GDP by Region as % of National Total 1981-1996   16
1.5   Employment Rates of Women, 1976-97   19
1.6   Average Real Annual Earnings ($ 1997) of Men and Women, 1967-1997   19

1.7   Change in Real Annual Earnings by Decile, Women and Men,
       1981-1995   20
1.8   Change in Real Annual Earnings by Decile, Men Only   22
1.9   National Unemployment Rate   24
1.10   Incidence of Job Lay-Off   28
1.11   Average Family Income Before Transfers (Families with
       Children) ($1996)   30
1.12   Weeks Worked in Year   31
1.13   Average Weekly Earnings (Constant 1993 Dollars)   31
1.14   Change in Median Annual Earnings, 1983 - 1992   33
1.15   Transfer Payments as % Income — All Families   35
1.16   Family Income Shares: Before and After   35
1.17   Incidence of Low Income   37
1.18   Average Income by Source of Families with Children Living
       in Poverty   38
1.19   Income Distributions Compared   42
1.20   The Structure of Earnings Compared   43

Figures
1.1   Unionization Rates, 1967-1997 (Union members as % of Paid
       Workers)   26

CHAPTER 2: **Unemployment, Underemployment
            and Precarious Jobs**   **47**

Job Shortage or Skills Shortage?   47
The Unemployment Squeeze   49
Unemployment   51
"Hidden" Unemployment   53
The Pattern of Job Creation in the 1990s   56
Self-Employment   58
Temporary Jobs   61
Part-time Jobs   62
Jobs in Small Business   67
Workers of Colour and Aboriginal Canadians in the Labour Force   69
Workers With Disabilities   71
Conclusion   72

Tables

2.1	The Unemployment Rate in the 1990s	51
2.2	Provincial Unemployment Rates, 1989-1999	52
2.3	Average Duration of Unemployment (Weeks)	53
2.4	Labour Force Participation Rates, 1989-1999	54
2.5	Participation Rates in Canada and the U.S., 1989-1997	55
2.6	Employment by Class of Worker (000s)	56
2.7	Changes in Employment 1989-98 (000s)	57
2.8	Annual Earnings by Class of Worker (1995)	59
2.9	Average Earnings for Self-Employed Men and Women, 1996	60
2.10	Growth of Self-Employment By Type, 1989-98 (000s)	60
2.11	Employed in Temporary Jobs	61
2.12	Who is Working Part-Time? (May 1999) %	63
2.13	Reason for Part-Time Work (1998) %	63
2.14	Work-Schedules: "Flexible" for Whom?	65
2.15	The Part-Time Hourly Wage Gap (1997)	65
2.16	Workers in Low Wage Jobs (%)	66
2.17	The Part-Time Benefit Gap (1995) (% of Workers Covered)	66
2.18	Average Annual Job Gains and Losses, by Firm Size, 1978-92	68
2.19	Small is Ugly: Average Hourly Wages and Benefits of Full-Time Workers (1997)	68
2.20	Workers of Colour and Aboriginal Workers: Average Earnings (1995)	70

Figures

2.1	Distribution of Employment by Firm Size, 1989-97	67

CHAPTER 3: **The Wonderful New World of Work: Wages and the Quality of Jobs in the 1990s**   **75**

What Kinds of Jobs?	75
The Attack on the Public Sector	78
Low-Paid Jobs	80
The Changing Structure of Earnings	80
Access to Benefits	82
Wages vs. Profits	83
Job Quality in the 1990s: The Growth of Long Hours	85
Changing Shift Schedules	88

Balancing Work and Family		89
Stress and Work Satisfaction		91
Conclusion		94

Tables

3.1	Employment by Occupation (as % Total)	76
3.2	Median Hourly Wages by Selected Occupation (1997)	77
3.3	Public Services Jobs	79
3.4	Public vs. Private Sector Jobs	79
3.5	Workers in Low Paid Jobs (1997) (< 2/3 National Median Wage i.e. less than $9.24/hour)	80
3.6	Distribution of Annual Earnings of Men and Women (constant $ 1997)	81
3.7	Access to Benefits (% Workers Covered)	82
3.8	Paid Vacation Leave 1995	83
3.9	The Corporate Recovery	83
3.10	Changes in Real Wages and Productivity	84
3.11	Long Weekly Hours in Main Job (% Employees, Age 25+)	85
3.12	Incidence of Overtime (% Workers) (1997)	86
3.13	Work Schedules	88
3.14	Work Arrangements of Women	89
3.15	Time-Stressed Population, 1992 and 1998 (%)	90
3.16	Average Time Spent on Selected Activities, Married Parents Employed Full-Time, 1998 (Hours per day)	90
3.17	% Workers Reporting Stress in Work Environment	91
3.18	Job Insecurity	92
3.19	Work Satisfaction (Strongly Agree)	93
3.20	Physical Work Environment	93

CHAPTER 4: **The Union Advantage**	**95**

Collective Bargaining Coverage Today	97
The Union Wage Premium	99
Incidence of Low Pay	101
Wage Inequality / Polarization	103
Non-Wage Benefits	103
Equality Issues and Collective Bargaining	106
Looking to the Future	109

Tables

4.1 Union Coverage in 1998 98
4.2 Average Hourly Wages of Women and Men, by Unionization and Selected Characteristics, Canada 1995 100
4.3 Change in Hourly Wage Associated with Unionization, Canada, 1995 By Sex and Occupation 101
4.4 The Union Advantage in 1998 101
4.5 Share of Women and Men in "Low-wage" Jobs, by Unionization and Selected Characteristics, Canada 1995 102
4.6 Dispersion of Hourly Wages, by Sex and Unionization, Canada 1995 ($) 103
4.7 Non-wage Benefits, by Sex, Union Status and Selected Characteristics, Canada 1995 104
4.8 Vacation Entitlements in Major Collective Agreements (% employees covered by provision in 1998) 105
4.9 Job Security Related Provisions In Major Collective Agreements (% employees covered) 106
4.10 Collective Agreements and Equality 107

CHAPTER 5: **The Changing Distribution of Income: Poverty and the Declining Middle Class** **113**

Does Inequality Matter? 113
Earnings Inequality 114
Family Income and Inequality: Long-Term Trends 115
Trends in the 1990s 118
Family Income and Government Transfer Payments 122
After Tax Income 124
Inequality and Seniors' Incomes in the 1990s 126
Poverty 129
Poverty in Canada 131
Conclusion 138

Tables

5.1 Change in Average Annual Income After Income Taxes 120
5.2 Market Incomes of Families by Decile, 1989-97 ($1997) 121
5.3 Incomes of Families with Children After Government Transfers by Decile, 1989-97 ($1997) 123

5.4	Incomes of Families with Children After-Tax by Decile, 1989-97 ($1997)	123
5.5	Percentage Increase in Family Income as a Result of Transfer Payments	125
5.6	Average Income of Elderly Households, 1973-1996	126
5.7	Low Income Cut-offs of Family Units, 1997	133
5.8	Poverty Rates by Family Type in Canada, 1989 and 1997	134
5.9	Provincial Poverty Rates, 1989 and 1997	137

Figures

5.1	Share of Total Family Income (before income tax) by Decile	115
5.2	Percent Change in Share of Total Family Income by Decile	116
5.3	Share of Total Family Income (Before Income Taxes) by Income Class, 1970 and 1997	116
5.4	Share of Families With Children Under 18 by Income Class, 1973-1996	118
5.5	Average Family Income, 1989-1997	119
5.6	Average Market Income of Families, 1995	120
5.7	Change in Transfer Payments to Families by Quintile, 1989-97 ($1997)	124
5.8	Change in After Tax Income by Quintile, 1984-89 and 1993-97	125
5.9	Share of Persons with Incomes Below 50% of Median Income	131
5.10	Poverty Rate by Age of Household Head, 1989 and 1997	134
5.11	Incidence of Poverty, Men and Women (1997)	135

CHAPTER 6: **The Shrinking Social Wage**	**139**
Rolling Back the Welfare State	140
Health Care	144
Post-Secondary Education	148
Social Assistance	149
Unemployment Insurance	152
Housing	154
Child Care	156
Pensions and Seniors' Income	157
Social Well-Being	161
Index of Social Health	163
Conclusion	165

Tables

6.1   Federal Program Spending (% of GDP)
6.2   Federal Cash Transfers to Other Levels of Government,   142
       1989/90 to 1998/99 ($1998 per capita)   143
6.3   Growth of Real Government Current Expenditures on
       Goods and Services per Capita   143
6.4   Average Household Expenditures, Selected Items,
       1986-1998 ($1998)   144
6.5   Growth of Real Public Spending on Health per Capita   144
6.6   Private and Public Per Capita Health Expenditures,
       1990-1998 ($1992)   145
6.7   Total Health Expenditure in Canada by Use of Funds,
       1975-1998 ($1992 per capita)   146
6.8   Public Expenditures on Post-Secondary Education
       by Province, 1989/90 to 1997/98 ($1997 per capita)   148
6.9   Average Undergraduate Arts Tuition Fees, 1990/91 to 1999/2000   149
6.10   Average Debt at Graduation, 1982-95 ($1995)   149
6.11   Welfare Incomes as Percent of Poverty Line,
       1990-1996   151
6.12   Estimated Annual Salary of Minimum Wage
       Workers by Province, 1976, 1992 and 1999 ($1992)   152
6.13   Number of Regular UI Beneficiaries by Age and
       Sex - monthly average   154
6.14   Social Housing Completions, 1989-1998   155
6.15   Participation in Early Childhood Programs
       by Household Income   157
6.16   1996 Source of Income of Elderly (Constant 1996 Dollars)   158
6.17   Life Expectancy at Birth, 1961-1996   161
6.18   The Well-Being of Aboriginal Peoples   163
6.19   Components of the Index of Social Health   164

Figures

6.1   Federal Program Spending as % of GDP, 1961-2001   141
6.2   Estimated Federal Cash Transfers for Health, 1989-99   147
6.3   Percentage of Unemployed Receiving UI Benefits, 1989-1997   153
6.4   Infant Mortality Rates, Selected OECD Countries (1996)   162
6.5   Index of Social Health and GDP, 1970-95   165

CHAPTER 7: **The Tax System**   **167**

Canadian Taxes in the International Context   167
Personal Income Taxes   171
The Personal Income Tax System and Well-Being   176
Regressive Taxation   178
Who Bears the Burden?   181
Corporate Taxation   188
Conclusion   192

Tables

7.1   Tax Revenue as a Percentage of GDP, 1996   169
7.2   Percentage of Average Gross Earnings Paid in Income Tax
       and Employees' Social Security Contributions, 1997   170
7.3   Average After-Tax and After-Transfer Income,
       1989-97 (% of Gross Pay)   171
7.4   Percentage of Household Budget Spent on Four Major
       Categories, 1998   172
7.5   Average Effective Federal Tax Rate by Income Class
       1987, 1988 and 1989 (%)   174
7.6   Personal Income Tax Distribution, 1996   175
7.7   Percentage Distribution of Benefits by Income
       Levels, 1996 Tax Year   176
7.8   Income Gap Among Canadian Families with Children,
       1989-1997 (Income Ratio of Highest to Lowest Decile)   177
7.9   Gini Coefficient, 1989-97 (Families)   177
7.10   Taxes Paid by Three Families, British Columbia, 1998   179
7.11   Taxes as Share of Family Income, British Columbia, 1998   180
7.12   Income Sources and Tax Subsidies for High Income
       Taxpayers, 1996   181
7.13   RRSP Contributions by Income Class, 1996   182
7.14   Average Family Income Tax Rates by Quintiles, 1979-1997   183
7.15   Percentage Change in Average Real Market Income
       and Effective Tax Rates by Quintile, 1989-97   184
7.16   Federal Income Tax Payable, 1988 and 1998
       (in constant $1988)   185
7.17   1999 Budget Tax Reduction Measures, Single Taxpayers   188
7.18   Statutory Corporate Income Tax Rates for G-7 Countries (%) 189
7.19   Corporate Taxes as a Share of GDP, 1996 (%)   189

Figures

7.1	Taxes and Growth	168
7.2	Taxes and Productivity	169
7.3	Average Effective Income Tax Rate by Income Class, 1996	175
7.4	Effective Personal Income Tax Rates as % of Broad-Based Income, 1988	179
7.5	Federal Income Tax Threshold, 1980-2003 ($1998)	186
7.6	Percentage Increase in Income Taxes by Income Class as a Result of Partial De-Indexation, Single Taxpayer (1998)	186
7.7	Percentage Increase in Income Taxes by Income Class as a Result of Partial De-Indexation, Two Earner Couple with Two Children, 1998	187
7.8	The Tax Mix, 1961-1998	190
7.9	The Corporate Tax Mix as % of GDP, 1950-1995	191

CHAPTER 8: The State of Working Canada in the New Millenium   195

Slow Growth in Wages Continues	196
The Vulnerability of Working Households	197
Will the Expansion Continue?	198
What About Tax Cuts?	200
The Lost Decades	202

Figures

8.1	Unemployment Rate by Province, December 1998 to December 1999	196

Falling Behind

Introduction and Acknowledgments

This study was loosely inspired by the biennial publication of the Economic Policy Institute (EPI) in the United States, *The State of Working America* (Cornell University Press). Like the Canadian Centre for Policy Alternatives, the EPI is a progressive research institute with close links to the labour movement and the academic community.

The State of Working America has documented key U.S. social and economic trends from a perspective which judges social progress largely on the basis of what is happening to the great majority of U.S. citizens. Over the years, the publication has charted such key trends as the stagnation and decline of wages for most workers, increasing wage and family income inequality, the distributional impacts of the tax system, the increasing concentration of wealth, and the implications of an increasingly "precarious" labour market for working people and their families. *The State of Working America* has become a valued and respected reference tool for social activists, the media, academics and students.

We hope that this publication will be equally useful, equally respected as a source of objective information, and that it will be published on a regular basis in the future to chart major social and economic trends in Canada from a progressive perspective.

We trust that readers will find this study interesting to read as well as useful, but it should be noted that the primary intent is to provide a compilation of data and a close empirical analysis of major trends. The text is deliberately very "data heavy" in order to provide a ready reference source, and to facilitate later updating. A detailed description of the contents of each chapter and a list of tables and charts has been provided to facilitate access to data on specific topics.

Falling Behind: The State of Working Canada 2000 is a joint project of the Canadian Centre for Policy Alternatives and the Canadian Labour Congress (CLC). The CLC contribution came in the form of the time of Bob Baldwin, Andrew Jackson, and Cindy Wiggins, respectively Director, Senior Economist and Senior Researcher with the CLC's Social and Economic Policy Department. Andrew Jackson, also a Research Associate with the CCPA, was the primary author of Chapters 1 through 4. Cindy Wiggins was the primary author of Chapter 5 and contributed material throughout. Bob Baldwin contributed material on elderly Canadians and pensions to Chapters 5 and 6.

David Robinson, a Research Associate of the CCPA and Director of Public Policy and Communications with the Canadian Association of University Teachers, and Andrew Jackson were the primary authors of Chapters 6 through 8, and edited the text to make it more coherent and accessible.

Bruce Campbell, Executive Director of the CCPA, was closely involved in the inception and execution of the project. Credit is also due to Ed Finn, Kerri-Anne Finn, and Diane Touchette at the CCPA for their work on the production. Thanks to Andrew Sharpe, Executive Director of the Centre for the Study of Living Standards for providing comments on the draft text and correcting errors.

It should be acknowledged from the outset that this kind of study would not have been possible if it had not been for the prior work of Statistics Canada. In the first place, the vast majority of the data we have used have been gathered by Statistics Canada in the form of regular surveys, such as the Labour Force Survey, the Survey of Consumer Finances, and the Census. This study draws heavily not only on published data from these and other surveys, but also on unpublished data provided to us by Statistics Canada. (Note that the Labour Force Survey data for years before 1999 in this report do not reflect the most recent historical revision and were derived from the historical data available in and before 1999. The revision minimally affects the absolute level of some numbers, but does not change trends.)

Second, Statistics Canada regularly publishes research papers and special studies in publications such as *Perspectives on Labour and In-*

come and the *Canadian Economic Observer*, in order to analyze in depth and disseminate the results of its surveys. We are grateful that the agency has taken an active interest in many of the topics in which we are most interested—such as inequality and poverty and the changing nature of work—and much of the justification for this publication lies in the fact that it condenses and pulls together a lot of the very valuable work that has been done by Statistics Canada staff in recent years. Statistics Canada enjoys a reputation second to none in terms of the quality of data provided, the use of special surveys, and the depth of internal analysis of its own results.

That said, one significant data weakness needs to be noted. We are aware that any generalities about working people must be qualified by analysis of trends according to age, sex, and other key demographic variables. Below, we have attempted to separate out different trends among women and men, and to pay some attention to the experiences of different generations. Unfortunately, few Statistics Canada surveys provide separate data for workers of colour, Aboriginal workers, and workers with disabilities. Some limited data are provided in the Census, but it would be useful if the Labour Force Survey were changed to provide information on a regular basis.

Canada is, to state the obvious, also a very diverse country in geographical and political terms. Most of the data we have analyzed are available on a provincial basis, but, as a practical matter, it would have been impossible for us to multiply every table by ten. We have paid only limited attention to inter-provincial differences, except to occasionally highlight some particularly important differences.

It should finally be noted that much of the data on which this analysis was based is available only through 1997 and 1998. The grim picture of developments in the 1990s which emerges has to be qualified by more positive developments at the end of the decade. These are briefly covered in the conclusions.

Ottawa, 2000

Preface

By Kenneth V. Georgetti
President, Canadian Labour Congress

Falling Behind: The State of Working Canada 2000 does not make for happy reading. The study draws upon a wealth of statistical data to spell out a highly disturbing message: working people and their families have not been making much progress in the "lean and mean" Canada of the 1990s. Indeed, by some measures, the living standards of most Canadians have pretty much stood still since the mid-1970s. Astonishingly, measured in terms of growth of real income per person, the 1990s have been the worst decade for Canadians in our history—as bad as the Great Depression decade of the 1930s.

The real wages of men have stagnated for a very long period of time, while the real wages of working women have caught up only very slowly with those of men and remain far from equal. Families have had to work longer and longer hours in order to maintain the same level of earnings from employment, and the idea of an affluent "leisure society" made possible by technological progress has become little more than a bad joke. Workers who are fortunate enough to hold steady jobs are working longer and harder under more stressful conditions than ever before.

Jobs have not only been scarce; they have also become much more precarious. High unemployment has increased the risk of temporary and permanent layoffs. And unemployment has been accompanied by a steady growth of poorly paid and insecure part-time jobs and short-term contract jobs. In short, reasonably well-paid and secure jobs, the kind most Canadians count on, have become hard to find and to hold. This has been particularly true for women, young people, workers of colour, Aboriginal Canadians, and workers with disabilities.

The "restructuring" of the labour market has been driven by employers. "Downsizing" and contracting-out have eliminated jobs, and made the remaining jobs more intense or more precarious. Yet the promised benefits in terms of competitiveness and efficiency have gone to the business bottom line, not to workers.

The market economy has failed to deliver rising living standards through higher earnings. Instead, it has delivered more insecurity and stagnant incomes for the great majority. But the evidence shows that very high income groups have been insulated to at least some degree from slow economic growth. The market has failed to grow the pie, but the rich have taken a larger slice in inflated senior management salaries, stock options, and the capital gains inflated by the boom on Bay Street.

Fortunately, working people were protected to a significant degree through the recession of the late 1980s and into the 1990s by social programs such as Unemployment Insurance and public pensions and social assistance, which had been built up in an earlier period of economic growth. Unlike the United States, the growth of inequality and poverty generated by a failing labour market was held in check by transfer programs, paid for by a relatively progressive tax system.

Canada does not look like a very fair or equal society compared to many social democratic countries, but social programs have made a very real difference. Unfortunately, as this study shows, the effects of sweeping program cuts in the 1990s are now showing up in rising inequality and rising poverty.

This study clearly underlines the importance of a healthy labour market in creating a fair and secure society. And it underlines the importance of a strong labour movement in sustaining good jobs. The evidence shows that unions raise wages, expand access to benefits, enhance job security to the extent possible in a market economy, and take the edge off the huge differences in income and wealth generated by the market.

The fact that the Canadian labour movement has remained strong, and still represents more than one in three workers, has made a real difference for all working people. At the same time, unions have to take on with even greater determination the task of organizing and bringing the gains of collective bargaining to the growing proportion of workers who are in low-paid and insecure jobs, most of them in small businesses.

This study makes it clear that living standards are more than dollars in the pocket, important though these are. A high standard of living includes access to security in retirement, to decent health care, to quality public education, and to basic public services. Collectively, these make up the "social wage." Again, the depressing message of this study is that we have been falling behind, that past achievements are threatened, and that new social problems and challenges are not being responded to as they should.

The labour and progressive social democratic movement has to take on the challenge of convincing all Canadians that a strong public sector is good for all of us, and that tax cuts purchased at the price of service cuts and social programs are a step backwards from building the kind of society we want.

This study documents and analyzes what has been happening to working Canadians, and does not delve too deeply into the underlying causes. Nor does it offer detailed prescriptions for change. But some lessons do come to the fore.

First and foremost, Canada must commit itself to regaining full employment, defined as decent jobs for all who want to work. Business and the right-wing media tell us all the time that we can have insecure low-paid jobs, or no jobs at all. That is a false choice for workers, and it will be rejected. The market economy must be shaped to deliver good jobs. Certainly, a large part of the answer lies in making job creation the key objective of economic policy, not least of interest rate and government spending policies.

Governments must also play their essential role in a mixed economy by investing in areas like research and development and education and skills and public infrastructure, all of which help the private sector create good jobs. The Canadian Centre for Policy Alternatives and Choices! have helped develop these kinds of policies in recent Alternative Federal Budgets and other studies.

Governments must also turn their backs on policies which put corporate interests first. Business constantly argues that workers must be "flexible," that wages must be kept low in relation to productivity, and that corporate taxes should be cut. But the experience of many other countries tells us that there is no contradiction between wanting economic growth and having a strong labour movement, good social programs and progressive taxes. Countries like the Netherlands, Austria, Denmark, Ireland and Norway have grown as fast as the US in the 1990s without adopting the lean and mean US social model.

It is surely worth noting and pondering the fact that all of the key policy changes of the 1980s and 1990s—free trade, deregulation, privatization, zero inflation, deep cuts to public spending, and cuts to social pro-grams—were justified on the basis that they would ultimately make us all better off. But the right-wing business prescription has not delivered faster growth, and it has most certainly failed to deliver rising living standards for working people. Unleashing the so-called forces of the "free market" has given us more inequality and less security, with no gain in terms of growth.

To be sure, creating an economic and social model that works for working people will involve more than a change in policies here in Canada. In "the new world order," the market will have to be placed in a social context through international means as well, not least through reforming very one-sided and unbalanced integration agreements such as NAFTA and the World Trade Organization.

The key point that has to be made is that the market economy can deliver progress, but only if the market is embedded in society. That means putting real limits on the power of business, building strong non-market mechanisms such as social programs and public services, and greater equal-ity of bargaining power between business and workers.

The CLC helped initiate this project because labour and social activists need a good reference source on basic indicators, and a good analysis of the economic and social trends which are so radically shaping and reshaping the lives of working people. Ultimately, however, the pur-pose of good information and analysis is that it helps inform and sustain a broad movement for social change. Hopefully, this study will make at least a modest contribution in that direction.

CHAPTER 1

From the "Golden Age" to the "Great Canadian Slump":

The Declining Economic and Social Well-Being of Canadian Working People

What does it mean to say that working people are becoming better or worse off over time, or to argue that society as a whole is making progress? Attempts to define well-being inevitably arouse a host of conceptual and philosophical questions which are debated at length by academics and working people alike. Is money the key to happiness? Are we better off if our income goes up but we work longer hours in more precarious and more stressful jobs? Are we better or worse off if we are making progress, but our neighbours, family and friends are sinking into poverty? Are we better off if our taxes are cut, but the social programs and public services provided by government are reduced? Are even steadily employed working people better-off if they get some crumbs from the corporate table in a world where Bill Gates and a handful of global billionaires accumulate massive wealth? Is society richer if GDP rises while the natural environment becomes unliveable, and the quality of life in our community erodes as a result of crime, vandalism and the other diseases of a divided society?

While dollar income is a critically important indicator of living standards, there are clearly important measures of well-being that are not captured by GDP. Some of these have been identified and included as key components in measures of well-being that attempt to go beyond GDP, such as the Genuine Progress Indicator or GPI, the Index of Social Health (see Chapter 7), and the Index of Economic Well-Being which has been developed by Lars Osberg and Andrew Sharpe of the Centre for the Study of Living Standards, (available from *www.csls.ca*). Broader measures of well-being include the level of security, access to free time, the level of poverty and inequality in a society, the quality of community life, and the environmental and social legacy which is passed on to future generations.

Despite the value judgments which are rightly central to this debate, basic dimensions of well-being are relatively easy to define, are enduring over time, and can be measured. The approach taken throughout this book views the level of real income as measured by GDP and other indicators, such as family income and wages, as very central indicators of social progress, along with the availability of social programs, public services, security, and free time to working people. Further, it is assumed that most people prefer to live in a society where extremes of income and life chances are limited, and where our fellow citizens need not endure poverty, either in the form of absolute or relative deprivation. To be poor is not just to be deprived of basic needs, but also to have much less ability to consume than the social norm.

A preference for equality as a goal is not just altruistic to the considerable extent that working people face a real risk of experiencing periods of low income over a lifetime. Statistics Canada recently reported that there is a turnover in the number of households living in poverty (i.e., below the low income cut off line) of about 50% each year and that, while one in 20 Canadians were poor throughout the 1993-1996 period, one in five Canadians and one in four children experienced at least one year of poverty over that period. (Statistics Canada Cat. 75F0002-MIE. *To What Extent are Canadians Exposed to Low Income?*). The costs of inequality are also to be counted in terms of crime, divided communities, and the high costs of poverty in terms of spending on social programs and health.

This Chapter provides a general overview of two key dimensions of well-being—income and inequality—by tracing the changes in those dimensions from the 1950s and the 1960s, the *"Golden Age"* of post-war capitalism, to the 1990s. This study does not examine indicators of environmental well-being or of community health, though these are important. This overview also serves as an introduction to the more detailed examination of specific trends in the 1990s which is taken up in later chapters.

INCOME
THE COMPOSITION OF INCOME

Most working people would put income at or near the top of the list of determinants of their well-being. Money may not be everything, but, in a market society, most of our needs and wants are met through purchases in the marketplace. To be poor, in terms of income, is to experience limited access to even such basic needs as food, shelter and clothing. By contrast, to be affluent and to enjoy a rising real income over time means that one can buy more goods and services, provide greater opportunities to one's children, and enjoy access to leisure and a measure of security. The accumulation of the savings needed to buy a house, to enjoy a decent retirement, and (increasingly in today's Canada) to finance education and training is closely linked to income.

In all contemporary market or capitalist societies, money income is distributed to people in three main ways: as wages and salaries, as income from investments, and as income transfers from governments, such as old age pensions, and unemployment insurance and social assistance benefits. In Canada, in 1997, more than $7 of every $10 of before-tax personal and household income (71%) came from wages and salaries, another 7% came from income from self-employment, 3% came from investments (excluding income earned in RRSPs and pension plans), and 13% came from government transfers. Income from transfers is concentrated among the elderly and the non-working poor, while income from investments in stocks and bonds is concentrated in the hands of the highly affluent and, to a lesser extent, among retirees.

Table 1.1 presents the composition of household income by income group showing the very high level of dependence on wages for middle and higher income households, and the high level of dependence on transfers for low income households. Even high income households depend much more on wages and salaries than on investment income (though the figures in the Table are low since investment income, as reported here, excludes income earned in tax sheltered RRSPs, pension plans, and unreported income). Overall, 12% of personal income in Canada comes from investments (1997 National Accounts data). Investment income is clearly distributed on generational lines, with older households and the elderly typically depending more on income from savings. Table 1.2 shows the

---

Table 1.1
The Composition of Household Income by Income Group (1997)
(Families and Individuals Combined)

Income Group	Wages and Salaries	Self-Employment Income	Investment Income	Transfers
Low $10,000- $15,000	21.5%	3.3%	2.5%	68.6%
Middle $50,000- $55,000	75.4%	5.8%	2.4%	9.5%
High $100,000 plus	77.6%	11.5%	4.6%	2.2%

SOURCE: Statistics Canada Cat. 13-207-XPB. *Income Distribution by Size in Canada, 1997.* Table 42. "Other" money income brings totals to 100%.

share of the three major sources of personal and family incomes, which go to the highest income 10% of Canadian families, further broken down, and to the bottom 90% of families. The figures are for 1990, when average family income was $51,300, the top 10% made more than $99,100, and the top 1% made more than $185,000 (and averaged $295,000). The top 10% made just over $2.50 in every $10 of wage and salary income, almost $6 out of every $10 of self-employment income (all those high-paid doctors, lawyers and accountants), and more than $4 out of every $10 of investment income. The very affluent, the top 1%, had a much smaller share of wages and salaries than of income from business or investments, and collected $1 in every $4 of self-employment income, and almost $1 in every $5 of investment income.

Table 1.2
The Distribution of Income Among Families by Major Source (1990)

	Top 1%	Share of Next 4%	Next 5%	"Bottom" 90%
Wages and Salaries	4.2%	10.2%	10.8%	74.8%
Self-Employment Income	23.9%	23.0%	9.9%	43.2%
Investment Income	17.5%	15.5%	9.7%	57.4%
Government Transfers	0.6%	2.3%	2.8%	94.3%

SOURCE: Abdul Rashid. "High Income Families," *Perspectives on Labour and Income*. Statistics Canada. Winter, 1994.

To state the obvious, the vast majority of working people and working families are very heavily dependent upon wage and salary income, so the wages provided by jobs are an absolutely crucial determinant of working-class well-being. Transfers are very significant for lower income households, while investment income is of limited importance for the great majority with the partial exception of the elderly.

THE LEVEL OF OVERALL INCOME

It is true and important to say that national income or GDP per person is a limited measure of well-being which has to be supplemented by other indicators. But the fact remains that income is probably the single most important measure of living standards over time. If real (that is, inflation-adjusted) GDP per person increases, then most of the increase in national income will go to working people in the form of higher wages and salaries, and in the form of better public and social services paid for through taxes. It is true that the division of national income between working people and profits is an important distributional issue, but the portion going to wages has changed relatively little over time, and no permanent significant increase in working class living standards can be won through redistribution from investment income.

Higher GDP and higher real wages give people the ability to consume more goods and services, to collectively pay more in taxes for better public services and social programs, and to save more for the future. It is also easier for society as a whole to deal with pressing social problems, such as the quality of the environment and poverty, if total income is rising. In the 1960s and 1970s, when key Canadian social programs such as Medicare, the Canada Pension Plan, the Canada Assistance Plan, and accessible higher education were being put in place, the proportion of income going to taxes was rising at a faster rate than wages. Working people seem to have generally supported paying higher taxes for better services, not least because their after-tax incomes were also rising. In short, the collective provision of public goods and services, the pursuit of broad social goals, and the redistribution of income and wealth are most likely to advance when real GDP is rising.

Table 1.3 provides a long-term overview of the income of Canadians in average per capita or per person terms. The first column shows real GDP per capita, the single most important indicator of Canadian liv-

Table 1.3 The Growth and Stagnation of the Income of Canadians 1961-1998		
(1) Real GDP per Capita	**(2) Personal Disposable Income Per Capita (1992 Constant Dollars)**	
1961 ($12,121)	$8,036	
1971 ($17,066)	$11,165	
1981 ($22,248)	$16,101	
1989 ($25,840)	$17,564	
1999 ($28,686)	$17,001	Sources: (1) (2) Centre for
Growth		the Study of Living
1961-73 3.66%	3.91%	Standards based on
1973-81 2.22%	2.97%	National Accounts data.
1981-89 1.89%	1.09%	$ are constant 1992
1989-99 1.05%	-0.33%	dollars

ing standards over time. As illustrated, the real income of Canadians has grown more slowly decade by decade since the 1960s. Over the 1989-1999 period, real GDP per capita grew by an average 1.05%, compared to 1.89%, 1981-89 and 2.22%, 1973-81. After tax income—personal disposable income per capita—fell by an average 0.33% in the 1989-99 period, compared to an increase of 1.09%, 1981-89, and 2.97%, 1973-81.

It was only at the end of the 1990s—from 1997 on— that Canada resumed a sustained "normal" real economic growth rate of 3% (which is itself only a 2% growth rate of income per person when 1% population growth is taken into account). Even this is well below the 4% average growth rate of the recovery in the 1980s. One telling indicator of the depth and duration of what economist Pierre Fortin has described as *"the Great Canadian Slump"* of the 1990s is the fact that the absolute number of full-time jobs which existed in 1989 was not regained until 1998. In other words, all net job creation over that period was in the form of part-time jobs or self-employment. (The trend to very precarious forms of employment is detailed in Chapter 2).

The real GDP long-term growth rate began to fall from about the mid-1970s, in part because the Canadian government, along with most other advanced industrial country governments, deliberately gave priority to fighting rising inflation through high interest rates, and abandoned full employment and strong growth as key objectives of macro-economic policy. The abandonment of pro-growth macro-economic policies coincided with—and some would argue caused—a slowdown in the rate of productivity growth, which is the most important determinant of longer-term growth rates. Most economists would agree that a major cause of falling productivity was a slump in business investment.

The Canadian experience was neither particularly poor nor unusual compared to other industrial countries in the 1970s and 1980s. Indeed, by some measures Canada did quite well over this period. Canada grew by an average 4% per year in the 1970s compared to 3% in the U.S., and the 3.2% average of the major industrial countries (OECD *Economic Outlook.* December, 1998. Annex Table 1.) Growth and job creation more or less matched U.S. performance in the 1980s. While Canada had a very deep recession in the early 1980s, largely because of the very high real interest rates imposed by Bank of Canada Governor Gerald Bouey, real growth in the 1983-1989 recovery period averaged a fairly healthy 4%, the same rate as in the U.S., and at least matched growth in the major European economies.

However, the 1990s have been an unmitigated disaster in terms of Canadian macro-economic performance. From 1989 to 1998, we experienced the slowest rate of GDP per capita growth of any major industrial country, and significantly lagged behind the U.S. in both growth and job creation. From 1989 through 1998, the Canadian real growth rate (not adjusted for population growth) averaged just 1.8% compared to 2.5% in the U.S. (notwithstanding the convergence with U.S. economic performance which was supposed to result from the Free Trade Agreement) and this was mirrored in a much worse job creation performance. Real GDP per capita did not grow at all from 1989 to 1994, and has grown very slowly since. The 1990s saw the worst performance of the Canadian economy since the 1930s. Indeed, Andrew Sharpe of the Centre for the Study of Living Standards has calculated that the 1990s were almost as bad as the Great Depression decade of the 1930s in terms of real income growth per person.

Column 2 of Table 1.3 shows the growth of *"personal disposable income per capita."* This refers to the income which is left in the hands of households after income tax and social security contributions. (Note, however, that GST and sales tax paid are not included in calculating disposable income per capita). Because governments in the 1990s dealt with the debt problem in a slow-growth economy by raising taxes on top of spending cuts (mainly by not fully indexing the income tax system to inflation), the average tax burden rose while incomes were flat or falling. As of 1999, after-tax real household incomes were still about 3% below the 1989 level.

A different indicator of the broad evolution of incomes is the level of real average pre-tax family income. Families in 1997 were, on average, almost $3,000 worse-off than in 1989 even before they paid income taxes ($57,146 in 1997 compared to $59,862 in 1989).

Real incomes do, of course, vary across Canada and there are important differences in household income between the richer and poorer provinces. However, differences in wage levels and employment are offset to some degree by transfer payments to households, and federal equalization payments serve to level up the tax base in the poorer provinces.

In 1996, the gap between per person after tax income across provinces was more narrow than one might imagine—varying between a low of $14,000-$15,000 in Atlantic Canada, to a high of between $17,000 and $18,000 in the "have" provinces of Ontario, Alberta and British Columbia. Moreover, the distribution of real GDP between regions has changed very little over the past twenty years. As shown in Table 1.4, despite suffering the most severe impacts in the recession of the early 1990s, Ontario's share of national GDP has grown since 1981 at the expense of all other regions. (In the 1990s, the West has increased its share somewhat.)

Table 1.4
Real GDP by Region as % of National Total
1981-1996

	1981	1996
Atlantic	12.5%	12.0%
Quebec	23.8%	22.3%
Ontario	38.4%	40.5%
Prairies	19.2%	19.0%
British Columbia	12.5%	12.0%

SOURCE: Statistics Canada, Canadian Economic Observer, cat. no. 11-010-XPB.

WHY DID CANADA DO SO BADLY IN THE 1990s?

Studies produced by the Canadian Centre for Policy Alternatives and leading Canadian economists, such as Pierre Fortin, Lars Osberg and Mike McCracken, have argued that Canada experienced a decade of stagnation in living standards mainly because the Bank of Canada imposed radically deflationary policies in the late 1980s. In an attempt to squeeze inflation to near zero, the Bank raised interest rates and overvalued the currency. The deep recession of the early 1990s, which resulted in the loss of about one in five manufacturing jobs over a little more than two years, and a peak unemployment rate of more than 11% in 1992 and 1993, combined with high interest rates to produce a rapid growth of public debt. Government spending cuts to deal with the debt problem in a slow-growth environment further lowered growth in the recovery. [On the macro-economic factors behind the Great Canadian Slump of the 1990s, see Lars Osberg and Pierre Fortin (Eds.) *Unnecessary Debts*. Lorimer. Toronto. 1996; *The Alternative Federal Budget Papers*. Canadian Centre for Policy Alternatives. 1997 and 1998; Brian MacLean and Lars Osberg (Eds.). *The Unemployment Crisis: All for Nought?* McGill-Queen's University Press. Montreal and Kingston. 1996.)] Even eminently "*orthodox*" and "right-wing" economic analysts now put the major blame for Canada's dismal economic performance in the 1990s on contractionary macro-economic policies. (See, for example, *OECD Country Reviews of Canada*.]

It can also be argued that the turn to pro-business and *"free market"* policies in the 1980s and 1990s did nothing to raise economic growth rates or close the productivity gap with the United States (see Andrew Jackson. "From Leaps of Faith to Lapses of Logic" *Policy Options*. June, 1999). By these measures, the introduction of the Free Trade Agreement and NAFTA, combined with privatization, deregulation, and the virtual abandonment of active, government-led, industrial and economic development policies, were a bust. Ironically, the tenth anniversary of the Free Trade Agreement—which was, above all, supposed to lead to stronger productivity growth—coincided with a raging national debate over Canada's poor productivity performance in the 1990s. The OECD, which sparked the debate, itself pointed out in the *1998 Country Review of Canada* that *"structural policies"* had to date done nothing to promote the needed shift to a more innovative and productive economy.

Conversely, it is often argued that Canada has not gone "far enough" in pursuing pro-market policies. Proponents of this view say that the strong growth of U.S. jobs in the 1990s shows the superiority of the U.S. *"model"* of highly *"flexible"* labour markets and small government, and that countries like Canada would do better in terms of growth and job creation if unions were weaker, if labour standards were lowered to U.S. levels, if taxes were cut, and if income support programs for the unemployed were severely cut. This was, broadly, the policy prescription presented in the major *OECD Jobs Study*, which is regularly parroted in the right-wing media.

As shown below, the U.S. model is associated with many less desirable features, notably very high rates of inequality and poverty, while countries with more generous welfare states, higher taxes, and stronger labour movements are much more equal. Is the choice, then, between growth and inequality; between efficiency and equity? The evidence suggests not. [See L. Mishel and John Schmitt (Eds.) *Beware the U.S. Model: Jobs and Wages in a Deregulated Economy*. Economic Policy Institute. Washington. 1995.] In fact, on close examination, U.S. growth performance is not terribly impressive in a comparative context, and much of the modest difference between U.S. and European growth rates in the 1990s can be explained by different macro-economic policies. The U.S. has been more relaxed about inflation, and budget cuts have been much less severe. Further, it is quite possible to find examples of countries which have created jobs at the same pace as in the U.S., but which still have strong labour movements, decent welfare states, and a reasonable level of equality. The Netherlands, Denmark and Norway are cases in point—all of which had higher per capita GDP growth rates than the United States from 1990 to 1998 and had very low unemployment rates at the end of the 1990s.

None of the advanced industrial countries has performed at all well in terms of growth since the mid-1970s. The consequences have been seen in different combinations of rising unemployment, stagnating wages, and increased inequality. The abandonment of full employment objectives bears the major part of the blame, though the downward pressures of *"globalization"* have also played a role.

EARNINGS FROM EMPLOYMENT

The fact that average real incomes of households have been growing ever more slowly since the mid-1970s, and have been stagnant in the 1990s, is mainly explained by changes in earnings from employment. The decline in incomes would have been far greater for low-income households if increased transfer payments from governments had not cushioned the fall in earnings which resulted from flat wages, combined with high rates of unemployment and underemployment in the late 1980s and 1990s.

Annual earnings depend on two main variables: the amount of time worked, and pay rates. Obviously, the annual earnings of a person will be lower if she or he is unemployed for part of the year, or works part-time, or for only part of the year. By the same token, the annual earnings of two-person households will be greater if both spouses work full-time for pay outside the home. As shown in Table 1.5, household earnings in the 1970s and 1980s were boosted by the increased participation of women in the paid workforce. Between 1976 and 1990, the proportion of adult women (age 25 and over) who were employed rose from 39% to 53%. (In both years, some women were also unemployed and seeking jobs.) An increased proportion of women who were working also moved into full-year, full-time jobs. (Other women who would have liked to move into full-time jobs were unable to do so because of labour market conditions.)

Further, as shown in Table 1.6, through the 1970s, 1980s and, above all, in the 1990s, the pay gap between women and men closed as women moved closer to the still distant goal of pay equality. From 1967

Table 1.5
Employment Rates of Women, 1976-97

	Employment Rate of Adult Women	Percentage of all Women Working Full-Year, Full-Time
1976	39%	—
1980	44%	45%
1990	53%	51%
1997	53%	51%

SOURCE: Statistics Canada. *The Labour Force Survey.*
Statistics Canada Cat. 13-217, *Earnings of Men and Women.*

to 1997, the pay gap between women and men working full-year, full-time, closed from 58% to 72%, and the gap between women and men working on a non-full-year or part-time basis closed from 51% to 79%. It is very important, however, to note that only about half of all working women, even today, work full-time on a full-year basis compared to two-thirds of men—so a large part of the annual earnings gap between women and men is produced by time worked rather than by pay rates. Some of the gap in time worked is explained by the high level of involuntary part-time employment among women.

The closing of the gap was the result of increased time worked by women, falling or stagnant wages of men, and modest increases in the earnings of women as noted below. The increased paid work-time of women—offset to a modest degree by the tendency of men to retire earlier—made a major contribution to the growth of household incomes in the 1970s and 1980s, cushioning the impacts of slower wage growth com-

Table 1.6
Average Real Annual Earnings ($1997)
of Men and Women, 1967-1997

	Full-Year, Full-Time Workers			Other Workers
	Men $	Women $	Women as % of Men	Women as % of Men
1967	32,057	18,725	58.4	50.6
1975	42,635	25,664	60.2	50.6
1980	42,586	27,405	64.4	61.4
1989	42,328	27,928	66.0	73.7
1997	42,626	30,915	72.5	78.6

SOURCE: Statistics Canada Cat. 13-217-X1B, *Earnings of Men and Women.*

pared to the 1950s and 1960s. Clearly, many women wanted to work outside the home, and this shift was not caused solely or, even most importantly, by the desire to maximize household incomes.

It is striking that this trend for women to work longer hours came to a shuddering halt in the 1990s when both the employment rate of adult women and the proportion of women working full-time, full-year remained stuck. This almost certainly reflected poor conditions in the job market much more than any new-found desire on the part of women to return to the home. In any case, part of the story of the stagnation of working family income in the 1990s is the inability of women to work longer hours.

The second major factor behind the level of annual earnings is pay rates. Table 1.6 shows the average real annual earnings of workers who are employed year-round, full-time. Workers in these kinds of jobs are not directly affected by rising unemployment or by the shift to part-time and contract jobs. As shown, there was a very significant growth in the real wages paid in these *"core"* jobs between 1967 and 1975, the closing years of the *"Golden Age."* In those eight years, the real wages of men grew by 33%, and the real wages of women grew by 37%. Astonishingly, there has been no real wage growth at all for men working full-year and full-time since 1975, and wages have just about matched the growth of prices through both the 1980s and 1990s. (As will be shown below, much of the burden of this stagnation has fallen upon younger men.)

The story for women has been different. Earnings growth in permanent, full-time jobs has been slow, but it has nonetheless been real. Overall, however, the real earnings of the one in two women who work in permanent, full-time jobs rose by only 13% in the entire period since 1980.

When all paid workers are divided into 10 income deciles, (10 equal sized groups, ranging from the lowest to the highest paid) it can be seen that real average earnings fell between 1981 and 1995

Table 1.7
Change in Real Annual Earnings by Decile, Women and Men, 1981-1995

Decile	Women % Change	Men % Change
1	9.8	-31.7
2	17.1	-24.5
3	17.5	-21.6
4	13.6	-17.7
5	11.9	-12.3
6	13.4	-8.5
7	13.7	-4.7
8	16.1	-2.2
9	17.0	-0.5
10	17.9	6.2

SOURCE: Picot, Garnett. What is Happening to Earnings Inequality and Youth Wages in the 1990's? Statistics Canada. Table 1. July, 1998.

for the bottom 90% of male workers (See Table 1.7). By contrast, real earnings for workers in the top decile increased by 6.2%. The annual earnings of women increased across the whole earnings distribution, but by more at the very top. Most of the growing inequality in earnings was among men. Between 1981 and 1995, real earnings in the lowest wage decile of men dropped by a huge 31.7% and by 24.5% in the second lowest decile. The fall in lower income men's earnings was the result of a drop in hours and weeks worked, a decline in real wage rates, and an increase in the number of men with no earnings.

While the real annual earnings of women rose, it must be noted that much of this increase was due to more hours worked over the year. There is obviously much more to the quality of jobs than wages and, as will be documented in Chapter 3, workers have been working harder and longer in more and more stressful conditions in the 1990s.

SECURITY OF EMPLOYMENT AND INCOME

Security in a particular job or in work is another major dimension of well-being. A major defining feature of a market or capitalist society, going along with dependence on wage income, is insecurity of employment at the level of the firm. The vast majority of working people enjoy no real long-term job security through the terms of a contract or collective agreement, but remain employed only so long as it is profitable for their employer to continue in business with the same number of workers, or until the next round of corporate or public sector *"downsizing"* intended to produce more for less.

Unions have won important protections from layoff, notably through seniority provisions in collective agreements, but most unionized workers are nonetheless subject to temporary and permanent layoffs. In the 1990s, at least, job security has been no greater in the public than in the private sector, and *"downsizing"* through layoffs has actually been more prevalent than in the large corporate sector where hiring freezes and waves of early retirement have been the preferred instruments.

Despite the lack of formal job security and the risk of layoff, a significant proportion of all workers are employed in reasonably steady *"core"* jobs, and average tenure in a job has actually increased in the 1980s and 1990s, mainly because of the lack of new hiring, particularly in larger workplaces. Meanwhile, many workers—particularly women, young workers and workers of colour—are employed in very precarious and unstable jobs which do not provide guaranteed hours in a week or in a month, let alone ongoing job security.

Clearly, the overall health of the job market or labour market is an absolutely crucial determinant of well-being. Employment security will be highest when unemployment is low and employment growth is high. This is true for two key reasons: 1) workers will be somewhat less likely to be laid-off from the job they currently hold in periods of expansion, and 2), most importantly, they will be much more likely to find a job if they are laid-off or are just entering the job market. The ability of workers to win wage increases is also much greater in a low unemployment economy where many employers are hiring workers, as is the ability to progress up career ladders.

The level of GDP growth is very closely linked to the level of employment growth and thus to the unemployment rate. While it is possible to have some brief periods of *"jobless growth"* in the early stages of an economic upturn, growth of GDP over and above the rate of growth of labour productivity—output per hour—inevitably results in increased demand for workers. As a very rough rule of thumb, employment growth will equal GDP growth less the trend rate of labour productivity growth, currently a bit above 1% per year. (The figure will vary depending upon how jobs are divided between full and part-time, and between paid jobs and self-employment.)

Increased employment will generally reduce the unemployment rate, though unemployment may remain high and even stable despite rising rates of hiring if more workers join the labour force. Historically, periods of strong job growth have pulled more people into the workforce. Given that productivity is growing by about 1% per year and that the population is growing by about 1% per year, it takes GDP growth in excess of 2% to have any impact on the unemployment rate.

Table 1.8 shows that the average rate of unemployment in Canada has been ratcheting upwards decade by decade in line with slowing economic growth, a growing population, and rising rates of labour force participation.

Table 1.8
National Unemployment Rate

1950s	4.2%
1960s	5.0%
1970s	6.7%
1980s	9.3%
1989	7.5%
1992	11.3%
1997	9.2%
1998	8.5%
1999	7.6%

SOURCE: Statistics Canada. Labour Force Survey.

The national unemployment rate averaged 9.3% in the 1980s, sharply up from the 4% level of the 1950s and the 5% level of the 1960s, and still stood at 8.5% in 1998 after six years of slow growth in the recovery from the recession of the early 1990s. It was only in late 1999 that the unemployment rate fell to near the 7.5% "low point" of the late 1980s.

Many people today have come to believe that "*full employment*" is an impossible dream. Yet Canada came close to providing a job for everybody who wanted one in the "*Golden Age*," and unemployment rates of 4-5% have been achieved in the 1990s not just in the U.S., but also in Japan before the recent slump and, in Europe, the Netherlands, Norway, Austria, Denmark and Ireland.

The widely cited headline unemployment rate represents average unemployment in the course of a *month*. Over the course of a *year*, a higher proportion of workers will experience at least one spell of unemployment. The likely length of a period of unemployment tends to vary in the same way as the unemployment rate, increasing when unemployment is high, and falling when unemployment is low. In the 1970s, and at the peak of the expansion of the 1980s, the average length of a completed period of unemployment was about 3 1/2 months. In the recessions of the early 1980s and early 1990s, the average length rose to almost five months, and the average length of a new unemployment spell today is a bit above four months. (Garnett Picot and Andrew Heisz, *Canadian Labour Market Performance in Historical Context*. Paper presented to the CSLS Conference on the Structural Aspects of Unemployment in Canada, 1999. Available from *www.csls.ca*.)

The "*turnover*" of the unemployed in Canada, as in the U.S., is very high compared to most European countries, and the proportion of workers who are unemployed for long periods of time is relatively low, while the proportion of workers hit by periods of involuntary unemployment over a year is correspondingly high. That said, some workers "*end*" a period of unemployment by giving up looking for work rather than by getting a job. The ranks of these "*hidden unemployed*" have been growing as jobs have dried up, as will be detailed later.

While long-term unemployment of permanently laid-off older workers has become a major problem in the 1980s and 1990s, much of the burden of unemployment falls upon young workers trying to enter or get a foothold in the job market, and on adult women trying to re-enter the job market after time spent looking after children. In periods of rising unemployment, the increase in the unemployment rate is driven more by the sharp fall-off in job creation than by layoffs of workers from existing jobs. Nonetheless, as shown in Table 1.9, the risk of layoff for workers is quite high, and there has been some increase in that risk over time. In 1994, a year of strong job growth, 19% of men were subject to a layoff, compared to 17.1% in 1978 (11.2% vs. 10.6% for women). Layoffs tend to be higher among men because of the higher concentration of employment in male-dominated industries such as construction, forestry, and manufacturing. As will be noted later, this is an underestimate of the recent increase in job insecurity, which is revealed not just in the incidence of layoff from paid jobs but also in the rapid growth of self-employment. Four in ten new *"jobs"* created in the 1990s (1989-99) came in the form of self-employment, and about one in five workers are now self-employed. For this large and fast growing group, there is a risk of losing the *"job"* through bankruptcy, but the greater risk is to have a low and very variable income. Income security for working people involves security not just against layoff, but also against loss of income due to unemployment. Unemployment Insurance is the key cushion against the impact of temporary unemployment, while social assistance only guards against destitution in the event of long-term unemployment. (Social assistance is a very poor cushion against loss of wages due to unemployment, not just because of low benefits, but also because unemployed workers qualify only if their liquid assets have been exhausted, and only if other members of the household are not working.)

Cuts to UI have greatly increased income insecurity for workers. In the 1970s and 1980s, about three in four unemployed workers qualified for UI benefits. This proportion fell very sharply in the 1990s, from 74% in 1990 to just 36% in 1997. And average weekly UI benefits have fallen

Table 1.9
Incidence of Job Lay-Off, 1978-1994

	Men Permanent	Temporary	Total	Women Permanent	Temporary	Total
1978	9.0	8.1	17.1	5.2	5.4	10.6
1981	8.6	9.1	17.7	4.3	5.7	10.0
1984	9.9	10.8	20.7	5.4	7.1	12.5
1989	8.1	8.6	16.7	4.1	5.6	9.7
1994	8.9	10.1	19.0	4.6	6.6	11.2

SOURCE: Statistics Canada Cat. 71-539-XPB, *Permanent Layoffs, Quits and Hiring in the Canadian Economy, 1978-1995.* Table 1.

from 60% of average weekly earnings in the early 1980s to 54% in 1995. (Data from Lars Osberg and Andrew Sharpe. An *Index of Economic Well-Being for Canada*, and Canadian Labour Congress *Left Out in the Cold.* 1998.) The erosion of UI in the 1990s has contributed in a very major way to decreased income security for working people and, as noted below, to increased poverty.

For working people, security also means protection against interruptions of wage income due to illness, disability, or old age. It is occasionally forgotten by progressives that a central purpose of the income transfer system is to provide *security* for working people against loss of income, a purpose which is distinct from its other important function of providing a *minimum level* of income to deal with poverty. In a society providing high levels of security for working people, transfers will tend to be significant, not just for low-income groups, but also for the broad ranks of the middle class.

Unionization affects worker well-being along many dimensions, and the *"union advantage"* in terms of wages, benefits, working-time, and other issues is considered at length below. While the union impact on wages is significant, the benefits of unionization are also experienced very importantly in terms of greater worker security. The protections of a collective agreement give access to grievance and arbitration procedures in the event of disciplinary action, making arbitrary individual dismissal much less likely. Seniority provisions provide some assurance of access to career ladders, and protection against layoff. Benefits provisions (e.g., employer-sponsored pensions, extended health plans) provide security against illness and old age above and beyond those provided through public programs.

As shown in Figure 1.1, the unionization rate in Canada has been remarkably stable over time, declining only marginally through the 1970s, 1980s and 1990s. Canadian experience contrasts sharply to that of other industrialized countries, notably the U.S., where the unionization rate has fallen from 30% at the end of the 1960s to less than 15% today. However, the overall stability of the unionization rate in Canada is mainly due to a major increase in public sector unionization up to the 1990s which was concentrated among women (who make up about two-thirds of the total public sector workforce). The unionization rate of men has fallen since the 1960s, in large part because of the shrinking proportion of jobs to be found in traditionally heavily unionized sectors such as the resource industries, manufacturing and construction. As will be explored in detail

Figure 1.1
Unionization Rates, 1967-1997 (Union Members as % of Paid Workers)

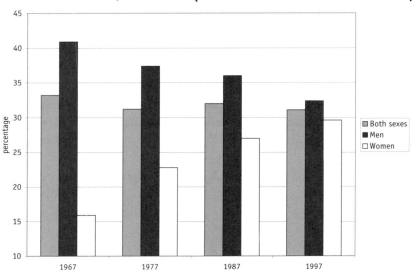

Source: Statistical Portrait of Unions, Perspectives on Labour and Income, Statistics Canada, cat. 75-001-XPE, Winter 1997.

below, access to the benefits of unionization has been very limited in the private service sector industries which have dominated job creation in the 1980s and 1990s.

POVERTY AND INEQUALITY

Other major dimensions of economic and social well-being are the level of poverty and inequality. All market economies deliver unequal outcomes to a greater or lesser extent in terms of the "primary" distribution of incomes which takes place through market mechanisms before government intervention. As noted above, income from investments tends to be highly unequally distributed in line with the concentration of wealth ownership in the hands of the few.

Most importantly, wages and salaries are also distributed very unequally, for three major reasons. First, unemployment and underemployment affect workers differently. Some remain in jobs right through an extended period of high unemployment while others are temporarily or permanently on the sidelines of the job market. Second, the hours of work vary between jobs. Third, and most important, the level of earnings varies a great deal from the top to the bottom of the wage distribution, with chief executive officers sometimes earning hundreds of times more than the average workers, who may themselves earn twice as much as very low-wage workers.

Pay differences are obviously related to skill, education and experience, and serve a necessary purpose in all economies. Few would question the need for some progress in terms of pay as workers progress up career ladders, and some jobs are more demanding or require scarce skills and thus merit higher pay. However, pay differentials also reflect bargaining power in the labour market; unionized workers have more power than non-union workers and thus typically enjoy a significant wage premium over otherwise comparable workers. Unions also tend to compress wage differentials in workplaces, and thus reduce wage inequality in the economy as a whole in countries where unionization rates are high (see Chapter 4).

Wage differentials also reflect various forms of segmentation and segregation in the job market. For example, women are typically paid less than men, even when they are similar jobs in terms of skills, and women tend to hold jobs which are less well-paid than the jobs of men. The structure of earnings is directly affected by the level of collective bargaining and labour standards, and differs between countries in major ways, as will be noted below. The wage distribution in Canada is quite unequal compared to that of many European countries, though not as unequal as that of the U.S.

Table 1.10 is based on Statistics Canada data taken from the widely publicized *Growing Gap* report released in 1998 by the Centre for Social Justice. It shows the distribution of market incomes for families with children, and thus removes the elderly—who typically have little earned income—from consideration. The table shows the average market incomes for the bottom 20%, middle 20%, and top 20% of the population for four years from 1973 to 1996 (further broken down into *"deciles,"* each representing one-tenth of the population). The following key observations emerge:

- The middle fifth of working families bear out the story of the average person and family told above. Overall, their incomes rose somewhat from 1973 to 1984 and 1984 to 1990, but fell in the 1990s. In 1996, real incomes were only slightly higher than in 1984.

Table 1.10
Average Family Income Before Transfers, 1973-1996
(Families with Children) ($1996)

	1973 $	1984 $	1990 $	1996 $	% Change 1973-90	% Change 1990-96
Bottom 5th						
Decile 1	5,204	2,062	2,760	435	-47	-84
Decile 2	19,562	14,930	16,599	11,535	-15	-31
Middle 5th						
Decile 5	40,343	42,495	46,477	42,829	+15	-8
Decile 6	46,136	49,664	54,561	51,494	+18	-6
Top 5th						
Decile 9	71,611	79,628	88,426	86,497	+23	-2
Decile 10	107,253	123,752	134,539	136,737	+25	+2

SOURCE: Statistics Canada *Survey of Consumer Finance* data from Armine Yalnizyan, *The Growing Gap*, Centre for Social Justice. October, 1998.

- The bottom fifth of working families experienced a major decline in income from 1973 to 1984, some recovery from 1984 to 1990, and then a huge income decline in the 1990s. The poorest 10% of families had very low market incomes throughout the entire period, and these shrank dramatically to just $435 per family in 1996, indicating almost complete marginalization from the job market. The poorest 10% of families clearly do not get even close to a survival income from the market, and poverty rates would be very high for the next 10% as well if it were not for social programs. (Almost all of the bottom 20% of families with children would fall below Statistics Canada's Low Income Cutoff or poverty line.) Clearly, rising unemployment and the growing precariousness of jobs have had major impacts upon the poorest one-fifth of families, undercutting their ability to survive from the market.

- The story for the top 20% of families is different again. Their market incomes rose by about one-quarter from 1973 to 1990. However, even this top group did not fare well in the 1990s. Only the very top 10% experienced a market income gain in the 1990s, and this was just 2% (1990-1996). Likely, very high-income earners—say, the top 1-2% who are successful lawyers and accountants or senior corporate executives—experienced much faster real income growth in the 1990s in line with the rise in corporate profits and the booming stock market. However, the Canadian experience is different from that of the

U.S., where increased inequality in the 1990s has been very much associated with rapid income growth at the top of the income distribution pyramid.

- Differences in market incomes are clearly profound. The top 10% of families have market incomes almost three times larger than families in the middle of the income distribution.

Overall, the data clearly bear out the now familiar picture of the *"shrinking middle class."* Middle-class working families gained a bit of ground in the upturn of the 1980s, but overall have market incomes only a little higher than in the mid-1970s. Families at the bottom have suffered large losses of market income, and the bottom 10% have become an underclass, all but expelled from the market and almost entirely dependent on transfers. Meanwhile, high income families have continued to experience rising incomes, though even they were by no means immune from the income disaster of the 1990s.

This polarization of market incomes is not explained by an overall shift of income from wages and salaries to profits, since the wage share of national income has changed little over time, tending to rise in recession and fall in recoveries. As of late 1999, the share of corporate profits in Canadian national income had just recovered to the level of the late 1980s, which was itself a bit below the level of the *"Golden Age."* The interest income share of national income has risen since the mid-1970s in line with the shift to high interest rates, but this has been mainly at the expense of other forms of business income.

The major driving force of greater market inequality in Canada has not been a shift of national income shares between capital and labour, but changes in the job market. Again, this is in contrast to the U.S., where the profit share of national income has indeed risen at the expense of wages and salaries in the 1980s and 1990s, in turn boosting the fortunes of senior corporate executives and stockholders.

One determining factor affecting the distribution of wages has been the increased impact of unemployment and underemployment on time worked. Table 1.11 shows the number of weeks worked in the year for adult (aged 25-54) men and women at the bottom, middle and top of the earnings distribution. As shown, men in the middle and at the top average very close to a full year's work, while men at the bottom have experienced, over time, a decline in the weeks worked in a year. 1981 and 1989 and 1984 and 1993 represent similar years in the business cycle. In 1993, men at the bottom of the income ladder were working about two

Table 1.11
Weeks Worked in Year, 1981-1993

		1981	1984	1989	1993
Men					
(Age 25-54)	Decile 1 (lowest)	31.0	24.0	28.7	21.9
	Decile 2	43.5	37.7	41.4	35.6
	Decile 5	50.5	50.2	50.4	49.9
	Decile 10 (highest)	51.6	51.6	51.7	51.7
Women					
(Age 25-54)	Decile 1 (lowest)	20.4	20.3	24.3	21.3
	Decile 2	31.3	32.4	36.9	35.8
	Decile 5	48.3	48.2	49.1	49.6
	Decile 10 (highest)	51.2	51.3	51.7	51.8

SOURCE: G. Picot *Working Time, Wages and Earnings Inequality Among Men and Women in Canada, 1981-1993* (1996).

weeks less than in 1984, a roughly similar year in the unemployment level. By contrast, women at the bottom and middle of the earnings ladder have increased the number of weeks worked per year, as noted above.

The second major factor behind increased earnings inequality has been increased inequality of wage rates. Table 1.12 shows average weekly earnings, again for adult (aged 25-54) men and women at the top, bottom and middle of the earnings distribution. The table indicates some increase in polarization as measured by the ratio of earners at the top to earners at the bottom. In 1993, men in the top 10% were earning $1,534 per week, up somewhat from 1981, while men at the bottom were earning just $301, much less than in 1981. The wage gap between top and bottom grew from a factor of 4.3 in 1981, to 5.1 in 1993.

Again, the story for women was different, with real wages growing from 1981 for all women, and the wage gap between top and bottom women workers remaining more or less the same. (The wage gap for women is higher than for men mainly because a much larger proportion of women work part-time). In fact, the overall distribution of wages in Canada would have become more unequal if it had not been for the increased participation of women in the work force, and the closing of the pay gap between men and women.

A very detailed analysis by Garnett Picot of Statistics Canada has found that increased inequality in terms of annual earnings has, for both men and women, been driven more by hours worked in a year than by hourly wage rates (Garnett Picot, *"Working Time, Wages and Earnings*

Table 1.12
Average Weekly Earnings of Adult Men and Women, 1981-1993
(Constant 1993 Dollars)

		1981 $	1984 $	1989 $	1993 $
Men					
(Age 25-54)	Decile 1 (lowest)	350	298	301	301
	Decile 2	493	431	454	437
	Decile 5	710	670	683	630
	Decile 10 (highest)	1492	1449	1569	1534
	D10/D1	4.3	4.9	5.2	5.1
Women					
(Age 25-54)	Decile 1 (lowest)	157	151	157	173
	Decile 2	233	235	242	241
	Decile 5	373	381	399	393
	Decile 10 (highest)	984	1002	1018	1069
	D10/D1	6.3	6.6	6.5	6.2

SOURCE: Picot (1996).

Inequality Among Men and Women in Canada, 1981-1993." Paper presented to the Conference on Labour Market Institutions and Labour Market Outcomes. Hamilton, Ontario. September, 1996). Unemployment and the shift to jobs with shorter hours have hit the lower paid hardest, while those in high-pay jobs have tended to work more hours per week.

Statistics Canada analysis has also shown that it is young workers who have been hit hardest by changes in the overall distribution of earnings. As shown in Table 1.13, the real median earnings of both men and women *"entry"* workers aged 20-24 fell by more than one-fifth between 1983 and 1992. This fall has been driven mainly by a fall in the hourly wages of young people. Somewhat older young workers also experienced a decline in relative earnings. Put another way, over time, younger people have become steadily worse off than preceding *"cohorts"* of young people were at a similar stage in their lives.

Table 1.13
Change in Median
Annual Earnings by type, 1983 - 1992

All Earners	2.1
Men	-1.6
Women	11
Younger Workers	
(Age 25-34)	
Men	-8.1
Women	-1
Entry Workers	
(Age 20-24)	
Men	-21.9
Women	-24

SOURCE: Ross Finnie. *Earnings Dynamics in Canada: Earnings Patterns by Age and Sex, 1982-1992.* Research Paper R-97-11E. Applied Research Branch, Human Resources Development Canada. 1997.

The labour market experience of those who first entered the job market in the later 1980s and 1990s has been worse than those who entered it in the 1970s and early 1980s—bearing out the usual picture of a dismal working life for those following in the wake of the "baby boomers." (However, demographics does not really explain what happened. As a relatively small generation, the post-baby- boomers should have had limited difficulties making their way into good jobs, particularly given the falling age of retirement of their grandparents. The problem was that very few new good jobs were being created as they entered and are still entering the job market.)

The key point is that the significant increase in the inequality of earned income has been driven by both high and rising unemployment, and by the decline in the relative earnings of lower-earning men. It seems likely that families with two wage earners have been protected to some degree by the increased annual earnings of women, which reflect an increase in time worked more than increased real wages.

Young workers and their families have suffered a particularly sharp erosion of their real earnings. It is important not to lose sight of the fact that increased market income inequality in Canada has been driven much more by the loss of income at the bottom and middle of the income ladder than by large absolute gains at the top.

THE TAX/TRANSFER SYSTEM AND LOW INCOMES

A major factor shaping the overall level of income inequality and the incidence of low income and poverty is the transfer system: payment of dollars by governments to people. Major transfers consist of public pensions (Old Age Security, the Guaranteed Income Supplement and the Canada/Quebec Pension Plan), Unemployment Insurance benefits, Social Assistance benefits, Workers' Compensation and child benefits, including the Canada Child Benefit now delivered through the income tax system. As briefly noted, transfers make up a very large share of the income of poorer households. Table 1.14 shows the significance of transfers as a share of disposable family income from 1980 to 1996. The already high transfer dependence of the poorest 20% of families has grown from just under half to almost 60% of income, and the dependence of the next poorest 20% has increased even more, from one-seventh to one-quarter of income. It is only the top 20% of families who have seen no increase in transfers as a share of income since 1984.

Table 1.14
Transfer Payments as % Income — All Families, 1980-1996

	1980	1984	1990	1996
Lowest Quintile	46.5	56.2	53.2	59
Second Quintile	13.8	21.3	21.5	25.5
Middle Quintile	6.9	10.3	10.5	12.8
Fourth Quintile	4.2	6.1	6.3	6.8
Top Quintile	2.3	3	3	3

SOURCE: Statistics Canada Cat. 13-210-XPB. *Income After Tax, Distributions by Size in Canada.* Text Table V.

The term *"dependency"* is often used to imply that the existence of a transfer program results in its use and abuse, and cuts to UI benefits and to social assistance have been explicitly justified on the basis that they create *"disincentives"* to paid work. In point of fact, to qualify for benefits, UI beneficiaries must become involuntarily unemployed, and are required to actively seek work. Benefit entitlements are modest and expire after very short periods of time, depending upon work history and the local rate of unemployment. The majority of UI recipients are on temporary layoff and will return to the same employer. Most others use UI as a bridge between jobs. UI *"dependency"* is, then, largely determined by the state of the labour market.

Many social assistance recipients do depend on benefits for extended periods of time, usually because they are temporarily or even permanently unable to work (e.g., persons with disabilities; single parents with children). Low wages in available jobs create a welfare *"trap"* for others. Single parents, for example, are often unable to find jobs that match the already well-below-poverty-line incomes provided by social assistance, let alone cover child care costs, drug costs, and so on. Even so, there is very significant movement between low-paid jobs and social assistance and, again, *"dependency"* is more due to the fundamental shortage of good jobs than to any alleged *"disincentives"* to work.

It can be easily shown that both UI and social assistance caseloads ratchet up in times of recession, and fall in times of recovery. The fact that declines in the 1980s and 1990s have not matched the increases in periods of recession is yet another indicator of the fundamental problem: the lack of jobs that can provide a steady, adequate income. As noted above, the overall level of employment in the economy is determined by the demand for labour, which is a function of economic growth and productivity growth.

Increased *"dependency"* was the result of economic failure, not some sudden surge of worker disinterest in holding jobs.

Dismantling UI and social assistance, as advocated by right-wing economists, could perhaps starve more of the unemployed into accepting jobs at extremely low wages. Such a strategy might even create some new jobs by lowering the price of very labour-intensive services, and thus increasing demand for those services. In many developing countries, for example, there is close to *"full"* employment, but a huge proportion of the workforce work for a minimal income in the informal economy, and the wealthy can hire many servants at very low wages. The availability of desperate, underemployed workers, in turn, pulls down the wages of all workers, perhaps with the exception of the very highly skilled. If it were not for the availability of transfer income, Canada's unemployed and underemployed would be even more desperate, further worsening the position of those employed at low wages, and in turn worsening the position of even steadily employed workers.

From the point of view of all workers, then, using taxes to compensate the unemployed and underemployed for the lost wages and low incomes caused by economic failure is preferable to the right-wing model of bringing back *"full employment"* on the basis of a highly *"flexible"* labour market in which workers have very little bargaining power. (In the textbook world of many economists, full employment can be achieved quite simply by cutting wages to a *"market clearing"* level. What these economists forget is that this *"solution"* did not work in the Great Depression—when the welfare state barely existed—and that working people will rightly reject an economic system that forces them to choose between starvation and working poverty.)

Transfers, in combination with taxes, make a huge difference to the overall distribution of family income. Table 1.15 compares the distribution of family income by the market with the distribution after the intervention of the tax/transfer system. The income shares of the bottom 40%, and particularly the bottom 20%, are increased (more than trebled in the case of the bottom 20%), mainly at the expense of the top 20%. The top 20% receive more than 20 times more market income than the bottom 20%, but "only" five times more in terms of total after-tax income. The gap would be narrower still if public services consumed were added to after-tax income.

In the 1980s, and in the 1990s to 1992, there was no change in the inequality or polarization of the overall distribution of disposable (after-

Table 1.15
Family Income Shares: Before and After Taxes and Transfers

	Market Income	Income After Tax and Transfers
Lowest Quintile	2.1	7.4
Second Quintile	10.1	13.2
Middle Quintile	17.7	18.1
Fourth Quintile	25.8	23.9
Highest Quintile	44.3	37.5
Ratio of Highest/Lowest	21.1	5.1

SOURCE: Statistics Canada Cat. 13-210-XPB. *Income After Tax, Distributions by Size, 1997.* Table 1.

tax and transfers) family income in Canada. Over this period, the top 20% more or less consistently received about five times more than the bottom 20%, and the overall distribution of disposable income (as measured by the Gini coefficient and other technical measures) did not change. (See Caledon Institute for Social Policy, *"Government Fights Growing Gap between Rich and Poor,"* 1995.) Setting aside fluctuations in periods of high unemployment, transfers alone almost offset increased inequality in the distribution of market income.

Further, as shown in Table 1.16, overall poverty rates—as defined by Statistics Canada's Low Income Cutoffs—have changed rather little in the 1980s and 1990s. The incidence of poverty rises in periods of high unemployment and falls in periods of recovery, but there was little change between 1985 and 1993, which are roughly comparable years. However, the child poverty rate has remained stubbornly high in the 1990s, reflecting increased poverty among young families, while the poverty rate among the elderly has been declining over time. As explored later in Chap-

Table 1.16
Incidence of Low Income, 1980-1997

	1980	1985	1990	1993	1997
All Persons	16	17.7	15.4	18	17.5
Children	15.8	19.5	17.8	21.3	19.8
Elderly	34	28	21.3	22.8	18.7
Families, Head (Aged 25-34)	12.1	15.8	15.1	21.1	18.7

SOURCE: Statistics Canada Cat. 13-207, *Income Distributions by Size in Canada.* Text Table III and Table 66.

ter 5, the poverty rate has fallen only very slowly in the 1990s recovery, particularly for families with children.

John Myles and Garnett Picot of Statistics Canada [Garnett Picot and John Myles, *"Social Transfers, Earnings and Low Income Intensity Among Canadian Children,"* 1981-1996. Statistics Canada, May, 1999] recently noted that poverty lines which separate the poor from the non-poor provide only limited information on changes over time since they ignore the *intensity* of poverty, that is, the extent to which people with low incomes fall short of the poverty line. As the Nobel Prize-winning economist Amaryta Sen argued, the proportion of the population living in poverty in a country could be reduced just by redistributing income from the very poor to those just below the poverty line, pushing some out of poverty at the expense of much deeper poverty on the part of others. The fall in the poverty rate which results is clearly not a true indicator of social progress.

Myles and Picot use a broader indicator to show that, until 1993, transfers were not only offsetting the impact of falling market earnings on low-income families with children, but were also reducing the intensity of poverty among such families. This is a further *"good news"* story to add to the proven success of the transfer system in terms of reducing poverty and the depth of poverty among Canada's elderly. However, progress in terms of fighting poverty among families with children came to a halt from about 1993, when cuts to social assistance and UI benefits really began to bite, offsetting the modest increase in child benefits targeted to low-income families.

The overall stability in the overall distribution of disposable family income as the result of the tax/transfer system shows that government policies can and do have a very large impact on inequality and on the incidence of low incomes. Though not without many defects (such as poverty traps) and gaping holes, the welfare state has served Canadians relatively well in terms of holding market-driven inequality at bay, and has stopped Canada from becoming a highly unequal and polarized society like the U.S. Ironically, this fact has been celebrated by right-wing think tanks like the C.D. Howe Institute, which have nonetheless championed cuts to precisely those programs that made this result possible. The left has correctly pointed to the success of social programs, and the enormous implications of cuts in terms of dealing with poverty and increasing market-driven inequality. However, the fact remains that the task of cushioning the impact on incomes of unemployment, precarious employment, and the stagnation and increased inequality of market incomes has been very expensive, and has run into limits.

It is difficult to finance redistributive social programs in a high unemployment economy with a very insecure labour market because of mounting costs. Further, the growth of UI and social assistance benefits in the 1980s and into the 1990s was (in the context of slow growth, high interest rates, and a deep recession inflicted by macro-economic policy) a major cause of rising public debt, which squeezed government budgets. Further, the tax revenues needed to fight the erosion of market incomes (and to service the growth of debt) undoubtedly played a major role in sparking the cut-taxes/slash-social-spending policies adopted by most Canadian governments in the 1990s.

Recent spending cuts have begun to bite with a vengeance, placing in question the long-standing overall stability of poverty rates and the overall distribution of disposable family income in Canada. Table 1.17 shows the average level of income from various sources of families living in poverty in 1993 and 1996. (These figures cannot be added up to get an average income, since not all families receive income from all these sources.) The main story that emerges is that, while market earnings and other transfers (e.g., child benefits) have grown very modestly in this period of recovery, social assistance and UI benefits have been cut quite deeply. The result has been almost no decline in the child poverty rate in

Table 1.17
Average Income by Source of Families with Children Living in Poverty

	1993 $	1996 $
Two-Parent Families		
Market Earnings	8107	8276
Social Assistance	5518	4747
UI Benefits	2560	1436
Other Transfers	4574	4738
Lone-Parent Families		
Market Earnings	3777	4075
Social Assistance	7676	6103
UI Benefits	922	489
Other Transfers	3287	3579

SOURCE: John Myles and Garnett Picot. *Social Transfers, Earnings and Low Income Intensity Among Canadian Children, 1981-96*. Statistics Canada. May, 1999.

a period of recovery, and an increased depth of poverty. The *"cut-taxes/ cut-social-spending"* solution is obviously no solution at all for the poor, and no solution to the overall social problems of poverty and inequality.

Canada in an International Context

In assessing the well-being of working people, it is useful to look at Canada in a comparative international context, in meaningful terms. Our political leaders have frequently hailed Canada's No. 1 place in the United Nations Human Development Index, while glossing over the fact that the Index is very narrowly based. Canada's ranking drops significantly when income distribution and the relative position of women are taken into account. Put bluntly, Canada may well rank very highly for relatively affluent men, but we are a more unequal and insecure society than many continental European countries. They have done better by having more regulated labour markets and stronger welfare states.

Table 1.18 presents a comparison of the overall distribution of disposable (after-tax and transfer) income for a number of advanced industrial countries for the most recent year in which comparable data are available (usually the early to mid-1990s). For each country, the total population has been divided into 10 equally-sized groups or deciles, ranging from the top (highest income) 10% to the bottom (lowest income) 10%. (The data have been adjusted to take into account differences in family composition and other factors, and are from the Luxembourg In-

Table 1.18
National Income Distributions Compared

	Top/Bottom Decile	Bottom as % Middle	Top as % Middle	Child Poverty Rate (%)
U.S.	6.44	34	219	22.7
Canada	3.93	47	185	13.9
U.K.	4.56	46	210	17.9
Germany (W)	3.84	46	177	8.7
France	4.11	45	185	7.5
Netherlands	3.05	57	173	4.1
Sweden	2.78	57	159	2.7
Industrial Country Average	3.53	52	181	na

SOURCE: Luxembourg Income Study data in Timothy Smeeding. *"Income Inequality: Is Canada Different or Just Behind the Times?"* Paper presented to the 1999 meetings of the Canadian Economics Association.

come Study, an academic research body which has, for many years, been compiling national data on the computer system of the Government of Luxembourg, making the data as comparable as possible, and sponsoring comparative research studies.)

The first column of the table presents the ratio between the income of a person in the top 10% of the national income distribution compared to a person in the bottom 10%. (It is actually an underestimate of the gap between the richest and poorest, since the ratio calculated is between the top income of the bottom 10% and the bottom income of the top 10%, rather than between the average in each decile.)

As expected, the U.S. clearly emerges as the most unequal society, with the top 10% having incomes almost six times greater than the bottom 10%. The U.S. is very different from the most equal societies, Sweden and the Netherlands, where the top 10% have incomes only about three times larger than the bottom 10%. By this measure, the Scandinavian countries and the Benelux countries (Belgium, the Netherlands, and Luxembourg) stand at the high-equality end of a wide income distribution spectrum, with the U.K. and the U.S. standing at the other end. A similar pattern emerges when more technical measures of inequality are used.

Canada is a somewhat more unequal society than the average among industrial countries, with the top 10% having incomes almost four times larger than the bottom 10%. However, it is clearly a much more equal society than the U.S. or that other central paragon of *"free market"* capitalism, the United Kingdom.

The second and third columns of the table compare the bottom and top 10%, respectively, to the mid-point of the income distribution (median income). In most countries, the bottom 10% have incomes about half the middle level, but the U.S. again stands out as having a very poor underclass with incomes only one-third as high as the middle. In most industrial countries, the top 10% have incomes roughly twice as large as the middle, but the U.S. gives much more to its most affluent citizens than the average. If $50,000 was the median family income, the top 10% in the U.S. would begin at $109,500, the top 10% in Canada would begin at $92,500, and the top 10% in Sweden would begin at just $79,500.

Finally, the table shows dramatic differences in child poverty rates (with poverty defined as living in a family with less than half the middle income). A child is far more likely to live in poverty in the U.S., the U.K., and in Canada (where the current poverty rate is one in five by the Statistics Canada measure of low income) than in the continental European countries, and child poverty is of minimal proportions in Sweden and the Netherlands.

The dry statistical detail of the table disguises visible and tangible differences between countries. If a Canadian drives around any large U.S. city, she will be struck by the fact that there are fewer middle-class neighbourhoods than at home, and correspondingly more upper-class neighbourhoods with huge houses and new model cars, and more very low-income areas where the poor are concentrated and deprivation is clearly present. In many European countries, there are much smaller visible variations in living standards, with the great majority of the population living in apartments or modest houses.

It is sometimes argued that inequality is the price we have to pay for higher rates of growth and thus higher incomes. But, as noted above, per capita GDP growth rates in the U.S. in the 1980s and the 1990s have averaged no higher than those of other industrial countries. And the gap in incomes between the U.S. and other industrial countries—when adjusted for real purchasing power to eliminate the effects of fluctuating exchange rates—is modest at best. According to the Luxembourg Income Study, median income in Sweden and the Netherlands in the early 1990s was 86% and 83% of the U.S. level. Real GDP per hour worked in these countries is only a bit below the U.S. level, so that most of the modest U.S. income premium is paid for through longer hours of work.

We Canadians are highly inclined to compare ourselves to the U.S. and, in doing so, often forget to take into account the much greater extent of income inequality south of the border. It is true that Americans, on average, have somewhat higher incomes than Canadians. However, almost all of the extra income goes to the well-off and does not benefit the average working family. A recent study by Michael Wolfson of Statistics Canada found that, on average, U.S. families have an annual after-tax income $2,200 more than Canadian families. (This figure is in Canadian dollars, with the comparison made to equalize differences in purchasing power in the two countries.) While American families are better off "*on average*," a family at the precise mid-point of the income distribution in Canada is actually better off than an American family at the mid-point of the U.S. income distribution to the tune of $700. In fact, it is only the most affluent 20% of Canadian families who are significantly "worse off" in Canada than in the U.S.

Moreover, that income advantage for ordinary working families in Canada is supplemented by much higher levels of access to free or cheap public services, notably Medicare, but also higher education, public recreational facilities, and so on. (See Mark MacKinnon, *"The Myth of the Rich American," Globe and Mail Report on Business*, December 21, 1998.) Put simply, if a family on Planet Krypton were trying to decide where to send their future son, Superman, to be raised on Earth, they would be better off to aim his rocket at Canada (or, better still, at Sweden) since the absolute income advantage of the U.S. is monopolized by the very well-off in that society. Inserted randomly into the U.S. income distribution, Superboy would face much higher odds of growing up in poverty than in Canada or in continental Europe.

As discussed above, there are two major forces shaping the distribution of income and the level of low income and poverty in any country: 1) the *"primary"* distribution of income by the market, above all in the form of wages and salaries, and 2) the subsequent reshaping of the market distribution of income through the tax and income transfer system run by governments. The first of these factors is critical because wages and salaries make up such a large share of total income. It is very hard to create a relatively equal society with low rates of poverty if the *"primary"* distribution of income is highly unequal, since the scale of the redistribution required through government will be very large.

Relatively equal countries like Sweden and the Netherlands do have good social programs which redistribute income to some degree, but a lot of the work of the welfare state in those countries is concerned with taxing middle-class people in order to provide them with public benefits, rather than taxing them to provide benefits for others. It turns out that countries like Sweden are quite equal mainly because wages and salaries are distributed in a relatively equal way.

Table 1.19 provides some data on the structure of earnings in the countries considered above. The first column shows the ratio between the cut-off point for the top 10% of all full-time earners and the median wage (the wage earned by a full-time worker at the middle of the distribution of earnings). The figure of 2.04 for U.S. men means that the top 10% of male earners have wages or salaries at least 2.04 times the earnings of the median worker. The gap between top and middle male workers is somewhat lower in Canada at 1.73, and lowest in Sweden at 1.62. Thus, if an average worker made $30,000 per year, top earners in the U.S. would make at least $61,200, compared to $51,900 in Canada and $48,600 in

Table 1.19
The Structure of Earnings Compared

	Ratio of Top to Middle (Full-Time Earners)		% Incidence of Low Pay	
	Men	**Women**	**Men**	**Women**
U.S.	2.04	2.03	19.6	32.5
Canada	1.73	1.78	16.1	34.3
U.K.	1.86	1.82	12.8	31.2
Germany	1.64	1.59	7.6	25.4
France	1.60	1.60	10.6	17.4
Netherlands*	1.66		11.9	
Sweden	1.62	1.4	3.0	8.4

SOURCE: *OECD Employment Outlook.* July, 1996. Tables 3.1, 3.2. Low Pay defined as less than two-thirds median earnings. * No separate data for women and men.

Sweden. It is interesting to note that the structure of earnings is little different for women and men, and differences between countries follow the same general pattern.

The more significant difference between countries, as shown in the second column, is the incidence of low pay, defined as earnings by full-time workers which are less than two-thirds of the median full-time wage. The incidence of low pay is very high at about one in three for women working full-time in the U.S., Canada and the U.K., and is significant for men working full-time. The level of low pay is generally much lower in continental European countries, and is particularly low in Sweden. The major factors which counter low pay are the level of collective bargaining coverage, and the level of minimum wage protection. Overall, the data show that Canada is closer to the U.S. model when it comes to the structure of earnings of full-time workers. The gap between high earners and the middle is appreciably less than the U.S., but the incidence of low pay is quite comparable.

The second major determinant of income distribution differences between countries is the tax/transfer system. A major role of governments in all countries is to use the proceeds of the tax system to deliver programs and services to all citizens, and to supplement low incomes. In all countries, public pensions are crucially important for maintaining incomes and reducing poverty among the elderly, who no longer work, and transfers will largely determine whether or not the unemployed must endure poverty and low incomes. Further, transfers are becoming increasingly important as a means to raise the incomes of the working poor, that is, of people who are working but at very low wages.

Table 1.20 provides one indication of the different role played by the tax/transfer system in different countries. It shows the proportion of the population who fall below a poverty line defined as one-half median income, before and after transfers. As shown, the poverty rate for all households in Canada is cut in half, from 22.9% to 11.2%, by transfers, and transfers also cut the child poverty rate in half. The impact in Germany, France and Sweden is even more dramatic, indicating the high level of dependence on public spending by the elderly and the unemployed. The transfer system plays a major role in reducing poverty among working families with children in Canada, France and Sweden. These data clearly illustrate the much more limited role of the transfer system in the U.S.

Table 1.20
National Poverty Rates — Before and After ˙
the Impact of Transfers

	All Households		Two Adult-Working Families with Children	
	Before	After	Before	After
U.S.	25.3	17.7	15.4	12.7
Canada	22.9	11.2	12.6	6.4
Germany	22.1	5.5	3.1	1.5
France	34.5	8.2	18.7	2.1
Sweden	33.9	6.5	9.6	1.4

SOURCE: OECD Economics Department Working Paper #189 *Income Distribution and Poverty in Selected OECD Countries* (1998). Tables 5.4, 5.7. Poverty defined as income less than half median.

The level and distribution of income in different countries is affected by more than the structure of earnings and the tax/transfer system. The levels of unemployment and job creation, linked to economic growth, are also important. Nonetheless, it is clear that public policies which impact on the structure of the labour market (such as support for collective bargaining and minimum wages) can, in combination with the welfare state, produce quite different societies. All of the countries considered above have been subject to the same stresses of "*globalization*" in terms of increased trade with developing countries, and in terms of increased competition between the developed countries. All have experienced more or less the same pattern of technological change. But the social contexts within which these changes have taken place have produced quite different outcomes for working people.

While no one model has solved the problems of working people, by any means, the greatly increased inequality and insecurity experienced in the 1980s and 1990s by some working people were not experienced by all. The OECD recently noted that, among the advanced industrial countries, only the U.S. and the U.K. experienced a significant rise in income inequality from the mid-1970s to the mid-1980s, while inequality was actually stable or falling elsewhere. However, more disturbingly, there was an almost universal shift to greater inequality from the mid-1980s to the mid-1990s (*OECD Report on Income Inequality and Poverty,* 1998).

CONCLUSION

Set against a historical backcloth, the 1990s appear as one of the worst decades for the well-being of working people since the Great Depression. The reason for this lies principally with the poor macro-economic performance of the Canadian economy, driven as it was by high interest rate policies and neo-liberal restructuring.

The tax and transfer system has done a remarkably good job of helping to counter poverty and market inequality in Canada in the 1980s and 1990s. However, it is not a viable long-term proposition to argue that the welfare state can indefinitely hold at bay the consequences of economic stagnation and market-driven inequality. The architects of the welfare state built up after the Second World War—notably Leonard Marsh in Canada and William Beveridge in Britain—as well as the labour movements and social democratic parties which championed the growth of public provision, always recognized and argued that a strong and redistributive set of social programs had to rest on the firm foundation of a well-functioning labour market. Full employment and decent and rising wages were viewed as the primary element of security for working people, to be supplemented as needed by programs to deal with temporary unemployment, disability, illness, and old age.

In the 1990s, the fundamental challenge of creating security and well-being for workers in a market society has increased, since the market economy is now not only failing to deliver anything close to full employment, but is also generating more and more precarious and badly-paid jobs. Increasingly, the welfare state has been pushed in the direction not just of replacing occasional losses of wage income, but of supplementing inadequate incomes from employment—as in the recent expansion of child benefits targeted at low- and middle-income families. (The welfare state has also had to cope with massive social changes, such as the huge increase in the proportion of single-parent families, headed mainly by women.)

Much of the political debate in Canada today is narrowly defined as one between those who would maintain social programs and those who would cut them and accept the social consequences. While progressives will clearly support the first position, they must also argue that fixing the labour market and the primary distribution of income by the market are of fundamental importance if we are to create a more secure and equal society.

CHAPTER 2

Unemployment, Underemployment and Precarious Jobs

The 1990s have been marked by the poorest level of labour market performance since the Great Depression of the 1930s. The official unemployment rate rose sharply from 7.5% in 1989 to over 11% in 1992, and continued to hover between 9% and 10% for the next five years. Against this backcloth of poor job prospects, many workers were pushed into part-time and contingent work situations. Others were forced to hold multiple jobs or join the growing ranks of the "self-employed" simply because no other job prospects existed.

This chapter looks at trends in unemployment and underemployment in the 1990s, and the rapid growth of "non-standard" or precarious jobs: part-time jobs, contract work, and self-employment. The story that emerges is one of growing employment instability for large numbers of working people, and particularly for women, young people, Aboriginal people, and workers of colour.

JOB SHORTAGE OR SKILLS SHORTAGE?

Canada experienced a long recession in the early 1990s, followed by a very slow recovery. Unemployment has remained high over the period, although it has been falling since 1992. In a high unemployment economy, there are more job-seekers than jobs on offer from employers, and unemployment thus tends to be associated with the growth of jobs that offer less security to workers, provide lower pay, and reflect employer needs.

The fundamental reality of a shortage of jobs in Canada in the 1990s is sometimes denied in the often told story of "skill shortages." The story line is that Canada is in rapid transition to a "knowledge-based economy," and that the basic cause of unemployment and low pay is that too many unemployed workers lack the education and skills required in available "high knowledge" jobs. In this story, the unemployed and underemployed are at least partly to blame for their own fate—having underinvested in their "human capital"—and the answer is held to lie in more education and training. "Structural" unemployment is said to exist when there is a mismatch between the skills required in available jobs and the skills of unemployed workers, rather than a shortage of demand in the economy. For example, if unemployed workers are poorly educated and available jobs demand a high level of education in, say, computer programming, then stimulating the economy won't solve the problem. Yet, even people (like those in the Department of Finance and the OECD) who believe that Canada's level of "structural" unemployment is high accept that a significant part of the unemployment problem in the 1990s was a fundamental shortage of jobs.

An important recent study by Lars Osberg of Dalhousie University and Zhengxi Lin of Statistics Canada calculates that only about one percentage point of the unemployment rate in 1998 was the result of skills mismatches. Very, very few job vacancies go unfilled because of a shortage of qualified applicants. (L. Osberg and Z. Lin "How Much of Canada's Unemployment is Structural?" Paper presented to CSLS Conference on Structural Aspects of Unemployment in Canada. 1999. Available from www.csls.ca.) Further, recent research studies from the Departments of Finance and Human Resources Development show that the increase in Canadian unemployment in the 1990s is not due to accelerating technological change and rapid movement towards a "knowledge-based economy." Jobs are indeed demanding higher levels of skills and education, but this shift is no more rapid than in previous periods. (Tim Sargent "Skill Biased Technical Change and the Canadian Economy," Department of Finance, 1999 and Y. Gingras and R. Roy. "Is There a Skill Gap in Canada?" Department of Human Resources Development, 1998.) There may be isolated skills shortages in some areas, but the reality in Canada is that there are usually more than enough applicants to fill available jobs, and this has been true through the 1990s.

The real story in Canada is not one of "skill shortages," but of an ever more highly educated workforce chasing fewer and fewer jobs that actually demand high levels of qualifications. It is true that there has been a growth in the proportion of jobs requiring higher levels of education—driven not just by computers and high tech, but also by the growth of health care and education—but that growth has been outstripped by the surge in education and credentials among the workforce. Young people entering today's labour market are by far the highest educated generation in Canadian history. (Indeed, they are perhaps the most highly educated in the world.) Far too many are unemployed or underemployed, not because they lack skills, but because there are far too few jobs of any description.

THE UNEMPLOYMENT SQUEEZE

The existence of a high level of "cyclical" unemployment in Canada has meant that employers have had a lot of power in the labour market. The impact of unemployment on the power of employers to squeeze wages and vary the terms of employment in their own interests is not talked about a lot in polite company, but it is an important premise of current economic policy. The Bank of Canada has long been concerned to maintain unemployment at a high enough rate, above 8%, to keep wages in check and thus to achieve very low rates of inflation. The concept of a NAIRU (a Non-Accelerating Inflation Rate of Unemployment), on which this policy has been based, is disguised in technical jargon, but the basic idea is that a high level of unemployment is needed to keep workers in line. This perverse doctrine has been an important guide to Canadian economic policy and is partly responsible for unnecessarily high unemployment in the 1980s and 1990s. (See Andrew Jackson, "The NAIRU and Macro-Economic Policy in Canada," CLC Research Paper #12, 1998.)

To its credit, the Bank of Canada did keep interest rates low in 1998 and 1999 as the economy closed in on what had once been thought to be "full employment"—reflecting the view of the Bank that "hidden" unemployment remains high.

Beyond keeping a tight lid on wages, high unemployment has given employers a lot of room to radically restructure employment relationships in the 1990s. With many workers seeking the few available good jobs, employers have been able to "downsize" their workforces and require those left behind to work harder and longer. They have also been able to hire "contingent" workers, offering short-term contracts or part-time jobs with very variable hours instead of permanent, full-time jobs. The very rapid growth of self-employment in the 1990s has also been driven by the ability of large business firms and governments to contract out work in the knowledge that there would be a lot of competition for the contracts, and lots of savings to be achieved compared to having permanent full-time workers doing the work in-house.

It is increasingly recognized in the popular media that jobs have become more precarious and unstable with the rise of "lean" organizations and the rapid growth of "downsizing" and "restructuring." Lean production techniques mean that a shrinking group of "core" workers are kept in permanent jobs, but typically work harder as different job tasks are combined and as "unnecessary" labour is eliminated. Many "core" workers are also working longer, more variable hours in the form of both unpaid and paid overtime, as discussed in Chapter 3.

Meanwhile, the ranks of "peripheral" workers with a more tenuous and contingent relationship to employers have been growing apace. Workers are constantly told that full-time permanent jobs with a single employer are a thing of the past, and that they must be ready to move from job to job and from contract to contract. It is held to be unreasonable to expect a steady job. All we can "reasonably" expect in this new millennium, apparently, is some training to foster "employability" through a series of short-term contracts (though few workers in precarious jobs actually get much formal training at all).

This shift to precarious work is presented as something that is closely related to technological change and globalization, driven by anonymous and overwhelming forces which are somehow beyond human, let alone government, control. Lost in all of the rhetoric is the reality that precarious jobs have become the norm much faster in some countries than in others, and that the process is driven less by rapid "structural" change in the economy than by high unemployment combined with a largely deregulated labour market.

In much of Europe, unions and employment legislation have—at least until very recently—limited the growth of contract work and substandard part-time work. For example, in the Netherlands, which is recognized to have one of the most "flexible" labour markets in continental Europe and is often favourably contrasted with Germany and France, part-timers get equal wages and benefits with full-timers, and contract workers must be given a permanent job within a defined period of time. In the U.S., precarious work grew rapidly in the 1980s, but its growth has been limited (compared to Canada in the 1990s) by low unemployment. In Canada, the combination of high unemployment and weak employment standards has led to a particularly rapid growth of precarious forms of employment in the 1990s. There were, however, signs that this might have begun to change with stronger economic growth in 1998 and 1999.

All that said, it should be acknowledged that not all part-time jobs and not all forms of self-employment are precarious, and some of the growth does reflect the preferences of workers and not just the demands of employers.

UNEMPLOYMENT

In the monthly Statistics Canada Labour Force Survey, and in line with international conventions, a person is counted as unemployed if he or she is not working in the reference week (not even for a few hours) and is actively seeking a job. This is a reasonable though narrow definition, as Statistics Canada itself acknowledges through the occasional publication of broader measures. It leaves out of the picture those who are working in jobs which do not provide the hours of work desired, and also leaves out people who have given up looking for jobs because they believe—often quite reasonably—that no jobs are out there to be found.

As shown in Table 2.1, the national unemployment rate rose from 7.5% in 1989—the "low" point reached at the end of the 1980s economic expansion—to a high of 11.3% in 1992. In the subsequent recovery, it has fallen gradually to 8.3% in 1998 and to below 8% in 1999. At the end of 1999, the national rate fell below 7%. There was a substantial improvement in both 1997 and 1998 in line with improved economic growth of 3.8% in 1997 and 3.0% in 1998, and this continued into 1999.

The unemployment rate for men was lower than for women in 1989, but rose more rapidly in the recession. This reflected the fact that job losses in the 1990-92 recession were heavily concentrated in male-dominated sectors, notably manufacturing—where one in five jobs were lost—and construction. The rise in unemployment was disproportionately borne by young

Table 2.1
The Unemployment Rate in the 1990s

	1989	1992	1997	1998	1999
National Unemployment Rate	7.5	11.3	9.2	8.3	7.6
Men	7.3	12.1	9.2	8.5	7.8
Women	7.8	10.4	9.2	8.1	7.3
Age 15-24	11.2	17.8	16.7	15.2	14.0
Adults	6.6	9.9	7.8	7.0	6.3

SOURCE: Statistics Canada. *Labour Force Survey.*

people, who were entering a labour market where jobs were generally not available, least of all to those without experience. The youth unemployment rate peaked at 17.8% in 1992. As shown in Table 2.1, unemployment among adults has fallen back to close to the 1989 level, but in late 1999 it remained significantly higher among young people than in 1989.

Table 2.2 provides data on unemployment rates by province. The rise in unemployment from 1989 to 1992 was particularly severe in Ontario, reflecting the wave of plant closures which hit industrial communities as a result of the overvalued dollar and restructuring under the Canada-U.S. Free Trade Agreement. Quebec was also hit by the large loss of manufacturing jobs. Atlantic Canada saw already high unemployment rates increase in the recession, while lower unemployment rates in the West also increased.

The recovery from 1992 to 1998 has been strongest in Ontario—the major beneficiary of the fall of the dollar to realistic levels—and in the West. By 1998, unemployment rates in the West had fallen to below 1989 levels, while Ontario, Quebec, Newfoundland, and Nova Scotia had unemployment rates higher than in 1989. Only by late 1999 had unemployment across the country just about returned to the 1989 level.

Table 2.2
Provincial Unemployment Rates, 1989-1999

	1989	1992	1998	1999
Newfoundland	15.7	20.2	17.9	16.9
PEI	14.0	17.9	13.9	14.4
Nova Scotia	9.9	13.1	10.7	9.6
New Brunswick	12.4	12.8	12.1	10.2
Quebec	9.3	12.8	10.4	9.3
Ontario	5.1	10.9	7.2	6.3
Manitoba	7.6	9.7	5.7	5.6
Saskatchewan	7.5	8.2	5.9	6.1
Alberta	7.3	9.5	5.7	5.7
British Columbia	9.1	10.5	8.9	8.3

SOURCE: Statistics Canada. Labour Force Survey.

Table 2.3 shows the average duration of unemployment (calculated with an upper limit on unemployment of 99 weeks). Average duration jumped, as is usual in a downturn, from 17.8 weeks in 1989 to 22.6 weeks in 1992. Unusually, there has been no fall-back to the 1989 level in the 1992-to-

Table 2.3
Average Duration of Unemployment (Weeks)
(Top code 99 weeks)

	1976	1989	1992	1997	1998
All	13.9	17.8	22.6	22.3	20.4
Men	14.1	18.9	23.8	23.9	21.6
Women	13.7	16.5	20.8	20.4	18.9

SOURCE: Statistics Canada. *Labour Force Survey.*

1998 recovery for either men or women, indicating that unemployed workers have continued to find it very difficult to find jobs. That said, there was an appreciable decline from 1997 to 1998, a period of strong job creation.

"HIDDEN" UNEMPLOYMENT

People who do not actively seek work are not counted as unemployed. It is generally accepted, however, that some "non-participants" in the labour force would take or seek jobs if they were available, but have become discouraged by the fundamental lack of jobs. A narrow definition of discouraged workers is provided by the Labour Force Survey, which counts the number of workers who report that they wanted to work but were not actively seeking work because they believed that no suitable work was available, or because they were awaiting recall to a job or a reply to a job application. In 1998, 155,000 workers fell into these categories, a fall from 188,000 in 1997. The "official" unemployment rate in 1998 would have been about one percentage point higher if these workers had been included with the unemployed.

There are, however, strong reasons to believe that this is a significant underestimate of hidden unemployment. Usually, when an economy is growing rapidly and creating jobs, more and more workers are drawn into the labour force, while a stagnant economy leads to the withdrawal of workers from the workforce. One indication of this is that the labour force participation rate (the proportion of the working-age population who are working or seeking work) varies across the country with the health of the job market. The participation rate in 1998 was above average in Ontario and the West, where job creation rates have been strongest, and below average in most of Atlantic Canada and Quebec. (The age structure of the population also plays a role in these differences.)

Table 2.4 shows trends in the participation rate in the 1990s. In-dicating the weakness of the recovery, the participation rate continued to fall from 1992 to 1997, and only began to recover to the 1989 level in 1998. Over the entire 1989-to-late-1999 period of recession and slow recovery, the proportion of the working-age population either working or actively looking for work fell from 67.5% to 65.5%. As is further shown in the table, this decline was mainly experienced by young people aged 15 to 24, and by men.

Table 2.4
Labour Force Participation Rates, 1989-1999

	1989	1992	1997	1998	1999 (Oct)
National	67.5	65.9	64.8	65.1	65.5
Men	77.1	74.0	72.5	72.4	72.5
Women	58.3	58.0	57.4	58.1	58.7
Age 15-24	70.6	65.3	61.2	62.0	63.8
Adults	66.7	66.0	65.5	65.8	65.8

SOURCE: Statistics Canada. *Labour Force Survey.*

If the labour force participation rate in 1998 had been the same as in 1989, there would have been another 375,000 unemployed workers, and the un-employment rate would have been 10.5% instead of 8.3%. There has been an ongoing debate over whether this kind of calculation is legitimate. It is noted by Statistics Canada—quite correctly—that the fall in the participa-tion rate since 1989 has been driven by factors other than the high unem-ployment economy, notably increased school enrolment and earlier retire-ment among men. (Deborah Sunter and Geoff Bowlby, *"Labour Force Participation in the 1990s,"* Statistics Canada Cat. 11-010-XPB. *Cana-dian Economic Observer.* October, 1998.) However, the picture gets murky because some increased school enrolment and some early retirement has probably been driven by the lack of jobs. In this context, it is useful to compare the Canadian and U.S. experiences, since it is likely that differ-ences reflect stronger growth in the U.S. rather than a lesser desire to work on the part of Canadians.

Between 1989 and 1997, the overall U.S. participation rate rose from 66.5% to 67.1%. As shown in Table 2.5, the fall in the participation rate for both young men and young women was much more marked in Canada than the U.S. In fact, it was twice as large among young men and about four times greater among young women. These differences do reflect increased enrolments in school and in post-secondary education. In Canada, the enrolment rate of young people aged 16 to 19 rose from 74% to 81% between 1989 and 1997, compared to an increase from 74% to 78% in the U.S. For young people aged 20 to 24, the enrolment rate in Canada rose dramatically from 28% to 39% in the 1990s, compared to an increase from 27% to 34% in the U.S.

Not only have more Canadian young people been attending school full-time, but the proportion of students working in part-time jobs or looking for work fell from 47% to 40% between 1989 to 1997. A reasonable conclusion to draw is that a large part of the plummeting youth participation rate reflects the lack of job opportunities, but that some of it is explained by an increased desire to stay in school longer and to acquire better qualifications.

Table 2.5
Participation Rates in Canada and the U.S., 1989-1997

	Canada		U.S.	
	1989	1997	1989	1997
Men				
Age 15-24	73.4	63.4	73.0	68.2
Age 25-54	93.8	91.1	93.7	91.8
Age 55-64	66.2	60.6	67.2	67.6
Women				
Age 15-24	67.8	59.0	64.4	62.6
Age 25-54	74.7	76.6	73.6	76.7
Age 55-64	34.4	36.5	45.0	50.9

SOURCE: Statistics Canada Cat. 71-005. Labour Force Update. Canada-U.S. Labour Market Comparison. Autumn, 1998.

As further shown in the Table, there has been a sharp fall in the labour force participation rate of older men in Canada in the 1990s—from 66.2% in 1989 to 60.6% in 1997. This has not taken place in the U.S. There has been a long-term trend to earlier retirement among Canadian men (though not among women) and the proportion of men aged 55-64 who are still working has fallen from 77% in 1976 to about 61% today. It is difficult to sort out how much of this reduction in the age of retirement, which clearly accelerated in the 1990s, is due to "push" as opposed to "pull' factors. In many cases, corporate and public sector "downsizing" was eased through severance and early retirement packages for older workers, some of whom accepted willingly, some of whom had no alternative, and some of whom likely accepted to save younger workers from layoff. The fact that the trend to earlier retirement among men has been so much more marked in Canada than in the U.S. is probably not due to the availability of better pensions as such, though early retirement incentives were likely used to a much greater extent.

It should finally be noted that the permanent layoff rate among Canadian men in the 1990s has been significantly higher than in the late 1970s (8.6% in 1994 vs. 6.9% in 1978), and that large numbers of older men in Canada clearly fell victims to the wholesale industrial restructuring of the 1990-92 recession. (Data from Sunter and Bowlby.)

THE PATTERN OF JOB CREATION IN THE 1990S

Table 2.6
Employment by Class of Worker (000s) , 1989-1998

	1989	1992	1997	1998	% Change 1989-98
Total Employment	13,086	12,842	13,941	14,326	9.5
Self-Employment	1,809	1,936	2,488	2,525	39.6
Paid Employees					
Full-time	9,449	8,937	9,349	9,679	2.4
Part-time	1,828	1,969	2,103	2,122	16.1

SOURCE: Statistics Canada. *Labour Force Survey.*

Table 2.6 shows changes in total employment by "class of worker" or type of employment in the 1990s. The employed are divided into three main groups: the self-employed, people working in full-time paid jobs with an employer, and those in part-time paid jobs with an employer. The most striking fact to emerge from this data is that the total number of full-time paid jobs which existed in 1989 was not regained until 1998. Thus, all of the employment created over that period was in the form of self-employment, or part-time paid jobs. Self-employment grew by 40% over the 1989-to-1998 period, growing through the recession and the recovery. By contrast, full-time paid employment grew by just 2.4% over the period. Part-time paid employment grew much more rapidly at 16.1%. It should be noted that full-time paid jobs did increase significantly from 1997 to 1998 and that self-employment fell in 1999, suggesting that employers have again begun to hire in line with the fall in the national unemployment rate towards more "normal" levels.

Table 2.7 looks at the same pattern in a way that shows changes for women and men. Overall, 58% of the new "jobs" of the 1990s through 1998 came in the form of self-employment, but this reliance on self-employment was greater for men than for women. As of 1998, the total number of full-time paid jobs held by men had still not regained the 1989 level. By contrast, one in three new jobs for women in the 1989-98 period still came in the form of full-time paid jobs. While women obviously did much better than men in the very weak job market of the 1990s, it is still striking that 42% of the new "jobs" for women came in the form of self-employment, and that 25% came in the form of part-time paid jobs. The absolute number of women entering self-employment was almost as great as the number of men entering such "jobs." Clearly, employment growth in the 1990s was heavily dominated by the growth of precarious jobs for both women and men.

Table 2.7
Changes in Employment 1989-98 (000s)

Change in Employment (1,240)
of which

		Contribution to Job Growth
Self-employment	716	57.7%
Part-time Paid Jobs	294	23.7%
Full-time Paid Jobs	230	18.5%

Change in Men's Employment (447)
of which

Self-employment	385	86.1%
Part-time Paid Jobs	97	21.7%
Full-time Paid Jobs	-37	-8.3%

Change in Women's Employment (794)
of which

Self-employment	330	41.6%
Part-time Paid Jobs	197	24.8%
Full-time Paid Jobs	267	33.6%

SOURCE: Statistics Canada. *Labour Force Survey.*

SELF-EMPLOYMENT

It is very difficult to generalize about self-employment, which is at least as varied a category as paid jobs. Certainly, not all of the self-employed are in truly precarious jobs, and a significant minority are extremely well-paid and have little or no trouble finding clients or customers. Successful lawyers, accountants, architects, and doctors are usually self-employed through partnerships or incorporated businesses, and they have been joined in the 1980s and 1990s by other highly educated, self-employed professionals in "new" occupations such as business consultants, computer consultants, and the like. The self-employed also include the owners of traditional small enterprises, such as farmers and fishermen, and the owners of stores and construction companies, among other small (and larger) businesses which will be variably successful. At the other end of the pay spectrum, there are self-employed care-givers for children and cleaners who earn very little, and may often have to scramble for work.

Rates of self-employment are high and generally rising in traditional areas such as construction and the retail trade, and growth has been particularly strong in the 1990s in a large category known as "business services." This consists of smaller enterprises selling services to other businesses. In this case, the growth of self-employment is a direct product of the trend to contracting-out of work as a direct alternative to hiring employees and conducting work in-house. As of 1998, one in five men and one in seven women in the Canadian workforce were self-employed (21% and 14%, respectively), though the growth of self-employment in the 1990s was equally divided between women and men.

The self-employed tend to be older than paid workers, and only 25% are less than 35 years of age. (Data from Statistics Canada, Labour Force Survey.) Typically, hours worked are longer than those for paid workers, averaging 42 hours per work compared to 36 hours per week in 1996. An interesting recent analysis has shown that there is a very high rate of turnover among the self-employed, with almost one in four of the self-employed just starting their own business in any given year in the 1990s, and with almost one in five of the self-employed winding up in their businesses in any given year. (See Z. Lin, G. Picot and J. Yates, *The Entry and Exit Dynamics of Self-Employment in Canada*, Statistics Canada, October, 1998.)

Analysis by Statistics Canada has shown that self-employment is more polarized between high and low earners than is paid employment.

Table 2.8
Annual Earnings by Class of Worker (1995)

	Employees	Self-Employed	
		Employer	Own Account (as % employees)
All Workers	33,700	41,000	22,900 (68%)
Men	40,100	44,900	27,200 (68%)
Women	26,800	28,800	14,800 (55%)

SOURCE: Statistics Canada Cat. 71-005-XPB. *Labour Force Update: The Self-Employed*. Autumn, 1997. Table 8. Data are for those with job tenure of more than 16 months, and excluding negative earnings.

As noted in Chapter 1, the self-employed are heavily represented in the ranks of Canada's top 1% of income earners. Self-employed "workers" who are themselves employers of other workers tend, unsurprisingly, to be the most highly paid. Data for 1995 (see Table 2.8) show this group had average annual earnings of $41,000, and 6.7% earned more than $100,000 in that year. (Statistics Canada Cat. 71-005-XPB. *Labour Force Update: The Self-Employed.* Autumn, 1997.) By contrast, "own account" self-employed workers—those who just worked for themselves—had average annual earnings of just $22,900 in 1995, and women "own account" workers had average annual incomes of just $14,800. Male "own account" workers averaged just 68% of the annual earnings of male paid workers, while women "own account" workers averaged just 55% as much as women paid workers. In 1995, only one in 10 "own account" self-employed workers earned more than $50,000, and six in 10 made less than $20,000. Few self-employed workers enjoy access to benefits or paid vacations.

The poorer performance of self-employed women has meant that the rapid rise in self-employment has slowed progress in closing the gender pay gap. The gap between men's and women's earnings is much more pronounced among the self-employed. As Table 2.9 reveals, the earnings gap between men and women who work full-time was 72.8% in 1996. Self-employed women with employees, by contrast, earned just 69.2% of their male peer's earnings, while the gap between male and female own account self-employed workers was even wider with women earning just 67.3% of men's earnings.

Almost 72% of women who are self-employed earn less than $20,000 a year, compared to 48% of women in paid employment. While almost 40% of women paid employees have earnings between $20,000

Table 2.9
Average Earnings for Self-Employed Men and Women, 1996

	Total ($)	Employees ($)	Self-Employed ($)			Self-employed earnings (% of employees)		
			Total	OA	Emp	Total	OA	Emp
Men	39274	40740	29816	25346	43891	73.1	62.2	107.7
Women	26091	27111	16814	15070	27642	62.0	55.6	102.0
Women as % of men	66.4	66.5	56.4	59.5	63.0			

OA- Own account self-employed   Emp - Employer
SOURCE: Karen D. Hughes, Gender and Self-Employment in Canada, Ottawa: Canadian Policy Research Network, 1999.

and $40,000, this is the case for only 17% of women who are self-employed. [Zhengzi Lin, Garnett Picot, and Janice Yates, "The Entry and Exit Dynamics of Self-Employment in Canada," (Ottawa: Statistics Canada Research Paper No. 134, March 1999)].

The massive growth of self-employment has sometimes been heralded as indicative of a welcome surge of entrepreneurship on the part of Canadians, and "making your own job" has been praised as the path to creative self-fulfillment. And it is true that self-employment has been driven by more than a shortage of paid jobs. It has grown in good times and bad times alike (though perhaps for different reasons), and there is no doubt that many people do prefer to work for themselves, particularly those who own successful enterprises. It may be the case that large workplaces, following restructuring and downsizing, have become so stressful that people are eager to get out just to escape the boss. However, the evidence clearly shows that the recent growth of self-employment has been overwhelmingly dominated by the growth of the relatively badly-paid "own account" jobs.

Table 2.10
Growth of Self-Employment By Type, 1989-98 (000s)

	1989	1992	1997	1998	Change 1989-98
1) Total self-employment	1809	1936	2488	2525	716
2) of which unincorporated, no paid help	822	904	1282	1351	529
2 as % of 1	45.4	46.7	51.5	53.5	

SOURCE: Statistics Canada. Labour Force Survey.

As shown in Table 2.10, three in four (73.9%) of the 716,000 new "jobs" that came in the form of self-employment between 1989 and 1998 were "own account" jobs where average earnings are much lower than in paid jobs. As a result, the proportion of all the self-employed who are "own account" workers rose from 45.4% to 53.5% of the total. The fastest growing occupations among the self-employed in the 1990s were providers of "non-institutional social services"—mainly child care—whose numbers jumped by 39%, from 1991-96, and providers of "services to buildings and dwellings"—i.e., janitors and cleaners—whose numbers jumped by 28% over the same period. (See "Shattering the Glass Box," Industry Canada. 1998. Available from www.ic.gc.ca.) This pattern is quite different from the 1980s, when only one-third of the growth of self-employment was driven by the increase in "own account" jobs. (For a detailed analysis, see *Labour Force Update: The Self-Employed*. Autumn, 1997.) The small decline in the number of self-employed workers in 1999 likely indicates that paid jobs will be taken by these "own account" workers as and when they become available.

TEMPORARY JOBS

As noted in Chapter 1, the likelihood of a new job lasting more than six months has been declining in the 1990s. This reflects a shift to short-term contract jobs. About one in eight paid workers now hold temporary jobs, that is, jobs with a formally defined end-date. As shown in Table 2.11, the incidence of such jobs in 1995 was slightly higher among women, and much higher (at about one in four) among young people. Temporary work is more common in the public than in the private sector (14% vs. 11% of all of the jobs in the sector), and is more common in small than large

Table 2.11
Employed in Temporary Jobs, 1991-1995

	1991 (%)	1995 (%)
All Paid Workers	4.9	11.6
Men	5.0	10.7
Women	4.8	12.6
Age 15-24	9.0	23.0
Public Sector	5.0	14.0
Private Sector	5.0	11.0

SOURCE: Statistics Canada Cat. 71-535-MPB #8. *Work Arrangements in the 1990s*. Tables 1.6a, 1.6b.

businesses. Governments, then, have driven the increase in contracting-out more than very large corporations.

Contract work is common in many non-managerial occupations, including professionals, though relatively rare among industrial workers. Temporary jobs typically provide both shorter hours and lower pay than permanent jobs; so weekly earnings in 1995 averaged $374 compared to $579 for those in permanent jobs. Unsurprisingly, pension coverage was much lower for those in temporary jobs (20% vs. 55% for workers in permanent jobs) and access to other benefits was similarly much lower. (Lee Grenon and Barbara Chun, *"Non-Permanent Paid Work,"* in Statistics Canada, *Perspectives on Labour and Income*, Autumn, 1997.) While some workers, particularly students, may be happy with temporary jobs, this is highly unlikely to be the case for many adults, and the growth of temporary work clearly reflects the unwillingness of employers to enter into permanent commitments (even though these are relatively easily broken).

The data in Table 2.11 indicate that the proportion of paid workers employed on temporary contracts grew very rapidly in the 1990s, from about 5% in 1991 to almost 12% in 1995. (This very sharp increase may partly reflect a change in definition, but another survey, the General Social Survey, put the incidence of temporary work in 1989 at 8%, so that the general pattern of change is quite clear.) The shift to contract jobs appears to be continuing: one in four of the new paid jobs created between May 1998 and May 1999 were temporary jobs. As with the growth of self-employment, the shift from permanent to contract jobs has been more marked in Canada than in the U.S.

PART-TIME JOBS

As noted in Table 2.6 above, part-time paid employment grew much more rapidly over the 1989-98 period than did full-time paid employment (16.1% vs. 2.1%). Almost six out of 10 new paid jobs created in this period were part-time, though full-time job creation did pick up speed in the higher growth years of 1994, 1997 and 1998. Part-time employment actually fell in 1999. (A part-time job is defined as one providing less than 30 hours work per week.) The heavy tilt of job creation to part-time is a continuation of a trend that dates back more than 20 years, though the proportion of workers working part-time held steady through the recovery period of the 1980s and accelerated again only in the recession of the early 1990s. Since the recession, the part-time rate has more or less held steady.

Table 2.12
Who is Working Part-Time?
(May 1999) %

All Workers	17.3
Young Workers (Age 15-24)	42.2
Men 25+	4.2
Women 25+	21.1
Permanent	14.5
Temporary	37.6
Workplace Size	
1-20	24.6
20-99	17.4
100-500	10.4
500+	8.5
Union Members	12.4
Non-Union Members	19.7
Health	25.9
Sales and Service	36.2

SOURCE: Statistics Canada. *Labour Force Survey*. Seasonally adjusted data for employees only.

Table 2.12 provides some basic data on who was working part-time in mid-1999. About one in six paid workers were in part-time jobs (17.3%). (The overall part-time rate is a bit higher at 18.1%, since the self-employed are somewhat more likely to work part-time than paid workers.) Very few adult men (4.2%) work in part-time jobs, and part-time work is heavily concentrated among young people (42.2%) and adult women (21.1%). As shown, part-time jobs are much more common in small work-places. There is a high level of over-lap with temporary jobs: 38% of tem-porary workers held part-time jobs. Part-time workers also tend to be concentrated in sales and service jobs, and in health care and other public services. One in five non-union workers are in part-time jobs, compared to one in eight union members.

The majority of part-time jobs are held by choice. As shown in Table 2.13, about one in four part-timers clearly report that they want part-time jobs. In addition, going to school and fulfilling family responsibili-ties are major reasons for working part-time. It should, however, be noted that caring for children and other family responsibilities may be a "con-

Table 2.13
Reason for Part-Time Work (1998) %

	All Part-Time Workers	Women (Age 25-44)
"Voluntary"		
Caring for Children; other personal/family responsibilities	14.7	37.4
Going to School	26.5	4.2
Personal Preference/Voluntary Decision	27.2	23.8
"Involuntary"		
Wanted Full-time/Business Conditions: looked for full-time	10.0	10.3
Wanted Full-time/Business Conditions: did not look for full-time	19.3	22.7

SOURCE: Statistics Canada. *Labour Force Survey*.

strained choice" for many part-timers, particularly adult women. Lack of affordable, quality child care, and the need to provide home care for the sick and elderly in the absence of other supports (including by men) partly determines this "choice" by women.

An increasing proportion of part-timers, particularly adult women, would, however, rather work full-time. Over the past 20 years, the proportion of part-timers who report that they work part-time because they could only find full-time work has ratcheted upwards, from 10.6% in 1976 to 20.1% in 1989, and to 29.5% in 1992. For "core age" women aged 25 to 44, the proportion of "involuntary" part-timers has increased even faster, from 9.1% in 1976 to 23.3% in 1989, and to 32.0% in 1992. (Labour Force Survey data.) Statistics Canada now further questions such involuntary part-timers as to whether or not they actively looked for a full-time job. If both those who looked and did not actively look in the reference week are counted as "involuntary" part-timers, it can be seen that, in 1998, about one in three part-timers—29.3% of all part-timers and 34.0% of adult women—were not working part-time by choice, and that the rate of involuntary part-time work has not fallen in the recovery period since 1992. Even on the basis of a very narrow definition, three in 10 part-timers are underemployed.

Clearly, the restructuring of work by employers has produced many more part-time jobs than there are workers who willingly want to work part-time. This conclusion is also suggested by the recent growth of multiple job holding. As of 1997, 10% of people working part-time in their main job held another part-time job. The combining of part-time jobs to get the desired total hours of work has grown particularly fast among women, and 5.9% of all working women are now multiple job holders, compared to 4.6% of men. An astonishing 8.8% of women in their early twenties were multiple job holders in 1997. (Deborah Sussman. "Moonlighting: A Growing Way of Life," Statistics Canada, *Perspectives on Labour and Income*, Summer, 1998.) Further, in 1995, 50% of part-time workers reported that they wanted to work more hours, suggesting that hours in part-time jobs (averaging 17 per week) are low even from the point of view of people who want less than 30 hours work per week. (Data from the 1995 Survey of Work Arrangements.)

It is often simply assumed by many commentators that the "flexible" part-time jobs offered by employers meet the needs of many workers for "flexible" hours. However, while it is true that part-time work takes up fewer hours per week in total, it is not at all the case that part-time hours are readily combined with family, school, and other activities. Table 2.14 shows the work schedules of full-time and part-time workers, further broken down by union and non-union status. As shown, an astonishing 37.9% of non-union part-timers and 26.3% of even unionized part-timers worked irregular shifts or on a purely on-call basis in 1995. The normal pattern in sectors like retail trade and restaurants is for shift schedules to be posted only days in advance, and workers who cannot meet the variable hourly demands of employers are often dismissed. Such variable hours are clearly unlikely to be desired by students, by workers looking after children, or those trying to hold more than one part-time job. High proportions of part-timers also work regular "unsocial" evening or night hours, and the great majority work on weekends. This may allow child care to be shared, but often at the cost of family life.

Table 2.14
Work-Schedules: "Flexible" for Whom?

	Full-Time		Part-Time	
	Union	Non-Union	Union	Non-Union
Worked Weekends	27.2	28.9	77.6	84.5
Regular Non-Day	23.4	12.1	27.7	22.4
Irregular, On Call	7.2	10.0	26.3	37.9

SOURCE: Statistics Canada. *Survey of Work Arrangements, 1995.* (unpublished data)

Even when workers want part-time jobs, wages and benefits usually leave a lot to be desired. In May 1999, paid part-timers earned, on average, $206 per week or $11.84 per hour for 17.4 hours of work (Labour Force Survey). The average hourly wage was 74% of that of full-timers, who earned an average $16.08 per hour. The pay and benefits gap is much greater among non-union part-timers. As shown in Table 2.15, non-union part-timers (three in four of all part-timers) earned just 64.4% of the wage of other non-union workers. As fur-

Table 2.15
The Part-Time Hourly Wage Gap (1997)

	Part-Time Wage as % Full-Time Wage	
	Union	Non-Union
All Workers	88.0	64.4
Men	83.4	55.8
Women	94.3	75.5
Firms		
< 20 workers	85.7	74.1
500+ workers	96.7	65.0

SOURCE: Statistics Canada. *Labour Force Study.*

Table 2.16
Workers in Low Wage Jobs (%)

	Full-Time Workers	Part-Time Workers
Women		
Union	7	15
Non-union	37	67
Men		
Union	4	na
Non-union	23	77

SOURCE: Statistics Canada. *Survey of Work Arrangements*. November 1995. (unpublished data) Low wage is defined as earning less than two-thirds the economy-wide median wage, i.e. jobs paid less than $9.33 per hour.

ther shown in Table 2.16, an extraordinarily high proportion of non-union part-timers—67% of women and 77% of men—were low-wage workers in 1995, earning less than $9.33 per hour. (This is two-thirds of the economy-wide median wage, or about enough to maintain a single person working full-time above the poverty line.) For the most part, then, part-time jobs are badly paid, the exception being unionized part-time jobs which are mainly found in public services, particularly health care, and in some unionized parts of the private services sector such as large stores and offices.

As also revealed in Table 2.17, there is a large benefits gap between full- and part-time workers, and very few non-union part-timers have access to non-wage benefits. Just 7.4%, for example, are covered by a pension plan. Entitlements to paid holidays are much less generous than those of full-time workers, when they are provided at all.

Table 2.17
The Part-Time Benefit Gap (1995)
(% of Workers Covered)

	Union		Non-Union	
	Full-Time	Part-Time	Full-Time	Part-Time
Pension	86.6	56.7	40.7	7.4
Health Plan	88.9	47.8	55.2	9.0
Dental Plan	81.7	44.2	52.2	8.0

SOURCE: Statistics Canada. *Survey of Work Arrangements.* November, 1995. (unpublished data)

Part-time work is not necessarily a bad thing. Many workers, particularly women with young children and young people, want to work part-time, if only for a few years. A minority of part-time workers, mainly those in unionized workplaces, get the same or close to the same hourly wages of equivalent full-timers and access to benefits plans. In a handful of union-ized environments—*The Toronto Star* newspaper is one example—full-timers can reduce their hours as a matter of choice, with a right to return to full-time work. That said, the great majority of part-timers work in badly-paid jobs which provide limited, if any, benefits, and many work very unpredictable hours. In this context, the disproportionate growth of part-time jobs in the 1990s counts mainly as bad news for working people.

JOBS IN SMALL BUSINESS

The constant propaganda of small business lobbyists would lead Canadi-ans to believe that small businesses are the major creators of new jobs, but—leaving aside the phenomenal growth of "own account" jobs described above—this is not the case. In fact, as illustrated in Figure 2.1, there has been a lot of stability in the distribution of private sector employment in the 1980s and 1990s, and the overall jobs share of very small businesses with less than 20 employees has modestly fallen in the 1990s.

There is, indeed, a very high rate of job creation each year in small firms, but this is almost matched by a very high rate of job destruc-

Figure 2.1
Distribution of Employment by Firm Size, 1989-97 (Business Sector)

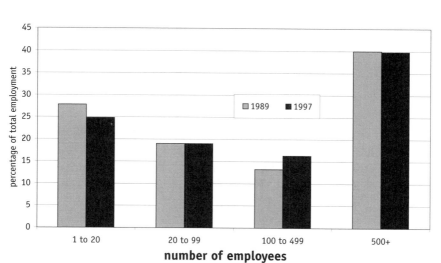

Source: Marie Drolet and René Morissette, Recent Canadian Evidence on Job Quality by Firm Size (Ottawa: Statistics Canada Analytical Studies Branch, Paper #128, 1998).

Table 2.18
Average Annual Job Gains and Losses,
by Firm Size, 1978-92

	Firm Size			
	1 - 19	**20 - 49**	**100 - 499**	**500 +**
Job Gains	23.4	15.9	12.2	6.8
Job Losses	-20.2	-14.2	-11.2	-6.6

SOURCE: G. Picot, J. Baldwin and R. Dupuy. *"Small Firms and Job Creation: A Reassessment."* Statistics Canada. *Canadian Economic Observer.* January, 1995.

tion. As shown in Table 2.18, job "churning" in the small business sector is much greater than among large firms. Large corporations may restructure, downsize and contract out, but they rarely disappear from the economic landscape, while very small firms are born in great numbers, but tend to have very short lives. What this means is that the number of new jobs "created" each year by small businesses is much higher than jobs created by medium and large business, but they tend not to last for very long. By contrast, jobs with large employers are not growing, but they tend to be more stable.

Table 2.19
Small is Ugly: Average Hourly Wages and
Benefits of Full-Time Workers (1997)

	Firm Size			
	1 - 19	**20 - 99**	**100 - 499**	**500 +**
Men				
Wage	$13.87	$15.30	$16.73	$20.16
Pension Coverage	13.3%	33.2%	53.5%	73.6%
Women				
Wage	$10.95	$11.72	$12.73	$14.93
Pension Coverage	5.7%	22.5%	34.0%	53.2%

SOURCE: Drolet and Morissette. (1998).

Jobs with large private sector employers tend to be much better jobs in terms of pay, benefits and even working hours than jobs with small employers. Table 2.19 provides data on hourly wage rates and pension plan coverage for men and women in the private sector by firm size. When other differences between large and small firms, such as unionization, are controlled for (which they are not in the Table), the pay gap between firms with less than 20 workers and those with more than 500 is still about 20%. This pay gap has been more or less constant, in the 1986-97 period. (See Drolet and Morissette, 1998.)

The overall stability of the total job share of larger firms is quite striking. The majority of private sector workers still work for firms with at least 100 workers. That said, very little of the job growth in the 1990s has been in the form of paid jobs with employers, as opposed to "own account" employment, and much of the job growth there has come in the form of part-time jobs.

WORKERS OF COLOUR AND ABORIGINAL CANADIANS IN THE LABOUR FORCE

Unemployment, under-employment, and the growth of precarious jobs have disproportionately impacted upon equality-seeking groups who have long faced discrimination and barriers to obtaining and keeping steady, well-paid jobs. While the situation of women is visible in the Labour Force Survey data, it is unfortunate that data for workers of colour and Aboriginal workers is only intermittently available from the Census.

About one in ten workers are defined as members of "visible minority" groups in the Census, of whom more than 80% were born outside Canada and are relatively recent immigrants. A number of studies have shown that, over the 1980s and 1990s, workers of colour who are immigrants have faced increasing difficulties closing the employment gap with native-born Canadians compared to earlier generations of immigrants, while even workers of colour born in Canada typically hold less stable and worse-paid jobs than other Canadians. In 1996, average income from employment for immigrants coming to Canada between 1986 and 1990 was 18% lower than the earnings of non-immigrants. For those arriving after 1990, earnings were 36% lower. (Statistics Canada, The Daily, May 20 1998).

These gaps remain even when differences such as age and education are taken into account. Typically, recent immigrants are younger than the workforce as a whole, but also more highly educated. Foreign credentials, however, are often not accepted in Canada, contributing greatly to the high concentration of workers of colour in relatively low-wage jobs. Overt racial discrimination, of course, also plays a major role.

As shown in Table 2.20, visible minority workers earned 15% less on average in 1995 than did all other workers, the same gap as in the 1991 Census. Full-time, full-year visible minority workers earned 14% less on average. Visible minority immigrants to Canada in the 1990s earned much less, averaging just over $15,000. Studies have found that the pay gap is much greater for visible minority men than women, though this should be placed in the context of the much lower level of earnings among women compared to men. The pay gap partly reflects the fact that only four in 10 recent immigrants are in skilled jobs, compared to six in 10 of all workers.

Table 2.20
Workers of Colour and Aboriginal Workers:
Average Earnings (1995)

All Workers	
National average	$26,474
Visible Minority Workers	$22,498
	(-15%)
of whom immigrated: 1976-85	$24,279
1986-90	$19,960
1991-95	$15,042
Aboriginal workers	$17,382

SOURCE: 1996 Census data. The Daily. May 12, 1998.

Low earnings reflect not just concentration in low-paying jobs, but also higher rates of unemployment. In 1995, visible minority workers experienced an unemployment rate of 14.2% compared to 10.1% for all workers (data from Statistics Canada 1996 Census). Black workers experienced an unemployment rate of 19.3%. Low earnings result in much higher poverty rates for workers of colour. The 1996 Census found that 36% of visible minority households lived in poverty in 1995, almost double the average level of 20%. 45% of Black households lived in poverty.

Self-identified Aboriginal workers make up just 2.3% of the working age population, but the Aboriginal population is growing very fast and already makes up a large share of the labour force in some Canadian cities. Despite very fast population growth, the proportion of the Aboriginal population who participate in the workforce has remained more or less constant in the 1990s. However, few move into steady, well-paid jobs. The 1996 Census data show that 59% of Aboriginal people reported employment income, not too much lower than 66% of the general population. However, only one in three Aboriginal people worked full-time, full-year, and this proportion was even lower for those living on reserves. The unemployment rate for Aboriginal workers in both 1991 and 1996 was a very high 24.5%, well over double the overall unemployment rate.

As shown in the table, Aboriginal workers earned, on average, just over $17,000 in 1995, or 34% below the Canadian average. About 44% of the off-reserve Aboriginal population lived in poverty in that year, and poverty rates on reserve are even higher.

Workers With Disabilities

Labour market data for workers with disabilities is not provided from most Statistics Canada surveys, but some limited information is available for 1991. (Gail Fawcett, *Living With Disability in Canada: An Economic Portrait*, Human Resources Development Canada, 1996.) In that year, the overall labour force participation rate of persons with disabilities was just 56.2% compared to 66.7% for the working-age population as a whole (and the gap was greatest among women.)

Disability does, of course, prevent some people from working. But 40% of persons with disabilities who were not in the labour force— and very often living in poverty or on low incomes from social assistance, Workers Compensation, limited CPP disability benefits and so on—reported that they could work. High rates of non-participation and unemployment for workers with disabilities thus reflect, to a significant measure, the continuing failure of employers and governments to address barriers, from physical access to workplaces, to transportation to work, to provision of special equipment in the workplace, to access to training.

Barriers also result in disabled workers being concentrated in low-wage jobs. The poverty rate of workers with disabilities who were in the labour force and employed in 1991 was 13.4%, compared to 8.2% of the employed population without disabilities. More than half of all of the working age population with disabilities had incomes below $15,000, and only one-third had incomes above $30,000. The labour force participation rate of workers with disabilities rose over the 1980s, suggesting some progress in addressing barriers to employment.

CONCLUSION

Unemployment and underemployment, fuelled both by the economic recession of the early 1990s and by the strict anti-inflation policies of the Bank of Canada, have imposed severe economic hardships on most Canadians in the 1990s. Poor job prospects have given employers considerable power to hold wages in check and to shift employees to temporary and part-time work with lower pay and fewer benefits than full-time jobs. Young people, women, workers of colour, Aboriginal Canadians and disabled workers have been disproportionately affected by these trends.

The 1980s, and particularly the 1990s, have also witnessed a major shift to temporary and precarious forms of employment. Employers have increasingly sought to create a "just-in-time" workforce by building peripheral layers of part-time and contract workers around a "core" of permanent, full-time workers (who themselves often work very variable hours because of required overtime).

It is often argued that "flexible" part-time and contract jobs match with the desire of some workers for "flexible" hours, but the reality is generally quite different. Jobs which are part-time or short-term may be quite acceptable in principle to some workers—particularly students and women with family responsibilities—but they would prefer that pay and benefits are comparable to similar permanent, full-time jobs, and that the hours of work are predictable.

Few people want to work at lower than regular wages on a casual, "on call" basis. Yet, outside unionized workplaces, equality of wages and benefits hardly exists, and many part-time and contract workers have very limited control of hours worked, and little or no opportunity to move into permanent jobs. The average pay of part-timers is 25% less than that of full-timers, and one in three part-time jobs provide no regular work schedule at all. By the end of the 1990s, half of all young people and a quarter of adult women— but just one in 20 adult men—were working part-time.

This fundamental shift in the labour market is often popularly characterized as the inevitable fall-out of either economic globalization or technological change. In truth, however, government policies have played a key role in this trend. In most European nations, the growth of precarious employment has been held in check by more stringent employment legislation that guarantees extended benefits to part-time workers and limits the use of contract employment by employers. In the United States, where the central bank has been less aggressive in targeting inflation, lower levels of unemployment have recently limited to a lesser extent the growth in contingent jobs.

For Canadians, slow job growth, high levels of unemployment and underemployment, and the increasingly contingent nature of jobs have together conspired to undermine their economic security and well-being. As will be shown in Chapter 3, the poor performance of the labour market has been the major reason why working people have witnessed a marked deterioration in wages and quality of work in the 1990s.

CHAPTER 3

The Wonderful New World of Work: Wages and the Quality of Jobs in the 1990s

This chapter examines what has happened to wages and the quality of jobs in the 1990s. The high levels of unemployment and underemployment, coupled with the growth in "bad jobs" detailed in the previous chapter, have clearly taken their toll on the pay cheques of working Canadians. The median earnings of men actually fell between 1989 and 1997, while women's earnings improved slightly, but still remained well below those of men. Overall, real wage rates (adjusted for inflation) for unionized workers in the business sector rose just 0.6% between 1989 and 1997. For public sector workers, real wage rates fell by more than 5% as a result of wage rollbacks and freezes by governments.

The labour market in the 1990s was more polarized with respect to the quality of jobs and wages. Consequently, the earnings gap between high-wage and low-wage earners has widened somewhat. About 25% of working Canadians are now in low-paid jobs, earning less than two-thirds of the median wage. One in three women earn less than $10,000 a year, compared to one in five men.

Overall, today's workplace has become a leaner and meaner environment. Working Canadians are putting in longer hours demanded by employers, while struggling to balance family and personal needs. Not surprisingly, working people are reporting higher levels of workplace stress.

WHAT KINDS OF JOBS?

Amid all of the hype today about the shift to a *"knowledge-based economy"*—not all of it untrue—it is easy to lose sight of the fact that a clear majority of workers are still engaged in relatively traditional blue and white collar occupations. Four in 10 men still work in *"blue collar"* jobs—that is, in non-managerial/non-professional (though often skilled) jobs in industry, construction, and transportation. While the proportion of production workers in the total labour force has fallen, the absolute number of manufacturing workers had, by the end of the 1990s, regained the level of 1989 when the mass wave of plant closures began, caused by the Canada-U.S. free trade agreement and an overvalued dollar. About another one in four men are in non-managerial/non-professional jobs in offices or in sales and services.

About six in 10 working women are in sales and service jobs, clerical jobs, or, much more rarely, in blue collar jobs. As shown in Table 3.1, there remains a high degree of occupational segregation between men and women, with men being more than four times more likely to work in *"blue collar"* jobs, and women being more likely than men to work in *"routine white collar"* sales, services, and office jobs.

Table 3.1
Employment by Occupation (as % Total)

	Men		Women	
	1989	1998	1989	1998
Managers	11.7%	11.9%	6.9%	8.5%
(of which Senior Managers)	(13.5%)	(12.8%)	(6.8%)	(6.1%)
Business, Finance, Administrative (of which, Professionals)	9.8% (22.7%)	9.5% (28.0%)	31.9% (6.5%)	26.9% (11.3%)
Scientific, Health, Social Sciences	13.3%	15.4%	17.9%	20.3%
Sales and Services	18.7%	19.6%	30.5%	31.5%
"Blue Collar"	44.4%	41.1%	10.0%	9.4%
	100%	100%	100%	100%

SOURCE: Labour Force Survey Data.

As illustrated, the ranks of managers have grown in the 1990s, especially among women. However, only a small proportion of managers, particularly women managers, are classified as senior managers, and some managerial growth likely reflects *"title inflation,"* which is a cheap way for employers to "compensate" employees.

The data in the table also indicate the strong growth of professional occupations, normally those requiring post-secondary qualifications. The proportion of scientific, health and social sciences jobs has grown for both men and women. This is a highly varied category of jobs, including the growing ranks of computer programmers, system managers and the like, but also consisting of jobs in health care and education as nurses, teachers, lab assistants, etc.

It is interesting to note the rather sharp fall from 32% to 27% in the proportion of women working in non-managerial jobs in business, finance and administration (i.e., clerical and technical office jobs). Within the context of the ongoing and large-scale erosion of routine clerical jobs, some women have moved into professional office jobs (though they remain heavily outnumbered by men in professional business jobs). Others have been forced to move into the growing ranks of sales and service workers. Within this broad category, the 1990s saw significant growth in mainly low-wage, part-time jobs. Almost one in three women and one in five men are sales and services workers. It is worth noting that the number of women engaged in just one of these occupations—child care and home support—grew by 83,000 between 1989 and 1998, contributing to about one in 10 of all of the new jobs created for women over the decade.

As in the 1970s and 1980s, there has been a modest tilt towards professional and managerial jobs at the expense of blue collar and clerical jobs over the past decade. Some of this shift has been bound up with the expansion of public and quasi-public services, though some is also due to the growth of the financial sector of the economy and to the increased employment of professionals in industry and in specialized firms selling services to business. Meanwhile, the ranks of sales and service workers have also grown.

There has, then, been some ongoing polarization in terms of the quality of new jobs with respect to skills as in earlier decades. Further, there has been some polarization with respect to wages brought about by changes in the occupational structure. Managerial and professional jobs tend to be reasonably well paid, while sales and service jobs (predominantly held by women) tend to be

Table 3.2
Median Hourly Wages by Selected Occupation (1997)

Managerial	
Administrative	$18.56
Professional	$18.68
"Blue Collar"	
Machining	$15.97
Construction	$15.50
Product Fabricating	$14.50
Clerical	$11.73
Sales	$8.75
Service	$8.00

SOURCE: Statistics Canada, Cat. 71-005XPB. Labour Force Update: A New Perspective on Wages. Summer, 1998. 50% of workers earn more and less than the median wage.

low-paid, averaging less than $9 per hour. "*Blue collar*" jobs tend to pay about average wages and provide full-time hours, and clerical jobs typically pay somewhat below average, but significantly more than the sales and service jobs held by such a large proportion of non-professional/managerial women.

Table 3.2 provides some detail on pay rates by occupation in 1997. The central point is that changes in the mix of occupations have tended to result in the growth of both "*good jobs*"—reasonably well-paid, permanent and full-time—and "*bad jobs*," relatively poorly paid and often part-time. As shown below, however, the "*good jobs/bad jobs*" distinction first put forward by the now defunct Economic Council of Canada in the mid-1980s ignores the deteriorating work conditions experienced even by those holding the supposedly "*good*" jobs.

THE ATTACK ON THE PUBLIC SECTOR

Another factor affecting wages and the mix of jobs in the 1990s has been the severe cuts to public services employment which began to bite seriously in 1992, and which still continue. In the early 1990s, about one in five of all paid workers in Canada were employed in public services, defined as *direct* employment by the federal, provincial and local governments, as well as employment in *directly* government-funded health, education and other social services. This definition excludes many workers in the broader publicly-funded sector, such as health and social service workers in arm's-length agencies and in private sector companies providing services to the public and paid for by governments (e.g., doctors and employees in doctors' offices, and workers in private health care labs). As shown in Table 3.3, the total number of public sector jobs fell by abour 100,000 between 1992 and 1997, and the proportion of all paid jobs which are in the public sector fell from 20.3% to 18.0%. Since 1997, total public sector employment appears to have stabilized.

The growth of public services employment in the 1960s, 1970s and 1980s was of particular significance to women who have held the majority of the growing number of skilled and reasonably well-paid jobs in the health, education and social services professions—particularly in the "broader" public sector of health and social services. Many working women have also held clerical jobs in public services, and the avenues of opportunity to move into managerial and administrative jobs have been greater in public services because of the adoption of formal employment

Table 3.3
Public Services Jobs (000's)

	Total	(% all employees)	MEN Total	(% all men)	WOMEN Total	(% all women)
1989	2,166	(19.2)	1,113	(18.2)	1,053	(20.4)
1992	2,219	(20.3)	1,098	(19.2)	1,121	(21.6)
1997	2,066	(18.0)	988	(16.4)	1,079	(19.9)

SOURCE: Labour Force Survey.

equity plans, which are still relatively undeveloped among even large private sector employers.

Table 3.4 compares pay in public and private sector jobs in 1995. Not only is average pay in the public sector significantly higher ($19.38 per hour vs. $13.85 per hour), but the proportion of very low-wage workers in the public sector is also far smaller. Some 41% of women in the private sector earned less than $10 per hour in 1995, compared to just 7% of women in public services, while 64% of part-time workers in the private sector (overwhelmingly women) earned less than $10 per hour, compared to 22% of part-timers in the public sector.

Pension plan coverage is very high at 90% for full-time public service workers, and significant (at 43%) even for part-time workers, compared to 51% and 15%, respectively, in private sector jobs. All of these

Table 3.4
Public vs. Private Sector Jobs

Average hourly wage		Public Sector	Private Sector
		$19.38	$13.85
Men	<$10/hr.	5%	25%
Women	<$10/hr.	7%	41%
Full-time	<$10/hr.	3%	25%
Full-time	$10-$15/hr.	18%	30%
Full-time	$15+/hr.	79%	45%
Part-time	$10/hr.	22%	64%
Pension Plan			
Full-time		90%	51%
Part-time		43%	15%

SOURCE: Data from Statistics Canada, 1995. Survey of Work Arrangements, reported in *"Public Sector Downsizing: The Impact on Job Quality in Canada"*. Canadian Council on Social Development, 1997.

advantages are heavily influenced by the much higher rate of unionization in the public sector, which is again of particular advantage to women workers (see Chapter 4).

LOW-PAID JOBS

One in four of all workers in Canada are low-paid, when defined as working in a job that pays an hourly wage of less than two-thirds the median wage for all workers. Of course, many low-wage jobs are also part-time, temporary and precarious, so that hours worked in low-wage jobs are also more likely to be lower than those worked in higher hourly wage jobs.

As shown in Table 3.5, women are more likely to be low-paid than men (almost one in three are low-paid compared to less than one in five men) while, unsurprisingly, many more young workers are in low-wage jobs. One in three non-union workers are in low-wage jobs, compared to just under 7% of unionized workers.

Table 3.5
Workers in Low Paid Jobs (1997)
(< 2/3 National Median Wage
i.e. less than $9.24/hour)

All workers	24.5%
Men	18.8%
Women	30.6%
Age 15-24	68.2%
Union	6.7%
Non-union	33.4%
Newfoundland	34.4%
PEI	41.4%
Nova Scotia	35.4%
New Brunswick	35.4%
Quebec	24.5%
Ontario	21.9%
Manitoba	31.4%
Saskatchewan	32.4%
Alberta	28.1%
B.C.	19.2%

SOURCE: Labour Force Survey (unpublished data).

The table shows that, on top of the significant differences in unemployment rates between the provinces noted in Chapter 2, there are major differences in the incidence of low-paid work. More than one in three workers in Atlantic Canada are in low-paying jobs, and close to one in three in Manitoba and Saskatchewan, compared to about one in five in both Ontario and B.C. The high level of low-paying jobs in Alberta likely reflects the very low level of the minimum wage in that province (see Chapter 7).

THE CHANGING STRUCTURE OF EARNINGS

Table 3.6 shows the distribution of annual earnings in 1989 and 1997 for women and men, indicating the proportion of both who fall into different earnings brackets. As illustrated, there remains a profound difference between the median earnings of women and men. (Median earnings are the earnings of someone at the precise middle of the earnings distribution, i.e., 50% earn more, and 50% earn less.)

Table 3.6
Distribution of Annual Earnings of Men and Women % (constant $1997)

	Men		Women	
	1989	1997	1989	1997
$10,000	19.1	20.1	33.6	31.6
$10-20,000	15.2	15.0	23.1	21.5
$20-30,000	15.0	15.7	20.8	19.8
$30-40,000	16.7	15.5	12.3	13.5
$40-50,000	13.3	11.9	5.6	6.8
$50-60,000	9.1	9.0	2.3	3.8
$60,000 +	11.5	12.8	2.3	3.0
Median	$30,441	$29,505	$17,207	$18,401

SOURCE: Statistics Canada, Cat. 13-217 XPB. *Earnings of Men and Women*. Table 1.

Other observations worth noting include:

- The median earnings of women in 1997 were just $18,401 compared to $29,505 for men, a pay gap of more than one-third. This pay gap reflects the high concentration of women in relatively low-paid jobs, the fact that a quarter of even adult women work part-time, and lower hours for full-time women workers.
- More than half of all women earners earned less than $20,000, and almost one in three earned less than $10,000.
- Strikingly, just 6.8% of working women earned more than $50,000 in 1997, compared to 21.8% of men, and 13.6% of working women earned more than $40,000 compared to 33.7% of men.

While many women have moved into managerial, professional and skilled technical occupations, very few are making above-average earnings (and many of those who do have been adversely affected by recent cuts to public and social services). That said, the "*good news*" in the table is that median earnings for women increased in the 1990s by more than $1,000, while median earnings for men fell by almost $1,000. Put another way, half of the closing of the pay gap in the 1990s was due to falling earnings among men, hardly a preferable route to equality, but half was driven by the modest progress of women into better- paying jobs (combined with longer hours).

The second major point to note from the table is the increased inequality of the earnings of men. There was growth in the numbers of men earning more than $60,000 per year—from 11.5% to 12.8%—indicating some wage growth for upper income earners, while the proportion of men with earnings of less than $30,000 increased from 49.3% to 50.8%. There was also a fall in the proportion earning an average wage of $30,000 to 40,000 per year.

ACCESS TO BENEFITS

Benefits, such as employer pension plans and various extended health benefits, are a very important part of total employee compensation, often accounting for as much as 20% of the total cost of compensation to the employer. As shown in Table 3.7, there was some decline in pension and extended medical benefits coverage in the first part of the 1990s, concentrated among non-union workers who already had a low level of coverage. In 1995, just 33% of non-union workers were covered by an employer pension plan, compared to 81% of unionized workers, while medical and dental plan coverage was about half as high. Most non-union managers and professionals working for larger companies are covered by benefits plans. Rates of coverage are extremely low for lower-wage non-union workers, particularly those working for smaller companies, as further detailed in Chapter 4.

Table 3.7
Access to Benefits (% Workers Covered)

	Pension Plan		Medical Benefits		Dental Plan	
	1989	1995	1989	1995	1989	1995
All	52.0	51.0	63.0	59.0	53.0	55.0
Men	54.0	54.0	68.0	64.0	57.0	59.0
Women	50.0	48.0	58.0	54.0	49.0	50.0
Union	77.9	81.0	78.2	83.0	80.1	76.0
Non-Union	36.8	33.0	47.3	44.0	46.4	42.0

SOURCE: 1989 Data from General Social Survey. 1995 Data from Survey of Work Arrangements. Cat. 71-535 MPB #8 Work Arrangements in the 1990s. Table 2-1.

Table 3.8
Paid Vacation Leave 1995

	10 days or less	11-15 days	16-20 days	More than 20 days
All	28	28	19	25
Men	27	27	18	28
Women	29	30	20	22
Union	16	23	24	36
Non-Union	37	32	15	16

SOURCE: Statistics Canada, *Survey of Work Arrangements* (1995).

Paid vacation leave is another important workplace benefit. Unfortunately, we do not have data to show changes over time, but, as illustrated in Table 3.8, unionized workers enjoy significantly longer paid vacation entitlements than do non-union workers, with 60% getting more than 16 days per year, compared to just 31% of non-union workers. More than one in three union workers received more than 20 days per year, compared to just one in six non-union workers.

WAGES VS. PROFITS

It was noted in Chapter 1 that the distribution of national income between wages and profits has been quite stable over time, with profits tending to fall in periods of recession and rise in periods of recovery. The 1990s have certainly been no exception. Corporate pre-tax profits plummeted from 10.5% of GDP to 4.6% of GDP between 1988 and 1992, and have since come close to recovering to the pre-recession peak level.

As shown in Table 3.9, corporate rates of return on equity (profits

Table 3.9
The Corporate Recovery

	Corporate Pre-Tax Profits as % GDP	Corporate Rate of Return on Equity (Real)
1988	10.5%	12.7% (8.0%)
1992	4.6%	0.18% (-1.8%)
1997	9.2%	8.9% (7.3%)
1999 (QII)	9.8%	8.7% (7.7%)*

SOURCE: Statistics Canada. National Accounts and Canadian Economic Observer Table 36. Corporate Finances. Rate of return data adjusted for consumer price inflation.*1998 (QIV).

as a percentage of shareholder equity) have also, when adjusted for inflation, just about returned to the 1988 level. A more detailed analysis would show that large corporations have shown a greater increase in profitability than smaller companies and that large corporations in manufacturing, finance, transportation and other major sectors are at or near record profitability. The average profit numbers were dragged down for much of the 1990s by companies selling to the depressed national market, such as retail chains and construction companies, and resource companies which suffered big hits in 1998 as a result of depressed global commodity prices.

A major reason for the return to high levels of profitability in the business sector has been that wages paid to workers have increased at a much slower rate than the value of the output produced by workers. Table 3.10 shows that, between 1989 and 1998, output per hour (which is adjusted for SDP inflation) rose by a total of 9.4% in the business sector, while average weekly earnings (adjusted for inflation) rose by just 2.8%. This 2.8% partly reflects some increase in hours worked. Base wage rate for unionized workers in the business sector rose in real terms by just 0.6% over the entire period. (This gap between productivity and real wage growth is partly accounted for by the fact that consumer prices tended to increase somewhat faster in the 1990s than the prices received by producers.) Note also that wages do not include benefit costs. Meanwhile, wage

Table 3.10
Changes in Real Wages and Productivity

	Average Weekly Earnings	Wage Settlements: Commercial	Wage Settlements: Non-Commercial	Hourly Labour Productivity
1989	0.1	0.0	0.3	-0.2
1990	-0.3	0.9	0.8	0.4
1991	-1.0	-1.7	-2.2	1.4
1992	2.0	1.1	-0.3	2.2
1993	0.0	-0.9	-1.3	0.7
1994	1.7	1.0	-0.4	1.2
1995	-1.1	-0.8	-1.6	0.5
1996	0.5	-0.1	-1.2	-0.7
1997	0.5	0.3	-0.5	2.9
1998	0.4	0.8	0.9	0.7
Total Change 1989-1998	2.8%	0.6%	-5.4%	9.4%

SOURCE: Statistics Canada. Canadian Economic Observer Historical Statistical Supplement. Hourly Labour Productivity data are for the Business Sector, from the Daily, July 21, 1998 and June 30, 1999. Wages deflated by the CPI.

rates for unionized public sector workers fell by 5.4%, the result of numerous freezes and rollbacks by governments. The lion's share of income gains in the economic recovery since 1992 have gone to profits, not to wages. This trend continued into 1999, though public sector wages have begun to increase in line with the private sector.

Economists agree that wages should, over the long run, increase in line with productivity, and that such increases do not cause inflation. This means that real wages should now be rising by about 1% per year. Yet, wage settlements for unionized workers in the private sector have increased by more than 1% in real terms only once in the 1990s. With profitability now restored to pre-recession levels, there is every justification for workers to claim their fair share of rising Canadian national income.

JOB QUALITY IN THE 1990S: THE GROWTH OF LONG HOURS

Historical progress in reducing working time ground to a halt from the end of the "Golden Age," and there can be little doubt that the trend to longer hours for "core" workers has continued and intensified in the 1990s. Between 1989 and 1995, the proportion of men working 41 hours a week or more rose from 21.4% to 24.3% and, in 1995, 13.9% of men worked more than 50 hours. While fewer women work very long hours, change was very much in the same direction. This trend to longer hours has been somewhat more marked among managers, but 21.6% of non-managerial men and 7.3% of non-managerial women worked more than 41 hour weeks in 1995 (Table 3.11).

Table 3.11
Long Weekly Hours in Main Job
(% Employees, Age 25+)

	1989	1995 (of which 50+hrs.)
41 hours or more		
Men	21.4	24.3 (13.9)
Women	7.3	8.6 (4.6)
Non-Managers		
Men	19.3	21.6
Women	6.4	7.3

SOURCE: *The Changing Workweek: Trends in Weekly Hours of Work.* Canadian Economic Observer. September, 1996.

In 1991, just 7.7% of workers reported that they worked overtime in the week of the survey: 9.7% of men and 5.6% of women. (Data from the 1991, Survey of Work Arrangements). By 1997, 18.6% of workers were working overtime and 23.4% of adult men and 17% of adult women were working overtime in any given week, averaging an extra 9.1 hours. In effect, one in five people are now working a six-day week. Strikingly, more overtime was unpaid than paid, with 10.7% of workers working unpaid overtime, and 8.4% working paid overtime.

As shown in Table 3.12, unpaid overtime was much more common in the public than the private sector and, reflecting that, was relatively more important for women than for men. Many public sector workers in jobs from teaching to social work, to other kinds of service delivery, work long hours just to get the job done, but find it very difficult to obtain paid overtime even when they are entitled to claim it. Unpaid overtime is, of course, also common among managers and professionals.

Table 3.12
Incidence of Overtime (% Workers) (1997)

	Paid	Unpaid	Total
All workers	8.4	10.7	18.6
	(av. 8.5 hrs.)	(av. 9.2 hrs.)	(av. 9.1 hrs.)
Adult Men	11.4	12.6	23.4
Adult Women	5.6	11.5	16.8
Youth	6.8	3.0	9.6
Private Sector	8.8	8.9	17.2
Public Sector	6.7	18.6	24.5

SOURCE: Statistics Canada. Cat. 71-005-XPB. Labour Force Update Hours of Work. Summer, 1997 *Total reflects fact that some worked both paid and unpaid overtime.

Unpaid overtime is, to state the obvious, highly advantageous to employers, who obtain extra hours at no cost. The high level of unpaid hours being worked today likely reflects the impacts of repeated rounds of "*downsizing*" and "*restructuring*." The survivors have to pick up the work of those who have left as a result of layoffs or early retirement, and fear of future job loss is a potent factor behind putting in long hours. In a "survival-of-the-fittest" corporate culture, long hours are viewed as evidence of effort and commitment. Undoubtedly, many workers also internalize the ethic of "*doing more with less*," particularly those who are serving the public and helping make up for cuts through unpaid work.

Paid overtime, by contrast, is heavily concentrated in *"blue collar"* jobs in mining (15.2% incidence), manufacturing (15.8%), transportation and communications (11.4%) and construction (10.7%). Such jobs are mainly held by men. Paid overtime is more common among unionized than non-union workers (10% vs. 7%), and more common in large firms.

High levels of paid overtime can be costly to employers in the sense that premium pay rates, such as time-and-a-half or double time, are generally paid for work after normal hours, but this is balanced by the fact that employers save on the many costs of hiring additional workers. These include recruitment and training costs, and the cost of non-wage benefits, such as pension and extended health benefits. Many employers, then, prefer to regularly require paid overtime than to hire new workers, and may do so for long periods of time.

Another factor is the rise of *"just-in-time"* production techniques and the minimization of inventories, which require hours worked to vary significantly from one week to another in line with changing demand. *"Just-in-time"* production tends to call for *"just-in-time"* workers.

Relatively few workers in Canada have the right to refuse overtime below certain limits, and even unionized workers generally do not have a right to refuse. (An often conditional right to refuse exists for only about one in four workers covered by major collective agreements, and maximum work weeks under employment standards legislation permit scheduled overtime well in excess of 40 hours). Some employers (notably in the auto industry and other large-scale manufacturing) regularly schedule weekend overtime shifts.

Surveys indicate that a lot of paid overtime is voluntary, and only 6% of workers report that they would prefer to work fewer hours *if* it meant a corresponding cut in pay (1995, *Survey of Work Arrangements*). However, this is a very narrow question, and in practice many workers choose to take an increase in their standard of living partly as higher wages and partly as shorter working hours. *"Voluntary"* overtime has to be placed squarely in the context of stagnant wages and heightened job insecurity in the 1990s. It is not surprising that many working people with falling real after-tax incomes who face regular unemployment would be willing to work longer hours when they land a steady job. However, a number of unions have taken on the challenge of limiting overtime and long hours through contract provisions, and there is a lot of evidence that workers who have achieved shorter hours will strongly resist any increase. (See

More Jobs, More Fun, Communications, Energy and Paperworkers of Canada, 1997, for some examples.) In recent years, some unions have put a strong priority on shorter working time by bringing the issue to the bargaining table, showing that gains can be divided between money and time-off the job.

CHANGING SHIFT SCHEDULES

Shift work is a reality for many workers, particularly those who do not work in offices. Manufacturing and primary industries tend to operate outside normal working hours, often through the night and on weekends, and about one in three industrial workers work a shift schedule as opposed to regular daytime hours. Many public services workers—from hospital workers to bus drivers—must work at night and on weekends. Most restaurant, hotel and retail workers must work in the evenings and/or on weekends.

Corporate restructuring to respond to a "*just-in-time*" world, the shift to much longer operating hours in stores and other parts of the service sector, and increased casualization of work have led to some changes in the shift schedules of workers. Between 1991 and 1995, there was a small decline, from 70% to 68%, in the proportion of workers working a regular daytime shift, and a corresponding small increase in the numbers of those working night or rotating/split shifts. Most strikingly, there was a big jump in the proportion of workers usually working on weekends, from 11% to 15% of all workers.

Table 3.13
Work Schedules

		Regular Shift Schedule					
		Regular Daytime	Evening	Night/ Graveyard	Rotating/ Split	Irregular	Usually Worked Weekend
All	1991	70	5	1	10	14	11
	1995	68	5	2	11	14	15
Men	1991	70	5	2	11	12	11
	1995	67	5	2	14	12	16
Women	1991	70	5	1	8	16	10
	1995	69	5	1	9	15	14
Union	1991	68	5	2	17	9	5
	1995	66	5	3	17	10	10
Non-Union	1991	71	5	1	6	16	13
	1995	69	5	1	8	17	18

SOURCE: Statistics Canada, Survey of Work Arrangements.

BALANCING WORK AND FAMILY

As was highlighted in Chapter 1, there has been a tremendous increase in the proportion of women who participate in the paid work force, and working women have also been putting in longer and longer hours. The reality today is that most couples with children hold down two jobs, and about half hold down two full-time jobs.

As shown in Table 3.14, three in four (73%) women in two-parent families with children now participate in the paid workforce. This figure is about the same for women with children aged 3 to 5 (72%) and only modestly lower for women with at least one child under age 3 (65%). More than two in three of these working women, even those with young children, work full-time, and about one in four have to deal with shift work. For single parent women, the participation rate in the work force is lower at 63% (38% with children under age 3), but the proportion working full-time is even higher than for two-earner couples.

Table 3.14
Work Arrangements of Women

	Women in Two Parent Families	Women Single Parents
Women with children in Labour Force	73%	63%
Who work full-time	73%	77%
Working Women*		
•with children under age 6	68%	71%
•with children age 6-15	70%	77%
Not Working Regular Day Schedule	26%	27%
•with children under 6	30%	37%
•with children age 6-15	25%	27%

SOURCE: Statistics Canada, Cat. 71-535, MPB#8. *Work Arrangements in the 1990s.* Tables 3.1, 3.2 *Paid Workers

Clearly, the majority of working couples with children have to balance work and family in complex ways. This task is hardly made easier by the shift to more irregular and unstable hours on the one hand, and to longer hours on the other hand. It is also complicated by the growth of elder care responsibilities and the task of caring for the sick in a period when public health provision is being sharply cut back. Women bear the brunt of the "*time crunch stress*" which results. In 1998, about 21% of all women aged 15 and over reported they felt time-stressed, up from 16% six years earlier (see Table 3.15). The proportion of men who are time-stressed increased from 12% in 1992 to 16% in 1998.

Table 3.15
Time-Stressed Population, 1992 and 1998 (%)

Age	Men		Women	
	1992	**1998**	**1992**	**1998**
15+	12	16	16	21
15-24	7	10	18	22
25-34	16	25	23	29
35-44	16	23	22	27
45-54	16	20	18	22
55-64	n/a	8	9	14

n/a - Amount too small to be expressed.
SOURCE: Statistics Canada, The Daily, November 9, 1999.

Not surprisingly, levels of time-stress vary with the number of duties and responsibilities individuals have to undertake. According to the most recent statistics, time stress levels were highest in 1998 for married women aged 25-44 who were employed full-time and had children at home. More than one in three women in this group reported they were time-stressed (Statistics Canada, *Overview of the Time Use of Canadians in 1998*, cat. no. 12-F0080XIE). Women with full-time jobs are more likely to feel time-stressed because, as Table 3.16 reveals, they are also more likely to do all of the housework. As a result, working women on average put in more hours of combined paid and unpaid work and enjoy less free time than do men.

Table 3.16 TIME USE
Average Time Spent on Selected Activities,
Married Parents Employed Full-time, 1998 (Hours per day)*

	Age 25-44		Age 45-64	
	Men	**Women**	**Men**	**Women**
Paid work	6.9	5.5	6.9	6.2
Unpaid work	3.3	4.9	3.0	4.1
Total paid and unpaid work	10.2	10.4	9.9	10.3
Free time	4.2	3.6	4.5	3.9

* Average over a 7-day week.
SOURCE: Statistics Canada, Overview of the Time Use of Canadians in 1998, cat. no. 12-F0080XIE, table 3.

STRESS AND WORK SATISFACTION

Today's workplace has become leaner and meaner. *"Downsizing"* and *"restructuring"* by corporations and public sector employers have resulted in workers having to pick up the slack for those who have been laid-off or not replaced. At the same time, many employers have been experimenting with so-called *"new forms of work organization"* such as team work and total quality management. While often described as means to *"empower"* workers, the reality is often nothing more than old-fashioned intensification of work.

Work re-organization may mean giving some workers more interesting jobs, but in many cases it just means doubling-up on various tasks. On close examination, a lot of so-called *"multi-skilling"* is really just *"multi-tasking."* For example, nurses have to make up for the reduced hours of hospital orderlies and practical nurses. Furthermore, in many workplaces, there is a lot of pressure to just work harder and faster, as in the supposed bygone days of *"Taylorist"* assembly lines in which workers were given highly fragmented tasks, and then required to do them in the shortest possible time.

Table 3.17 WORK STRESS
% Workers Reporting Stress in Work Environment from

		Too many Demands/ Hours	Poor Inter- Personal Relations	Harassment Discrimina- tion	Stress from Risk of Accident/ Injury
All	1991	27.5	12.8	7.3	7.5
	1994	32.8	18.5	-	13.9
Men	1991	27.6	12.7	6.7	9.6
	1994	31.0	17.7	-	16.8
Women	1991	27.4	13.1	8.0	5.1
	1994	34.7	19.4	-	10.7
Union	1991	29.1	14.8	8.9	12.7
	1994	35.8	23.9	-	20.8
Non-Union	1991	26.8	11.9	6.4	4.8
	1994	31.5	16.1	-	10.8
Managerial/ Professional	1991	40.1	16.6	7.1	5.9
	1994	44.6	22.5	-	9.7
Skilled/ Semi-Skilled	1991	21.1	11.0	7.3	7.8
	1994	26.8	17.3	-	15.0
Unskilled	1991	19.9	11.3	8.1	10.2
	1994	22.2	13.4	-	19.7

SOURCE: Statistics Canada. General Social Survey.

While it is impossible to generalize about the changing conditions of work, the reality of increased stress on the job is apparent in data which is intermittently collected by Statistics Canada's General Social Survey. Some key sources of workplace stress are summarized in Table 3.17. In 1994, one in three workers reported experiencing stress from too many demands or hours, with stress being somewhat higher among women workers. This fits with the evidence that stress tends to be highest in jobs that impose high demands on workers, combined with very little control over how the job is to be done. Almost one in five workers also experienced stress from poor inter-personal relations at work. In both cases, stress levels appear to have increased significantly between 1991 and 1994.

Reported stress from the risk of accident or injury increased significantly over this period. As would be expected, this source of stress is least important among managerial and professional workers, who experience higher rates of stress from other factors. Increased stress seems to have affected union and non-union workers about equally, and there is some evidence that unionized jobs may be more stressful, likely because of the relatively high concentration of unionized workers in large-scale industrial operations, and in rapidly "*downsizing*" public services.

Uncertainty in the labour market has also raised the stress felt by workers who increasingly worry about layoffs and job losses. As revealed in Table 3.18, the share of working people who said they experienced stress from the threat of losing their jobs rose from about 11% in 1991 to over 23% in 1994. This form of stress was most commonly felt by union members, with more than 34% reporting stress from the threat of layoff or job loss.

Table 3.18
Job Insecurity

	Experienced Stress from Threat of Lay-off/Job Loss	
	1991	**1994**
All Workers	10.9	23.5
Men	12.5	23.8
Women	9.0	23.1
Union	15.3	34.2
Non-Union	8.7	18.5
Managerial/Professional	10.6	26.3
Skilled/Semi-Skilled	10.7	21.4
Unskilled	12.3	22.8

SOURCE: General Social Survey 1991, 1994, and Statistics Canada, Cat. 71-539.

Increased stress on the job is also closely associated with intensified management control of work, and reduced worker autonomy. As shown in Table 3.19, between 1989 and 1994 there was a sharp fall in the proportion of workers who strongly agreed that they had a lot of freedom over how to work, from 54.0% to 40.4%, even

Table 3.19
Work Satisfaction (Strongly Agree)

		Job Requires High Level of Skill	Lot of Freedom over How to Work
All	1989	46.0	54.0
	1994	46.3	40.4
Men	1989	50.0	56.0
	1994	49.5	42.7
Women	1989	40.0	52.0
	1994	42.7	37.9
Union	1989	NA	NA
	1994	51.9	34.8
Non-Union	1989	NA	NA
	1994	44.1	43.5
Managerial/ Professional	1989	NA	NA
	1994	68.6	51.4
Skilled/Semi-Skilled	1989	NA	NA
	1994	37.4	34.8
Unskilled	1989	NA	NA
	1994	20.9	31.1

SOURCE: General Social Survey 1989 and 1994.

though the skill level of jobs (as reported by workers) did not change.

Very little information is collected on a regular basis about the physical conditions of work, but the *1991 General Social Survey* does provide a snapshot of recent conditions. A significant minority of workers are still engaged in physically dangerous jobs, with about one in six workers reporting continuing exposure to various hazards such as dust, dangerous chemicals, loud noise, and poor air quality. One in three of all workers reported some negative health impact from workplace hazards exposure. Again, the data indicate that exposure to such hazards is significantly greater for union workers and, unsurprisingly, for non-managerial/professional workers (see Table 3.20).

Table 3.20
Physical Work Environment

	Experienced Negative Health Impact from Workplace Health Hazard Exposure	Experienced Workplace Injury in Past Year	Risk of Injury Caused Worry	Exposure to Dust in Air Most of the Time	Exposure to Dangerous Chemicals Most of the Time	Exposure to Loud Noise Most of the Time	Exposure to Poor Quality Air Most of the Time	Negative Health Impacts from Exposure to Computer Screen
All	34.1	9.2	7.6	18.8 (45.0)*	7.5 (48.4)*	15.7 (42.1)*	15.3 (70.7)*	8.5
Men	36.0	11.9	9.6	23.0	10.6	22.9	14.0	6.7
Women	31.3	5.9	5.1	13.8	3.8	7.1	16.8	10.6
Union	41.2	11.5	12.7	24.4	9.7	23.1	20.8	9.1
Non-Union	30.0	8.0	4.8	15.9	6.4	11.8	12.5	8.1
Managerial/ Professional	35.4	5.8	5.9	14.0	5.0	8.3	17.6	12.0
Skilled/ Semi-skilled	33.1	10.5	7.8	20.9	8.8	20.4	14.6	6.7
Unskilled	34.0	11.1	10.2	21.5	9.4	17.7	14.0	6.8

*Figure in brackets is % of those exposed (most of the time or sometimes) reporting a negative impact on health.

SOURCE: General Social Survey 1991.

CONCLUSION

High levels of unemployment and underemployment throughout the 1990s have conspired to reshape the wage structure and quality of working life in Canada. Wages have grown at an anemic pace for most working people, and fallen in real terms for others, particularly among those employed in the beleaguered public sector. The pay gap between men and women, while remaining unacceptably wide, has narrowed somewhat. However, fully half of this improvement can be explained by the deterioration in the median wage of men. Moreover, there has been a continuing increase in wage inequality, reflecting the growing polarization of the labour force into "good jobs" and "bad jobs."

The 1990s have seen a major increase not just in paid overtime, but also in unpaid overtime as the survivors of corporate and public sector "*downsizing*" have been forced to pick up the slack. Working-time has also been restructured to meet the needs of employers rather than workers, with the result that regular day shift work is shrinking while night work, and particularly weekend work, expand in line with the growth of the "*non-stop*" economy.

More and more industrial operations operate night and weekend shifts, and long operating hours have spread deep into the service sector. Long, unsocial and frequently unpredictable working hours clearly make it difficult to lead a life outside the workplace, and to balance work and family responsibilities.

"*Time stress*" has also been greatly compounded by the continuing increase in the total working-time of households described above. In short, the historical progress towards a society offering much more free time to workers to spend with their families and in community activities seems to have come to a halt for many of today's "*core*" workers.

The new reality of work in the 1990s is thus one marked by increased stress as the economic security of working people has been weakened by poor wage growth and high levels of unemployment and under-employment. Together with the precarious nature of many of today's jobs, these factors have increased concerns about job loss and forced many working people to work longer hours. Working women in particular have been caught in this squeeze and report the highest levels of stress as they struggle to balance the needs of work and family.

CHAPTER 4

The Union Advantage

In previous chapters, comparisons between union and non-union workers have been presented, with the passing observation that unionized employees enjoy wage and benefit advantages. The purpose of this Chapter is to provide more background and detail on these advantages by exploring further differences between unionized and non-unionized jobs.

Overall, collective bargaining coverage raises pay and benefits for unionized workers compared to otherwise comparable non-union workers. This "*union wage premium*" is greatest for workers who would otherwise be low-paid. Collective bargaining also promotes greater equality of wages and working conditions within the unionized sector by compressing wage and benefit differentials.

The impact of collective bargaining on the incidence of low pay and on inequality in the labour market as a whole thus depends on the extent of collective bargaining coverage in the labour force as a whole. In most continental European countries, collective bargaining coverage is very high because of generally high unionization rates, and because many non-union workers are covered by informal or legal extensions of collective agreements. By contrast, unionization has been falling in the U.S. and in the UK, and this has been linked to increased inequality and increased incidence of low pay in the 1990s.

Historically, the gains of collective bargaining have been heavily concentrated among male, mainly blue collar workers. However, unionization rates for men and women in Canada are now quite comparable (34%

Footnote: This Chapter draws heavily on Andrew Jackson and Grant Schellenberg, "Unions, Collective Bargaining and Labour Market Outcomes for Canadian Working Women," in R.P. Chaykowski and L.M. Powell (eds.) Women and Work (Kingston: John Deutsch Institute, Queen's University, 1999). Data are from the 1995 Survey of Work Arrangements.

vs. 32%), in part because of the high unionization rate in public services, but also because of the growth of unions in private services. Nevertheless, unionization rates in the private service sector are low, and this has particularly negative impacts upon working women who make up the great majority of low-paid services workers. In recent years, the labour movement has recognized that organizing these workers is essential if the movement is to continue to effectively contribute to greater equality by raising the wage floor, and by closing the pay gap between women and men.

It is often argued that the gains of unionization come at the expense of jobs. However, a recent OECD analysis of low-paid work and earnings inequality found that there is little evidence to suggest that countries where low-paid work is less prevalent have achieved this at the cost of higher unemployment rates and lower employment rates for the more vulnerable groups in the labour market such as youth and women (OECD *Employment Outlook, 1996*).

Leading U.S.labour economist Richard Freeman has similarly concluded, on the basis of numerous recent studies, that union wage effects (higher wages, particularly for the low-paid, and greater compression in the distribution of wages) do not come at the expense of productivity and are not responsible for the aggregate level of unemployment, largely because collectively bargained wages respond to shifting market realities.

Similarly, according to the 1995 *World Employment Report* of the International Labour Organization (ILO), it is wrong to view unions or good labour standards as the fundamental cause of unemployment, and it is important to recognize the positive impacts for society in terms of greater equality and less poverty. The ILO report takes particularly strong issue with the widespread view that labour market "rigidities" have been an important source of the unemployment problem in Europe, and emphasizes the many negative features of "flexible" U.S.-style labour markets from the point of view of workers. Collective bargaining procedures which secure steady employment at decent wages in a relatively non-polarized labour market are seen as an important source of social well-being, rather than as a barrier to job creation. This analysis has been borne out by the low unemployment rates achieved in the late 1990s in some smaller European countries with high rates of unionization—notably, Denmark, the Netherlands, Norway, Austria, and Ireland.

COLLECTIVE BARGAINING COVERAGE TODAY

Table 4.1 shows the proportion of workers in various segments of the Canadian workforce who were covered by the provisions of a collective agreement in 1998. Overall, 33.3% of workers were covered, slightly higher than the 30.7% of paid workers who were union members. (Collective bargaining coverage is slightly higher than union membership because some workers who are excluded from a union are nonetheless paid the same wages and benefits as union members, and because a few workers choose not to be members for religious or other reasons.) Union members made up 32% of the paid work force in 1987, so that there has been only a very slight fall in the unionization rate from the late 1980s to the late 1990s. (Unionization data is now obtained form the Labour Force Survey, which replaces the old CALURA survey; so the series are not strictly comparable.)

Other observations illustrated in Table 4.1 include the following:

- Union coverage is slightly higher for men than for women (34% vs. 32%). Between the late 1980s and the late 1990s, there was a small decline in unionization among men, more or less offset by a small gain among women.
- Union coverage is much higher in the public than in the private sector (76% vs. 24%). This raises the unionization rate among women, but it is important to note that women union members are about evenly divided between the public and private sectors (52% vs. 48%). Male union members are much more likely to work in the private than the public sector (65% vs. 35%).
- Union coverage is very low among young workers (13% for those aged 15-24) and highest for those aged 45 to 54 (46%). This reflects the fact that there was very little new hiring in the 1990s into larger, unionized workplaces, while young workers—if they have found jobs at all—tended to find them in small firms in the private services sector where unionization rates are very low.
- Union coverage varies little by level of education, reflecting high unionization rates among well-educated workers in health, education, social services and public administration.

Table 4.1
Union Coverage in 1998 as % of Paid Jobs

	Density		Density
Both sexes	33.3%	**Occupation**	
Sector		White-collar	30.8
Public	76.3	Managerial and administrative	18.0
Private	23.9	Professional	51.8
Sex		Clerical	31.1
Men	34.4	Sales	9.2
Women	32.0	Service	26.9
Age		**Blue-collar**	39.9
15 to 24	13.3	Primary	17.3
25 to 54	36.9	Processing, machining and fabricating	41.2
25 to 44	33.6	Construction	46.3
45 to 54	45.9	Transport equipment operating	41.4
55 and over	37.8	Material handling and other crafts	38.9
Education		**Workplace size**	
Less than Grade 9	34.5	Under 20 employees	14.0
Some high school	27.1	20 to 99 employees	33.6
High school graduation	29.9	100 to 500 employees	48.6
Some post secondary	25.3	Over 500 employees	60.5
Post secondary certificate or diploma	37.0	**Job tenure**	
University degree	38.7	1 to 12 months	15.7
Province		Over 1 year to 5 years	22.6
Newfoundland	41.5	Over 5 years to 9 years	36.9
Prince Edward Island	29.8	Over 9 years to 14 years	45.5
Nova Scotia	31.2	Over 14 years	59.6
New Brunswick	30.9	**Job status**	
Quebec	40.5	Permanent	34.1
Ontario	29.6	Non-Permanent	26.3
Manitoba	36.8		
Saskatchewan	36.4		
Alberta	25.3		
British Columbia	36.4		
Work Status			
Full-time	35.5		
Part-time	29.6		
Industry			
Goods-producing	33.3		
Agriculture	4.1		
Other primary	27.3		
Manufacturing	34.5		
Construction	28.3		
Utilities	67.5		
Service-producing	33.9		
Transportation, storage and communication	48.0		
Trade	13.1		
Finance, Insurance and real estate	10.3		
Community, business and personal services	36.2		
Government services	70.8		

SOURCE: Labour Force Survey

- By industry, union coverage is high in utilities and transportation industries, about average in manufacturing, and has declined to below average in construction. (However, many unionized construction workers work in non-union jobs some of the time.) Coverage is low in trade, finance, and in business services.
- Union coverage is highest in professional (52%) and blue collar jobs (40%), and lowest in sales jobs (9.2%).
- Union coverage is very low (14%) in small workplaces with less than 20 employees, but high in very large workplaces (60% in workplaces with more than 500 employees).

Generally, union coverage is dominant or significant in most of the public sector, broadly defined, and in larger private sector firms, particularly in transportation, utilities, communications and manufacturing. Union coverage is present in retail trade and elsewhere in the private service sector of the economy, but low in sectors dominated by small workplaces.

The 1993 Survey of Labour and Income Dynamics (SLID) found that the unionization rate for workers of colour was a below-average 26%, partly reflecting the low rates of hiring into unionized workplaces in recent years when immigration levels have been significant.

The Union Wage Premium

Evidence from the 1995 Survey of Work Arrangements (SWA) confirms the existence of a union wage premium. The average wage of women in unionized jobs was more than $5.00 (or 31%) higher than the average wage of women in non-unionized jobs, while for men the wage difference was about $4.50, or 24%. The wage premium associated with unionization is shown for selected subgroups of women and men in Table 4.2. The wage premium tends to be higher for less educated workers, though this is more clearly the case for men than for women. This is consistent with the fact that highly paid managerial and professional occupations in the private sector have very low rates of unionization.

The "*pure*" union wage premium is smaller than these figures suggest, since union membership overlaps with a number of other job characteristics associated with higher pay, such as working in larger workplaces, working in professional jobs, being an older worker, and having longer job tenure. The positive impact of unionization on hourly wages can,

Table 4.2
Average Hourly Wages of Women and Men,
by Unionization and Selected Characteristics, Canada 1995

| | WOMEN | | | MEN | | |
	Union	Non-Union	"Union Premium" %	Union	Non-Union	"Union Premium' %
All	16.68	11.58	30.6	18.98	14.45	23.9
Age 15 to 24	11.23	8.11	27.8	11.83	8.64	27.0
Age 25 to 44	16.92	12.71	24.9	18.79	15.80	15.9
Age 45 to 69	17.37	12.71	26.8	20.93	18.15	13.3
Less than high school	12.16	8.30	31.7	16.23	10.80	33.5
High school grad.	14.60	10.73	26.5	17.34	12.40	28.5
Certificate/Diploma	16.56	12.05	27.2	19.87	15.45	22.2
University degree	21.38	17.18	19.6	23.12	21.73	6.0
Full-time	16.90	12.61	25.4	19.29	15.60	19.1
Part-time	15.95	9.62	39.7	12.71	8.52	33.0
Managerial/Admin.	18.59	16.51	11.2	23.00	21.41	6.9
Professional	19.49	15.45	20.7	22.47	18.49	17.7
Clerical	14.47	11.21	22.5	16.55	12.26	25.9
Sales	12.04	9.09	24.5	13.51	10.90	19.3
Services	12.18	7.40	39.2	16.20	8.93	44.9
Blue Collar	12.87	9.37	27.2	18.32	13.17	28.1
Firm size less than 20	12.42	10.41	16.2	16.48	11.62	29.5
Firm size 20 to 99	15.03	11.13	25.9	17.00	13.12	22.8
Firm size 100 to 500	16.36	11.99	26.7	18.39	15.92	13.4
Firm size + 500	17.53	13.10	25.3	19.82	18.06	8.9

The "union premium" is simply the difference between the average union and non-union wage divided by average union wage, expressed as a percentage.

SOURCE: Survey of Work Arrangements

however, be confirmed using technical statistical techniques (regression analysis) which hold these other factors constant.

Using this analysis reveals that unionization in 1995 carried a pure wage premium of $1.24 per hour for women and $1.15 per hour for men. Unionization has a positive impact on hourly wages for women within all five occupational categories, with this generally in the range of $1.00 to $2.00. Similarly, unionization has a positive effect on the hourly wages of men in all categories, with the exception of those in professional occupations (Table 4.3).

Table 4.3
Change in Hourly Wage Associated with Unionization, Canada, 1995* By Sex and Occupation ($)

	WOMEN	MEN
Professional	1.11	NA
Clerical	1.62	0.83
Sales	0.85	1.53
Services	2.37	1.47
Blue Collar	1.67	2.25
All workers	1.24	1.14

Table 4.4
The Union Advantage in 1998*

	Hourly Wage $	
	Union	Non-Union
All workers	18.53	14.09
Men	19.45	15.81
Women	17.40	12.28

SOURCE: Statistics Canada Cat. 71-005. Labour Force Update: A New Perspective on Wages. Summer 1998. Table 15.
*Data are for workers covered by a collective agreement.

Looking at more recent data, Table 4.4 shows that the union advantage remained strong in 1998, with unionized workers averaging $18.53 per hour compared to $14.09 for non-union workers.

INCIDENCE OF LOW PAY

The incidence of low-wage employment among women and men in union and non-union sectors in 1995 is shown in Table 4.5. While almost one-half of all non-unionized women work in low-wage jobs, this is the case for less than 10% of women who are unionized. Striking differences are evident when comparisons are made between union and non-union women in specific age groups, and in specific occupations (e.g., 85% of women in non-union services jobs are low-paid compared to 26% of those who are unionized). The same pattern is evident among men, although non-union-ized men stand a better chance than non-unionized women of finding jobs

Table 4.5
Share of Women and Men in "Low-wage" Jobs, by
Unionization and Selected Characteristics, Canada 1995 (%)

	WOMEN		MEN	
	Union	Non-Union	Union	Non-Union
All	9	47	6	32
Aged 15 to 24	47	76	40	72
Aged 25 to 44	6	36	5	19
Aged 45 and over	5	41	na	18
Less than high school	22	78	11	50
High school/Some post-sec.	13	50	7	39
Certificate/Diploma	5	39	na	22
University Degree	na	16	na	11
Full-time	7	37	4	23
Part-time	15	67	na	77
Managerial/Admin.	na	14	na	7
Professional	na	20	na	18
Clerical	8	40	na	36
Sales	na	70	na	51
Services	26	85	na	72
Blue Collar	21	68	5	29
Firm size less than 20	na	56	na	42
Firm size 20 to 99	12	50	12	35
Firm size 100 to 500	9	44	6	26
Firm size more than 500	6	37	5	22

* Low wages jobs are those which pay less than 2/3rds of the economy-wide median wage. This includes jobs paying less than $9.33 per hour.

SOURCE: Survey of Work Arrangements

above the low-wage cut-off. As well, the incidence of low pay among non-union men tends to be somewhat lower than among women, particularly in sales and service occupations.

The importance of unionization as a protective factor against low-wage employment can again be confirmed with statistical techniques which reveal that, after factors such as age, education and firm size are taken into account, unionization still significantly reduces the *relative odds* of working in a low-wage job.

Wage Inequality / Polarization

As noted above, there is evidence that unionization rates and collective bargaining coverage have a positive impact on the overall distribution of earnings. We can show this by measuring polarization as the ratio between the top and bottom deciles of the earnings distribution scale (i.e., the top and bottom 10%). Table 4.6 presents an overview of wage distribution among unionized and non-unionized women and men in Canada. The ratio of the 9th and the lowest decile for unionized women is 2.50 compared to 3.30 for non-union women, ratios which are approximately comparable to those for men. Similarly, unionization lowers the gap between high and low paid workers and median earnings. This equalizing impact of union membership is a major reason why unionization is associated with reduced incidence of low pay.

Table 4.6
Dispersion of Hourly Wages,
by Sex and Unionization, Canada 1995 ($)

	WOMEN		MEN	
	Union	Non-Union	Union	Non-Union
Decile Limits ($s):				
Decile 9	25.00	19.78	27.00	25.48
Decile 5 (median)	16.00	10.00	18.75	12.50
Decile 1	10.00	6.00	11.00	7.00
D9/D5	1.56	1.98	1.44	2.04
D1/D5	0.63	0.60	0.59	0.56
D9/D1	2.50	3.30	2.45	3.64

Non-Wage Benefits

Occupational pensions, medical and dental plans and paid holidays are important aspects of the compensation package, and noticeable differences between workers in union and non-union jobs are evident (see Table 4.7). Indeed, non-wage benefits are more important than wage differences between union and non-union workers, since unionization is associated with a shift in the overall compensation package towards benefits.

Table 4.7
Non-wage Benefits, by Sex, Union Status
and Selected Characteristics, Canada 1995

	Women		Men	
	Union	Non-Union	Union	Non-Union
% WITH PENSION PLAN - All	79	31	83	35
Age 25 to 44	80	38	83	41
Age 45 to 69	83	34	89	46
Full-time	85	41	85	41
Part-time	60	9	31	na
Management/Administration	89	54	91	58
Professional	84	36	90	46
Clerical	81	32	88	39
Sales	na	21	57	33
Service	62	9	82	15
Blue Collar	61	22	80	27
% WITH MEDICAL PLAN - All	78	40	87	49
Age 25 to 44	80	48	88	56
Age 45 to 69	80	43	91	60
Full-time	86	54	89	56
Part-time	50	11	31	na
Management/Administration	88	69	94	77
Professional	79	45	88	60
Clerical	80	43	85	49
Sales	na	27	69	48
Service	61	13	84	21
Blue Collar	79	34	87	40
% WITH DENTAL PLAN - All	72	38	79	46
Age 25 to 44	75	46	81	55
Age 45 to 69	72	37	82	55
Full-time	80	51	82	53
Part-time	46	10	29	na
Management/Administration	87	65	81	73
Professional	71	44	77	58
Clerical	76	41	84	47
Sales	na	26	63	44
Service	54	12	79	19
Blue Collar	69	28	80	39

na - Sample size too small to provide reliable estimate.
SOURCE: Survey of Work Arrangements

For example, women in unionized jobs are more than twice as likely to be included in pension plans than are women in non-unionized positions, and the situation is similar when medical and dental plan coverage is considered. Like the union wage premium, differences between unionized and non-unionized workers remain when other factors, such as age, hours of work and occupation, are taken into account.

Table 4.8
Vacation Entitlements in Major Collective Agreements
(% employees covered by provision in 1998)

	Paid Holiday Days	
	less than 11 days	16.0%
	11 days	33.0%
	11-13 days	31.4%
	more than 13 days	7.8%
	Paid Vacations	
4 weeks	after 1 year	18.0%
	after 2-7 years	17.5%
	after 8 years	14.9%
	after 9-10 years	16.7%
	after 11-20 years	4.6%
	no provision	28.1%
5 weeks	after 1-10 years	6.4%
	after 10-15 years	24.2%
	after 15-20 years	25.2%
	after 20-25 years	13.2%
	no provision	31.9%

SOURCE: Department of Human Resources Development Workplace Information Directorate. Data are for all agreements covering 500 or more workers.

As shown in Table 4.8, unionized workers also enjoy favourable access to paid holiday time and paid vacation, with 71.9% qualifying for at least four weeks paid vacation (most commonly after 8-10 years of service) and 68.1% qualifying for five weeks paid vacation (most commonly after about 15 years of service). However, there has been a slight slippage in such entitlements since 1996.

Union membership generally conveys greater access to job security, though there are ultimately few if any cast-iron guarantees in a market economy. Seniority-based protection against layoff applies to 67.8% of unionized workers, up slightly from 1996, and recall rights are compa-

rable. Seniority-based promotion rights (usually qualified by job requirements) extend to about half of union members.

Direct employment guarantees (often very qualified) apply to only
about one in six union members, though the majority do enjoy some protection through advance notice of layoff. Wider employment security is
also promoted through collective bargaining, which provides some (usually qualified) access to paid training. As shown in Table 4.9, recent attempts at the bargaining table to preserve union jobs through restrictions
on contracting-out have resulted in protection for more workers.

Table 4.9
Job Security Related Provisions In Major Collective Agreements
(% employees covered)

	1996	1998
Some restrictions on contracting out	53.0%	62.9%
Technological change		
•advance notice	58.0%	50.0%
•right to retraining	25.7%	22.4%
Paid training on the job	47.9%	53.9%
Paid training-outside courses	34.0%	40.4%
Advance notice of layoff	55.2%	58.9%
(more than 100 days)	(3.2%)	(5.8%)
Seniority		
•on promotion	47.6%	50.0%
•on lay-off	66.8%	67.8%
•on recall	65.6%	65.7%
Employment guarantee		
—some provision	16.0%	16.9%

SOURCE: Department of Human Resources Development. Workplace Information
Directorate. Data are for all agreements covering 500 or more workers.

EQUALITY ISSUES AND COLLECTIVE BARGAINING

Differential pay and other forms of discrimination have been directly ad-
dressed in bargaining as union women have pushed forward an equality
agenda. Table 4.10 provides data on the incidence of collective agreement
provisions of particular importance to women, such as provisions regarding maternity leave, sexual harassment, and family responsibilities.

Half of workers covered by major collective agreements now have
the protection of a formal sexual harassment clause, more than double the
level of 1985, and 60.5% of major collective agreements contain a non-

discrimination clause. 27.6% of workers covered by major collective agreements have access to a provision calling for equal pay for work of equal value, compared to just 5.4% in 1985.

Many unions have negotiated formal job evaluation plans and the elimination or compression of pay grades occupied by lower-paid women.

Table 4.10
Collective Agreements and Equality
Per Cent of Employees Covered by Clauses Pertaining
to Selected Issues, Canada 1985 and 1998

Clauses Regarding:	1985	1998	% Point Change
Anti-Discrimination Provision	56.1	60.5	+ 4.4
Affirmative Action	5.9	11.8	+ 9.9
Sexual Harassment	20.6	51.7	+ 31.1
Equal Pay	5.4	27.6	+ 22.2
Job Sharing	2.6	9.5	+ 6.9
Flexitime	17.5	34.9	+ 17.4
Day Care Facilities	3.4	6.0	+ 2.6
Seniority During Maternity Leave	47.0	52.0	+ 5.0
Paid Maternity Leave UI/EI Supplement	37.0	52.8	+ 15.8
Max. Maternity Leave - With & Without Pay			
1 to 16 weeks	0.3	0.4	+ 0.1
17 weeks	16.6	22.8	+ 6.2
18 to 25 weeks	27.5	24.0	+ 3.5
26 weeks or more	17.6	21.5	+ 3.9
Length not specified	7.0	4.2	+ 2.8
No Provision	30.9	27.1	+ 3.8
Seniority During Adoption Leave	34.8	48.1	+ 13.3
Paid Adoption Leave UI/EI Supplement	20.3	30.2	+ 9.9
Max. Adoption Leave - With & Without Pay			
1 to 16 weeks	26.2	19.2	- 7.0
17 weeks	7.1	8.7	+ 1.6
18 to 25 weeks	3.4	13.9	+ 10.5
26 weeks or more	15.9	21.9	+ 6.0
Length not specified	0.9	1.8	+ 0.9
No Provision	46.3	34.5	- 11.8
Paid Leave - Illness in Family	22.5	24.2	+ 1.7
Unpaid Leave - Illness in Family	8.7	17.8	+ 9.1
Unpaid Extended Parental Leave	9.7	28.2	+ 18.5
Unpaid Extended Paternity Leave	21.7	47.2	+ 25.5
Unpaid Personal Reasons Leave	34.1	52.9	+ 18.8

SOURCE: Special tabulations prepared by Human Resources Development Canada, Workplace Information Directorate.

Bargaining has resulted in real progress on equity issues in the absence of legislative provisions, and has often made resolution of such issues subject to grievance and arbitration procedures.

Anti-discrimination provisions are common in collective agreements, but affirmative action provisions apply to only 11.8% of workers. Employment equity plans which would promote greater equality for workers of colour and other equality-seeking groups are relatively lacking and, even where they exist, rarely extend affirmative action to limit layoff or promotion based on seniority, and only apply to new hiring. Seniority rights, however, do limit discriminatory layoffs and promotions.

Another key area of progress has been with respect to paid maternity leaves. Today, the majority of workers covered by major collective agreements have access to such leaves, often with between 76% and 100% of normal pay. Provision for paid leaves in excess of 17 weeks have become increasingly common. Gains have been made in terms of provisions allowing workers to take time off work to attend to parental responsibilities and family care, although in most cases such leave has been provided on an unpaid basis.

With one in four adult women working part-time, provisions pertaining to part-time workers are particularly relevant to women. 70% of collective agreements have specific part-time provisions, up from 56% in 1985, and gains for part-time workers have been made on several issues, including sick leave, holiday time, severance pay, hours of work, health and welfare, and the pro-rating of benefits.

In 1997, as indicated by labour force survey data, unionized women part-time workers earned 94.3% of the hourly wage of full-time unionized workers, while non-unionized women part-timers earned just 75.5% of the hourly wage of non-unionized women full-time workers. The wage gap is lower for women than for men working part-time.

Unionization has also brought major gains with respect to benefits. 56.7% of unionized part-timers belong to a pension plan, below the 86.6% coverage for full-time unionized workers, but well above the pension coverage rate of just 7.4% for non-union part-time workers.

Unionization gives to all workers the normal protections of a collective agreement, notably access to a grievance and arbitration process regarding discipline, dismissal, and promotions; protection against layoff; and other rights and protections. In practice, even legislated minimum employment standards are much easier to access in a unionized environment. Most importantly, unions are an instrument of democratization, giving workers a collective, independent voice in workplace governance.

In 1993, the unionization rate for workers of colour was some-what below average at 26%. This group earned 27% more per hour than non-unionized workers of colour, showing that collective bargaining brings a significant advantage to groups facing pay and other forms of discrimination in the labour market. (Data from Statistics Canada, Survey of Labour Income Dynamics).

LOOKING TO THE FUTURE

A crucial challenge facing the labour movement today is to find ways to maintain and improve access to collective bargaining and to the benefits, rights, and protections it affords in the context of a structural shift toward low-paid and precarious employment. Whether Canada's unionization rate will rise or fall will be determined by the pace of structural change which adds and subtracts employment in unionized workplaces, and by the pace of new organization.

The obstacles to union organizing in the private service sector are not insuperable. Coverage is significant in some parts of retail trade, such as grocery stores and larger retail chains, and in the hotel industry. There have been successful and widely publicized recent organizing drives in fast food restaurants, small retail operations, and other small workplaces. Several unions have also made new organizing a major priority, and the relatively steady membership of most Canadian unions masks constant new organizing to replace lost members. The commitment of Canadian unions to new organizing has generally been significantly higher than in the U.S., although major changes in the U.S. may now be under way.

The overall picture, however, suggests that new organizing is running somewhat below the rate needed to maintain, let alone increase, the overall unionization rate. Where labour legislation has been reasonably facilitative of organizing, as in British Columbia today and as in Ontario under the NDP government, the number of new certifications has significantly increased, sometimes to at or near the level which would increase the unionization rate.

The fundamental reality is that union representation in the small firm, private services sector is low, and is likely to remain low, in the absence of public policy support. The key barriers are not worker rejection of unions or lack of union interest in organizing, but are rather structural (Alexandra Dagg, *"Workers' Representation and Protection in the 'New Economy'"* in Advisory Committee on the Changing Workplace 1997).

As a practical matter, it is extremely difficult to establish collective bargaining in sectors which are dominated by small firms and which are labour-intensive and highly competitive. A *"community of interest"* is hard to establish among workers where turnover is high, the hours of work are highly variable, and there is close supervision of workers by owners and managers. Further, small enterprise employers strongly resist unionization because of the loss of *"flexibility"* in hiring and firing and, most importantly, because unionization threatens to raise wages and benefits in highly competitive, labour-intensive sectors.

Employers have significant resources at their disposal to resist unionization: short-term and contract workers can be easily dismissed, the hours of part-timers can be changed, and work can be restructured through the use of franchisees, contractors, and sub-contractors in order to disguise the real nature of the employment relationship. Precisely because their jobs are so precarious, these workers fear employer reprisal or workplace closure if they join a union.

Unions themselves find it difficult to organize and to represent small bargaining units, given stretched staff and resources and the high costs of bargaining and representation in small units. The highly competitive reality of the small business, private service sector also means that it is difficult for unions to make significant gains for members. Wages, benefits and hours are an important part of the competitive equation unless they can be generalized across employers. A single fast food outlet or retail store will also be reluctant to raise wages above the prevailing industry level. Further, chains will be reluctant to make precedent-setting agreements in a single workplace.

A fundamental solution to this set of structural problems in the small firm, private services sector is to facilitate union organization and collective bargaining at a broader level than that of the individual firm and workplace, defined both sectorally and geographically. However, this is very difficult if there is no compulsion on employers to bargain as a group. In Canada, multi-employer or sectoral bargaining almost always requires the consent of both the employers and the unions involved (though there are important exceptions such as the institutional construction industry where multi-employer bargaining has sometimes been legislatively mandated).

Recently, proposals have been made to encourage, through facilitative labour legislation, the growth of the broader-based bargaining model in the small employer, private services sector where unions have been historically under-represented. Such legislative initiatives are needed to complement the organizing activities of unions themselves.

CHAPTER 5

The Changing Distribution of Family Income:
The Declining Middle Class and Trends in Poverty

This chapter explores how income disparities among Canadian families increased over the 1990s. A decade of high unemployment, social program cutbacks, downsized workplaces in both the public and private sector, and structural changes in the labour market have significantly increased poverty and inequality.

In particular, low- and middle-income familites with children experienced a marked decline in living standards in the 1990s. The number of children living in impoverished circumstances increased steadily, and the incidence of poverty rose dramatically among one-earner families and young families. Aboriginal people, people of colour, and persons with disabilities continue to face the greatest risk of low income within Canada, with incomes lagging far behind the average and rates of poverty far outpacing the national rate.

Overall, the picture that emerges from this analysis is gloomy. While the federal government claims victory over the deficit and now anticipates large fiscal surpluses, we have amassed a huge *social deficit*. The Canada of the 21st Century is becoming a decidedly more unequal society.

DOES INEQUALITY MATTER?

While many factors contribute to the quality of life, the degree of equality within society is an important measure of how well people are doing and of the overall well-being of the society in which they live. In fact, researchers are now discovering that greater social and economic inequality adversely affects life-long health outcomes, including mortality and life expectancy rates.

Recent research has found that improved health status is not merely a function of the amount of wealth produced in a country, but is also related to how income is distributed. While improvements in health and longevity do occur with increases in GDP per capita, there is a ceiling at which continued gains cease. Richard Wilkinson estimates the ceiling to be at about $5,000 income per capita. [Richard Wilkinson, *Unhealthy Societies: From Inequality to Well-Being* (London: Routledge, 1996)]. This explains why, despite increases in total income in industrialized countries, there has been little improvement in the overall health status of their populations over recent years. Indeed, the contrary may be true. In the United States, the richest nation on earth, life expectancy has actually decreased.

Once the income ceiling is reached, the degree of income inequality *within* a country becomes the major determinant of health status. Differences in health as a result of socio-economic status do not occur only between the very wealthiest in a society and the very poorest. They occur throughout the entire income ladder. The wealthiest are the healthiest, with a declining gradient in health status occurring all the way down the income scale. At the bottom of the ladder, statistics show that the poorest people in a society are the least healthy.

Empirical data comparing the average national health status between countries bears this out. Countries where income differences between the poor and the rich are larger tend to have worse health outcomes and lower life expectancy rates than in countries where the income gap is smaller. Life expectancy is highest in countries like Sweden, Switzerland and Norway, where the poorest 70% of the population receive a larger share of the income pie compared to what the poorest 70% receive in countries like the United States and the United Kingdom where the income gap is much larger. Equality matters.

EARNINGS INEQUALITY

As noted in Chapter 1, since wages are the largest source of income for most people, the distribution of earnings represents the greatest source of income inequality. Between 1950 and 1975, real incomes rose rapidly, resulting in increased standards of living. In turn, this was associated with declining or stable income inequality. Since then, real incomes have stagnated for most and inequality has tended to rise. Sustained high levels of unemployment, underemployment, growth in the precarious types of jobs discussed earlier, and changes in hours worked and hourly wages have all influenced the distribution of earnings.

Data also show that certain groups of Canadians face higher rates of low earnings. As noted in Chapter 2, recent immigrants, people of colour, Aboriginal Canadians, and women all have significantly lower earnings. As shown above, women still face very high rates of low pay. Moreover, the majority of welfare recipients without earnings are women: 27% are single-parent women, 21% are single women, together making up almost half of welfare recipients.

FAMILY INCOME AND INEQUALITY: LONG-TERM TRENDS

Figure 5.1 illustrates who received what share of total family income in 1995. The definition of income here is market income—wages, salaries, and investment income—plus transfers from governments. Each decile represents 10% of the population. The 10% of families in the bottom decile received only 1.5% of all total family income. The highest income 10% of families received 26.5% of all family income. The share of total income going to families in the bottom five deciles (50% of all families) was just 24% of total family income. On the other hand, families in the top three deciles, or 30% of families, commanded over half of all family income (55%).

In recent decades, the overall share of family income has become distributed less evenly; indeed, this has been the case since the end of the

Figure 5.1
Share of Total Family Income (Before Income Tax) by Decile, 1995

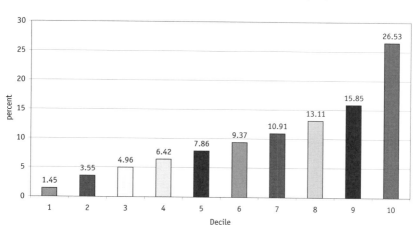

SOURCE: Abdul, Rashid, Family income: 25 years of stability and change, in Perspectives, Spring 1999, p 10.

"Golden Age." Families in the first seven deciles, or 70% of all families, have seen their share of the total income pie before tax decline between 1970 and 1995. The 30% of families with the highest incomes have seen their share of total incomes rise over that period. In short, the 30% at the top are increasing their share of the income pie, while the remainder are seeing their share decline (see Figure 5.2).

Figure 5.2
Percent Change in Share of Total Family Income by Decile, 1970-1995

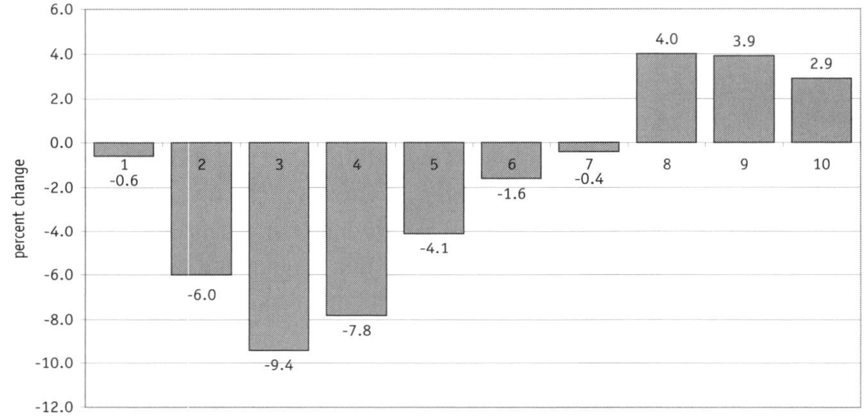

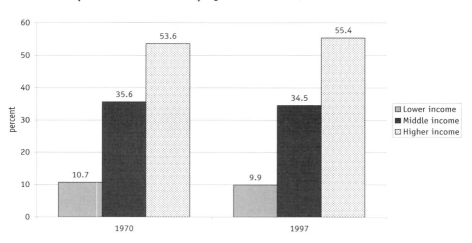

SOURCE: Abdul, Rashid, Family income: 25 years of stability and change, in Perspectives, Spring 1999, p 10.

Figure 5.3
Share of Total Family Income
(Before Income Taxes) by Income Class, 1970 and 1997

Lower-income and middle-income families today have a smaller share of the income pie than in the past. In 1970, as illustrated in Figure 5.3, families in the three lowest deciles received about 10.7% of all family income before income tax. By 1995, their share had dropped to 9.9%. The share of income going to families in the middle four deciles dropped from 35.6% in 1970 to 34.5% in 1995. Meanwhile, families in the top three deciles increased their share of family income from 53.6% in 1970 to 55.4% in 1995.

The changes in shares may not appear to be large until dollar values are attached. The decline in the share of income going to the fourth decile, for instance, meant a loss of $3,000 per family in 1995. At the same time, families in the highest decile increased their share of income by $4,200. In total, between 1970 and 1995 the decline suffered by families in the first seven deciles amounted to a transfer of about $8 billion from them to families in the top three deciles.

Who are those families in the first seven deciles that have been falling behind? In the bottom decile where annual incomes before income tax were less than $13,864 in 1997, 40% of the families are single-parent mothers with children. All families in the second income decile have incomes higher than the first decile limit, but lower than $22,066. Just over 71% of families in which a woman is the head of the family have incomes under $25,000 compared to 31% of families in which a man is the head of the family. In families where the head is under age 24, 52% have incomes under $24,999.

The average income before income tax of the fifth decile is $48,023. Of families in which the age of the head is over 65 years, 67% have incomes below $45,000. This is the case for 70% of families in which the head is over 70 years of age.

Families in the sixth decile had an average pre-tax income of $55,924 in 1997. 78% of immigrant families arriving in Canada after 1989 have incomes below this limit. Almost 54% of families with children under the age of 16 and 54% of families with children under 18 have incomes below $55,000.

Statistics Canada does not publish data on the distribution of family income by a disability category. However, we do know that the overall poverty rate for people with a disability was 22% in 1996 and 25% for women with a disability, so that their average incomes would be in the lowest or second lowest income decile.

Overall, it appears that the transfer of $8 billion in income from families in the seven lowest income deciles to those in the highest income deciles has come from the most vulnerable groups of people: single-parent families, young families, elderly families, immigrant families, people with a disability, and families with children. We can only imagine how much less poverty there would be today, how many fewer people would be using food banks, how many less homeless there would be, if governments had made greater income equality a priority.

TRENDS IN THE 1990s

The "Growing Gap" Report of the Centre for Social Justice showed that the 1990s have been a continuation of the recent past [see Armine Yalnizian, *The Growing Gap: a report on growing inequality between the rich and the poor in Canada,* Toronto: Centre for Social Justice, October 1998]. The analysis explored the changing distribution of market income among families with children between 1973 and 1996. Family incomes have become more polarized between rich and poor, with fewer families falling into the middle income class (see Figure 5.4). The Chart shows the proportion of families in 1996 on the basis of the income deciles of 1975. As illustrated, there was a large movement into the very bottom and very top of the income distribution and a "hollowing-out" of the middle-income groups over this period.

Figure 5.4
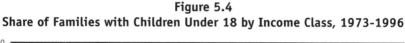
Share of Families with Children Under 18 by Income Class, 1973-1996

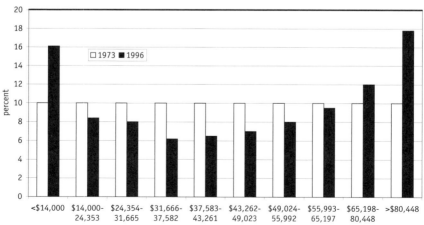

SOURCE: A. Yalnizyan, The Growing Gap (Toronto: Centre for Social Justice, 1998).

As shown in Figure 5.5, average family income was lower by any measure in 1997 than in 1989, even as the economy recovered from the severe recession of the early 1990s. Income before income taxes and transfers declined from $53,937 in 1989 to $50,672 in 1997, a drop of more than 6%. After government transfers, average family income fell from $59,862 to $57,146, or by almost 5%, over the same period. After income taxes and payroll taxes, the average real disposable income of families dropped more than 5%, from $48,311 to $45,605.

Figure 5.5
Average Family Income, 1989-1997

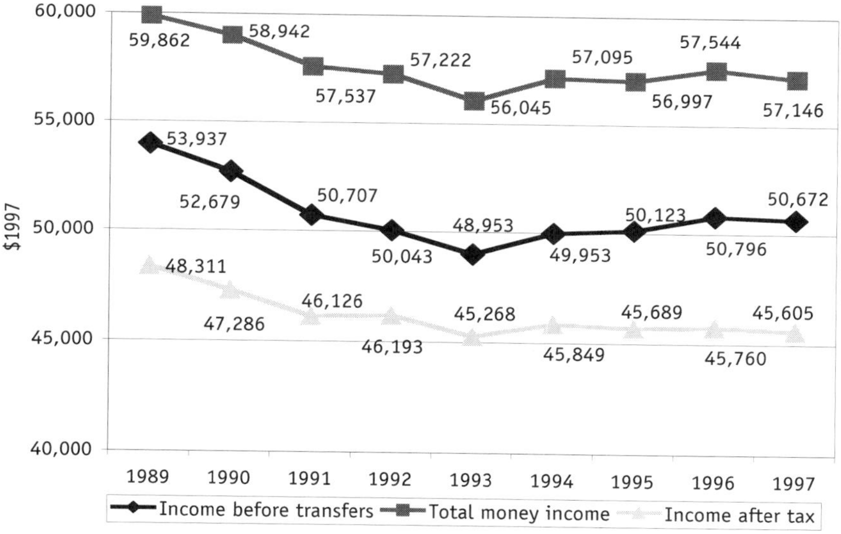

SOURCE: Statistics Canada, Income after tax, distributions by size in Canada, 1997, cat. 13-210-XP6

Table 5.1 shows the change in average after-tax income for various family types between 1989 and 1997 (adjusted for inflation). As shown, most family types experienced a decline in disposable income over this period. The only exceptions to this were very modest income gains made by two-earner couples without children (0.1%) and unattached elderly men (0.2%). Overall, the drop in after-tax income was particularly pronounced for men who are lone parents (-20.2%), one-earner two-parent families with children (-7.8%), and unattached, non-elderly men (-7.3%).

Table 5.1
Change in Average Annual Income After Income Taxes
by Family Type, 1989-1997*   ($1997)

Family Type	1989	1997	% Change
All Economic Families	48,311	45,605	-5.6
Elderly Families	36,669	37,124	-1.2
Married Couples Only	35,125	34,346	-2.2
Non-elderly Families	49,910	47,103	-5.6
Married Couples One Earner	39,261	34,674	-3.4
Married Couples Two Earners	50,411	50,484	0.1
Two-parent Families with Children	53,367	50,860	-4.7
One earner	40,151	37,002	-7.8
Two earners	52,249	52,007	-0.5
Lone-Parent Families	25,688	23,897	-7
Male Lone-Parents	39,675	31,670	-20.2
Female Lone-Parents	23,828	22,493	-5.2
Female, No Earner	14,010	13,225	-5.6
Unattached Individuals	21,406	20,333	-5
Elderly Male	20,802	20,836	0.2
Elderly Female	17,210	16,811	-2.3
Non-elderly Male	24,179	22,407	-7.3
Non-elderly Female	20,627	19,708	-4.5

SOURCE, Statistics Canada, Income after tax, distributions by size in Canada 1997, catalogue no. 13-210- XPB, Text Table VII.

The market income of families is strongly related to the ability of members to participate in the labour market, as well as the kinds of jobs they hold. As Figure 5.6 shows, two parent families in which both parents work

Figure 5.6
Average Market Income of Families, 1995

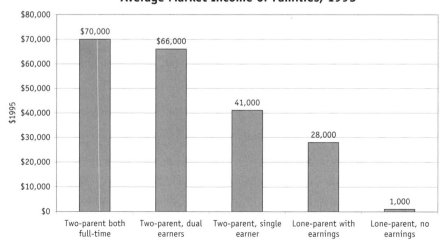

Source: Statistics Canada, 1996 Census

full-time have the highest market incomes. Lone-parents have the lowest earnings and lone-parents without work have almost no market income.

The change in average family income provides only part of the overall picture. We need to look more closely at how families in different income groups fared: that is, how total market income, income after government transfers, and income after tax was distributed between different income groups.

By dividing all families with children into 10 equal sized groups (deciles), we can see who bore the greatest burden of the decline in market income in the 1990s. This has been done by the Centre for Social Justice which examined trends in income distribution for families with children (since the income situation of the elderly is different and the income situation of children is of particular interest). As illustrated in Table 5.2, all deciles experienced a decline in market income, but this was not distributed evenly. Average incomes before transfers declined more than 66% between 1989 and 1997 for the 10% of families with the lowest incomes, and by about 30% and 18% for the second and third deciles, respectively. Families in the fourth and fifth deciles also experienced a significant decline in income, but for higher deciles the drop in income was less. The most modest drop in income was for families in the second highest decile.

The dramatic decline in market income for lower income families with children, coupled with more modest losses at the upper end, meant that income disparities among Canadian families grew in the 1990s. In 1989, the richest 10% of families with children had market income about

Table 5.2
Market Incomes of Families with Children by Decile, 1989-97 ($1997)

	1989	1991	1993	1995	1997	% change 89-97
Lowest decile	3,741	1,561	511	1,222	1,255	-66.5%
Decile 2	19,000	13,617	10,392	12,483	13,355	-29.7%
Decile 3	30,614	25,243	22,306	24,605	25,135	-17.9%
Decile 4	39,879	34,925	32,314	34,458	35,167	-11.8%
Decile 5	47,839	43,638	40,946	43,348	44,186	-7.6%
Decile 6	55,508	51,950	49,611	51,894	52,876	-4.7%
Decile 7	63,945	61,114	59,216	61,056	61,796	-3.4%
Decile 8	74,681	71,401	70,012	71,860	73,632	-1.4%
Decile 9	89,707	85,758	84,782	86,518	88,992	-0.8%
Highest decile	144,699	136,683	131,412	137,411	136,394	-5.7%

SOURCE: Centre for Social Justice using Statistics Canada, Survey of Consumer Finances, unpublished data.

39 times greater than the poorest 10%. By 1997, this gap had grown to nearly 110 times.

FAMILY INCOME AND GOVERNMENT TRANSFER PAYMENTS

Governments add to market income through transfer payments. These payments include Old Age Security, social assistance, Canada/Quebec Pension Plans, veterans' allowances, disability payments, Workers' Compensation, and training allowances. Also included in transfer income are the GST tax credit and the Child Tax Benefit. Since low- and modest-income families are the principal beneficiaries of transfers, these payments play an important role in bringing about greater income equality among families.

As a result of declining employment income and cuts to transfer payments, the average income of families with children after transfers declined between 1989 and 1997 (see Table 5.3). Families in the lowest income decile saw their incomes drop by about 11%, while families in the second and third lowest deciles experienced an even greater decline of about 16% and 14%, respectively. The incomes of families in the next three deciles dropped by 10%, 6.5%, and 4.7%. Proportionately, families in deciles 7, 8 and 9 experienced the most modest drop in incomes after transfers (between 1.7% and 4.1%), while the income of the highest decile fell by more than 6%.

Comparing Tables 5.2 as shown above and 5.3 highlights the critical importance of transfer payments, especially to families with lower incomes. Before transfers, families in the lowest decile received income of just $1,225 in 1997. After transfers, however, their income rose to $13,864—an increase of more than 11 times. Government transfers also very significantly improved the incomes of families in the second (+$8,711) and third (+$6,063) deciles. While the market income of the poorest 10% of families with children fell by 66% between 1989 and 1997, their actual cash income fell "only" 11% because of transfers. The contribution of transfers to the total income of families with children in 1997 was 21% for the lowest decile, 40% for the second lowest, and 19% for the third lowest—but less than 4% for the top 4 deciles.

As shown in Table 5.4—data for all families—transfers have a huge impact on the pre-tax incomes of all lower income families.

As a result of raising the incomes of poorer families, government transfers have been remarkably effective in dampening the growing gap in market incomes. In 1997, before transfers, the richest 10% of families

Table 5.3
Incomes of Families with Children After Government Transfers by Decile, 1989-97 ($1997)

	1989	1991	1993	1995	1997	% change 89-97
lowest decile	15,563	14,931	15,661	15,438	13,864	-10.9%
decile 2	26,252	22,843	21,418	21,798	22,066	-15.9%
decile 3	36,406	32,613	29,884	31,678	31,198	-14.3%
decile 4	44,359	40,874	38,592	39,492	39,926	-10.0%
decile 5	51,383	48,326	46,961	47,534	48,023	-6.5%
decile 6	58,688	55,710	53,654	55,791	55,924	-4.7%
decile 7	66,927	64,339	62,743	63,877	64,201	-4.1%
decile 8	77,101	74,371	72,763	74,280	75,540	-2.0%
decile 9	92,300	88,405	87,394	88,565	90,702	-1.7%
highest decile	146,888	138,891	133,187	139,057	137,942	-6.1%

SOURCE: Statistics Canada, Survey of Consumer Finances, unpublished data obtained from the Centre for Social Justice.

Table 5.4
Percentage Increase in Family Income as a Result of Transfer Payments

Quintile	Income Before Transfers	Income after Transfers	Percentage Increase
1	$8,199	$17,781	116.8
2	$25,979	$34,399	32.4
3	$44,627	$50,548	13.2
4	$64,450	$64,450	7.5
5	$110,113	$113,948	3.5

SOURCE: Calculations based on Statistics Canada, Income distribution by size in Canada, 1997.

with children had incomes nearly 110 times greater than the poorest 10% of families. After transfers, the gap narrowed dramatically to about 10 times.

Since the mid-1990s, however, transfer payments to families have declined as governments cut Unemployment Insurance and social assistance. Transfer payments as a share of average family income fell from a peak of 12.9% in 1993 to 11.3% in 1997. While this may seem like a small decrease, in dollar terms it has had a huge impact on families with lower incomes.

Figure 5.7 shows the decline in transfer payments between 1989 and 1997 by income quintile. Families with the lowest incomes lost $954 on average in transfer income, and families with the second lowest incomes lost $838. By contrast, the richest families experienced a more modest decline of $289, on average. This reflects again the importance of social assistance, UI, and income linked credits to lower income families.

Figure 5.7
Change in Transfer Payments to Families by Quintile, 1993-97 ($1997)

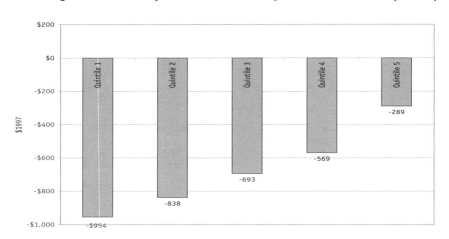

SOURCE: Statistics Canada, Income after tax, distributions by size in Canada, 1997.

The loss of $954 to a family with very low income is catastrophic compared to a loss of $289 for a family with a much higher income. For low-income families, it can mean the difference between having enough food to eat, or enough money to pay the rent. Single-parent families led by women face the highest incidence of poverty (56%), and have been hardest hit by the decline in transfer payments.

AFTER TAX INCOME

In 1997, the average income of families with children after income tax was $45,605, a decline of 6% from its highest point in 1989. Table 5.5 shows that after-tax income was lower in 1997 than it was in 1989 for all families with children.

As illustrated, the bottom 30% of families experienced the largest proportionate decline in average after-tax family income over the 1990s. The incomes of families in the lowest income decile, with average after-tax income of $13,806, dropped by more than 10%. Families in the 2nd and 3rd deciles fared even worse, posting declines of about 13%. Families in the fourth decile saw their average after-tax income drop by over 9%. For deciles 5 through 9, the decline was more modest.

Table 5.5
Incomes of Families with Children After-Tax by Decile, 1989-97 ($1997)

	1989	1991	1993	1995	1997	% change 89-97
lowest decile	15,396	14,822	15,581	15,359	13,806	-10.3%
decile 2	24,440	21,700	20,640	20,946	21,172	-13.4%
decile 3	32,302	29,247	27,429	28,841	28,275	-12.5%
decile 4	37,848	35,204	33,828	34,125	34,338	-9.3%
decile 5	42,623	40,151	38,748	39,589	39,693	-6.9%
decile 6	47,701	45,099	43,954	45,326	44,995	-5.7%
decile 7	53,758	51,012	50,083	50,652	50,850	-5.4%
decile 8	60,603	58,260	57,089	57,811	58,415	-3.6%
decile 9	72,017	67,957	67,199	67,558	69,178	-3.9%
highest decile	106,963	99,459	96,867	99,040	98,746	-7.7%

SOURCE: Statistics Canada, Survey of Consumer Finances, unpublished data obtained from the Centre for Social Justice.

Unlike the rebound in after-tax incomes following the recession in the early 1980s, the lowest income families have not to date benefited from the economic recovery in the 1990s. Figure 5.8 shows the changes in after-tax income for all families by quintile from 1983 to 1989 and from 1993 to 1997, comparing two periods of recovery. As illustrated, after-tax income for all families did increase in the 1980s and 1990s, and social programs in fact provided the biggest income gains for low income families in the 1980s. Average income after tax fell for families with the lowest incomes during the recovery of the 1990s, while other quintiles witnessed only modest gains when compared to the recovery of the 1980s.

Figure 5.8
Change in After Tax Income by Quintile, 1984-89 and 1993-97

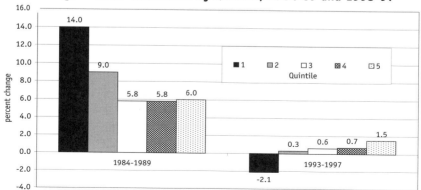

SOURCE: Calculations based on Statistics Canada, Incomes after tax, distributions by size in Canada, 1997 cat. No. 13-2100-XPB.

The evidence shows that the rising economic tide of the 1990s did not lift all boats.

If unchecked, this trend will lead to a significant rise in after-tax and transfer income inequality. This is of crucial concern because the transfer and tax system have to date been crucial in stabilizing growth of market income inequality. If the gap in market incomes continues to rise, and if governments fail to rebuild income support programs, then poor and working class families in Canada face the prospect of falling even further behind in the years ahead.

Inequality and Seniors' Incomes in the 1990s

As was the case with other household types, the 1990s were a period of declining real incomes for older households (i.e., households in which the age of the highest income earner in the household, or the household head, is 65 or older). As revealed in Table 5.6, the average income of older households declined by 3% between 1989 and 1996, from $32,667 to $31,834.

Table 5.6
Average Income of Elderly Households, 1973-1996

(Constant 1996 $)	1973	1981	1989	1996	1973-89	1989-96 % change	1973-96
Elderly families	$30,766	$37,225	$44,197	$42,759	44%	-3%	39%
Married couples	$25,372	$32,838	$40,347	$39,588	59%	-2%	56%
All other families	$40,611	$45,970	$53,306	$51,745	31%	-3%	27%
Unattached individuals	$12,669	$17,167	$19,683	$20,023	55%	2%	58%
Male	$13,998	$19,892	$23,330	$25,020	67%	7%	79%
Female	$12,084	$16,173	$18,527	$18,139	53%	-2%	50%
All households	$22,468	$27,367	$32,667	$31,834	45%	-3%	42%
Earnings	$7,712	$6,367	$6,816	$5,249	-12%	-23%	-32%
Investment income	$3,772	$6,755	$7,014	$4,113	86%	-41%	9%
Pension	$2,344	$2,864	$4,823	$7,098	106%	47%	203%
Other transfers	$894	$1,042	$1,286	$1,294	44%	1%	45%
OAS/GIS	$6,896	$7,695	$8,016	$7,887	16%	-2%	14%
CPP/QPP	$620	$2,227	$4,242	$5,678	584%	34%	816%
25-54 age group	$47,448	$53,360	$55,678	$52,214	17%	-6%	10%

	1973	1981	1989	1996
Senior households	$22,468	$27,367	$32,667	$31,834
Prime age households	$47,448	$53,360	$55,678	$52,214
Senior income as % of prime age	47%	51%	59%	61%

SOURCE: Statistics Canada. Survey of Consumer Finances.

Virtually all types of elderly households experienced the 3% decline in real incomes noted above (e.g., married couples, other family units, and unattached women). The only exception was unattached men, whose incomes actually increased by 7%. It is important to note, however, that the income of low-income households did increase between 1989 and 1996: from $13,173 to $13,485 (i.e., by 2%), and so did the incomes of older households with no earnings: from $24,956 to $25,823 (i.e., by 3%).

The improvement in the real incomes of low-income recipients was reflected in a modest decline in both low income rates and inequality among the elderly. Both of these developments in the 1990s reflect longer-term trends.

Low income rates stabilized for couples and families at just under 10%. For single elderly men, the low income rate declined from 36% to 33%, and for women from 57% to 53%. Bearing in mind that nearly 60% of all older women are single, compared to 25% of men, the extent of low incomes for older women is striking. It should also be noted that significant portions of the elderly have incomes just above and just below Statistics Canada's low income cutoffs. Thus, small income changes and/or changes in the low income lines can move significant numbers of people from one side of the low income lines to the other.

The only deciles of older income recipients whose share of total household income declined between 1989 and 1996 were the top two deciles. Their combined share of total income declined from 46.5% of total income to 44.9%. The share of total income received by the first decile was stable at 3.4%. The share of all other deciles increased slightly.

It is clear that the drop in average real incomes between 1989 and 1996 primarily reflected lower real incomes from investment and employment. The decline in employment income is part of a long-term trend, while the decline in investment reflects relatively lower interest rates in the 1990s and, likely to some small extent, a shift in savings from other forms of saving to RRSPs.

The decreased income from employment and investment was almost offset by increases in income from pensions and annuities, and the CPP and QPP. Increased income from these sources is part of a long-term trend. They have been the main sources of income growth for older Canadians in recent years, with the CPP and QPP being more important at the middle and lower end of the income spectrum, and workplace pensions at the middle and upper end.

Over the period 1981 to 1996, the absolute dollar income gap between individual older men and older women has increased, while women's incomes expressed as a share of men's has remained constant at 62%. More than half of the gap between older men's and older women's incomes in 1996 was accounted for by pension and annuity income. On average, men received $5,254 more than women from this source, compared to a total gap of $9,720. The other major sources of higher incomes for older men were the C/QPP ($2,002) and employment ($2,103). The average investment income of men added another $506 to the total gap, and OAS/GIS reduced the gap by $550.

The lower amounts that women receive from C/QPP and from pensions and annuities reflect the combined effects of lower percentages of women receiving income from the source, and lower amounts received per recipient which, in turn, reflect lower employment incomes. Of these two influences, lower percentages of women receiving income from the source is a slightly stronger influence in the case of C/QPP with its low level of maximum covered earnings, and a slightly weaker influence in the case of pensions and annuities.

Over the period from 1981 to 1996, the percentage of older women who receive pension and annuity income has been growing compared to the portion of men who receive income from this source. In 1981, only 7.8% of older women received income from pensions and annuities, compared to 39.9% of men. By 1996, the comparable numbers were 34.2% of women and 57.4% of men. But, over this period, the income received by women from pensions and annuities was declining in relation to that of men: from 68.8% in 1981 to 57% in 1996.

In the case of the C/QPP, there has been a significant narrowing of the gap in female and male incomes. The percentage of older women who received C/QPP benefits remained very stable between 1981 and 1989 at 35.2%, while the percentage of men who received C/QPP income increased from 72.2% to 83.2%. But, between 1989 and 1996, the percentage of older women in receipt of C/QPP benefits jumped to 70.3%, while the percentage of older men receiving C/QPP benefits increased to 89.4%. At the same time, the amounts that older women received from the C/QPP declined slightly compared to what men received: from 78.1% in 1981 to 75.7% in 1996.

In the case of both pension and annuity income and C/QPP income, it would be helpful to know what cannot be discerned from the

Survey of Consumer Finances—namely, the role played by survivor benefits in lowering average amounts received by older women.

In looking ahead, there is reason to hope that the percentage of older women who receive either or both of C/QPP income and pension and annuity income will come even closer to matching the male rates. For example, between 1989 and 1997, the gap between the percentage of employed men who belong to workplace pensions and the percentage of employed women who belong to workplace pensions declined from 11 percentage points (47 versus 36) to three percentage points (43 versus 40). In the case of the CPP, female contributors were only about half as numerous as men were in the late 1960s, but were 80% as numerous as men by the early 1990s. However, closing the coverage gap will still leave women with lower absolute incomes unless progress is also made on reducing the female/male earnings gap.

The income situation of today's elderly invites conflicting responses. On the one side, it is important to acknowledge the progress that has been made in reducing the incidence of low income and the closing of the gap between the incomes of older and younger households. The important role of public programs (OAS/GIS and C/QPP) in producing these positive results is also noteworthy. On the other side, the incidence of low incomes among the elderly is still too high; the gender-specific nature (i.e., female) of low incomes is not acceptable; and the cross-sectional data that are now available suggest a general decline in living standards for middle-income earners in old age (along with an increase in living standards for people with low incomes prior to age 65).

POVERTY

Most Canadians are aware that, for five years in a row, the United Nations Human Development Report has placed Canada first in its ranking of countries for their progress in human development. This is a broad measure of how well countries are doing, socially and economically.

Less well-known, however, is that Canada fares far worse when poverty rates are factored into the equation. In 1998, the UN added a new measure (the Human Poverty Index (HPI)) which analyzes how progress is distributed throughout the population and the extent to which citizens are excluded. The first year the index was published, Canada ranked 10th out of 17 industrialized countries and the UN Human Development Report specifically singled out Canada as having *"significant problems with poverty"*, and noted that *"progress in human development has been poorly distributed."* In 1999, Canada's ranking improved modestly to 9th place.

The HPI also ranks the wealth of countries. By this measure, we are the sixth wealthiest country of the 17 industrialized countries. Sweden has the lowest poverty rate, yet in terms of its overall wealth is third lowest. The United States is ranked as No. 1 when it comes to wealth, yet it is No. 17 according to the share of its population in poverty.

There is little relationship between the wealth of a country and its ability to reduce poverty. It is no coincidence that the seven countries with the lowest rates of poverty are the Scandinavian and European countries with a demonstrated commitment to equality, just as it no surprise that the countries with the highest share of people in poverty are the countries which have only a bare-bones welfare state and deregulated labour markets.

A study by the Organization for Economic Cooperation and Development (OECD) provides a graphic illustration of the difference between Canada and other countries when it comes to the share of the population with low incomes. The study calculated the share of persons with lower income, based on the proportion of people with incomes below 50% of median income (half of the population are poorer and half more affluent than the median). The proportion of the population falling below 50% of the median is a key indicator of poverty—measured relative to the rest of the population—and of inequality. As revealed in Figure 5.9, the countries with the lowest poverty rates by this measure are the Netherlands, Sweden, Germany, France, and Italy. It is notable that the countries which share income more equally have a much lower share of children in poverty. The United States, with the greatest share of people with incomes below 50% of the mid-income point, is ranked by the United Nations as the country with the highest degree of income inequality.

Figure 5.9
Share of Persons with Incomes Below 50% of Median Income

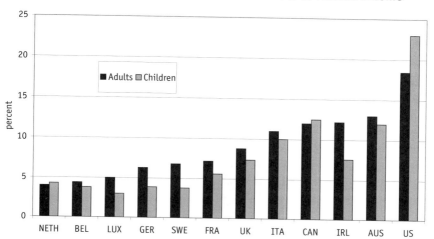

SOURCE: Forster, Michael, Measurement of Low Incomes and Poverty in a Perspective of International Comparisons, Labour Market and occational Papers, No. 14, Paris: OECD, 1994.

POVERTY IN CANADA

Growing income inequality has been closely linked to an increase in the number of families and single people in Canada who suffer the debilitating effects of poverty. Academic descriptions and statistics cannot capture the harsh reality of what it means to live in impoverished circumstances, but the thoughts and feelings of people living in poverty can paint a chilling yet thought-provoking landscape of what it really means to be poor (see Box).

Canada has experienced relatively high rates of poverty for many years and the growing income gap is reflected in the increasing number of families and people who are poor.

Poverty is defined here as an income falling below the Statistics Canada Low Income Cut-Off Line, or LICO. This widely used measure is based on how much a family spends on necessities compared to other families, and is thus a relative measure. The LICO lines are, however, very low in absolute terms. For example, as shown in Table 5.7, the low-income cutoff for a single person living in a large urban centre was just $17,409 in 1997.

In 1980, 13.2% of all families were poor. This dropped to 11.1% of all families by 1989 and moved up to 14% by 1997. However, over that time, the number of families increased, which affects the number of fami-

To live in poverty is a struggle for survival filled with tension, fear and frustration. It is to be robbed of pride, for people living in poverty can't afford the luxury of pride. To stand in line for food or Christmas toys or beg for a special clothing allowance leaves little room for pride.

It is the deep pain which comes with the knowledge that you must deprive your children of opportunities and experiences other children receive as their right.

It's the humiliation of going to your child's school to explain why you can't afford the expensive running shoes that don't mark the gym floor.

It's the look of sadness in your child's eyes when you say no to a school trip or to the purchase of school pictures. Young children don't understand the concept of money. As one parent put it, "They just think you don't love them as much as other parents love their kids".

Poverty is the dread lurking ever in your consciousness. Dread of the day your kids realize their family is different and somehow not as good. Dread of the day your children are ashamed of you. Dread of the end of the month with no money and no food.

Poverty is living a 'no-name, no frills' existence amidst a world in which materialism runs rampant. It's listening to non-poor people make false judgements about you, devalue your existence, question your integrity, label you 'poor' as though that's all there is to you.

Poverty is a demoralizing existence which saps the hopes and dreams upon which the rest of us build our lives.

**Reflections from working with the women
at the Ottawa Council for Low Income Support Services**

Table 5.7
Low Income Cut-offs of Family Units, 1997 ($)

Size of family unit	Size of area of residence				
	500,000 and over	100,000 to 499,000	30,000 to 99,000	less than 30,000	rural areas
1 person	17,409	14,931	14,827	13,796	12,030
2 persons	21,760	18,664	18,534	17,245	15,038
3 persons	27,036	23,213	23,050	21,448	18,703
4 persons	32,759	28,098	27,903	25,964	22,639
5 persons	36,618	31,409	31,191	29,023	25,307
6 persons	40,479	34,270	34,478	32,081	27,975
7 persons	44,339	38,032	37,766	35,140	30,643

SOURCE: Statistics Canada, Low income cut-offs, cat. no. 13-551- XIB.

lies actually living in poverty. In 1980, there were 856,000 poor families. By 1997, 306,000 more families had become poor. This is almost a 36% increase in the number of families living in poverty [Statistics Canada, *Income distributions by size in Canada 1997*, calculated from data in Table 1 and Table 66]. More of Canada's children became poor along with their parents. Child poverty increased from a little over a million children in 1980 to almost 1.4 million in 1997. The total number of poor people in Canada grew by 1.3 million between 1980 and 1997, an increase of 35%.

Poverty rates fluctuate with the rate of economic growth, rising during recessions when unemployment rises. It takes time for poverty rates to fall after recessions, as there is a lag between the resumption of economic growth and its effects on unemployment. However, as of 1997 and six years after the 1991 recession, the number of people who were poor was higher than at the peak impact of the recession in 1992. Moreover, in comparison to 1989 and the early 1980s, the rate of poverty had increased substantially for working-age Canadians. Poverty rates would have been higher if it had not been for offsetting trends. Among the elderly, there was falling poverty as the CPP/QPP was phased in while poverty has increased over time for the working age population, especially for families with children.

In the 1990s, it appears that economic growth has become increasingly unlinked from poverty reduction. In other words, we can no longer make the assumption that workers will share in the benefits of economic growth. Some will, to be sure, but the evidence is clear that a growing number of working class Canadians are not seeing their living standards rise. Indeed, living standards are dropping for many working class families. Poverty is structural in Canada now, and rising.

Figure 5.10
Poverty Rate by Age of Household Head, 1989 and 1997

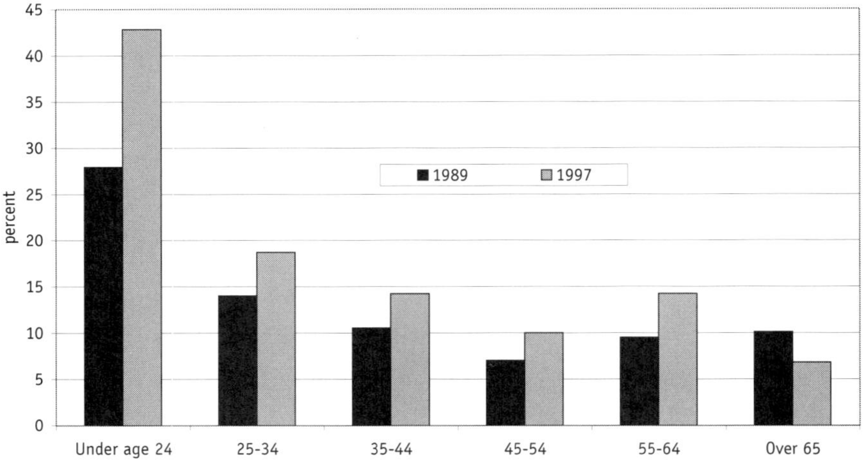

SOURCE: Statistics Canada, Income Distributions by Size in Canada, 1997.

Figure 5.10 shows the incidence of family poverty in 1989 and 1997 by the age of the head of the household. As shown, the rate of poverty has increased among all families, with the sole exception of families where the head is over 65 years of age. Most striking is the increase in the proportion of young families (head under age 24) who live in poverty. In 1989, about 27% were poor. By 1997, this had increased to almost 43%.

Of equal concern is the rise in poverty among families where the head is between the ages of 25 and 34: up from 14% in 1989 to almost 19%

Table 5.8
Poverty Rates by Family Type in Canada, 1989 and 1997

Family types	1989	1997
Married Couples	7.3	10.6
Two-parent families with children, 1 earner	19.5	25.6
Two-parent families with children, 2 earners	5.8	6.6
Lone-parent families, total	52.9	51.1
Lone-parent, female, total	52.9	56
Lone-parent, female, 1 earner	43.9	42.6
Lone-parent, female, no earner	95.2	95.7
Elderly families	10.1	6.8
Elderly, single, male	35.5	33.3
Elderly, single, female	56.6	49.1
Non-elderly, single, female	37.2	40.9

SOURCE: Statistics Canada. Income Distributions by Size, 1997.

in 1997. This is the age bracket where most families begin to have children.

Table 5.8 shows the rates of poverty in 1989 and 1997 for different types of families. There was a substantial rise in the poverty rate for two-parent families with only one-earner, increasing from 19.5% in 1989 to 25.6% in 1997. Lone-parents continued to have extremely high rates of poverty. Fifty-six percent live in poverty with their children, and 96% of single-mothers not in the labour force live in poverty with their children.

Things are not much better for single individuals, particularly for those under 24 years of age. The poverty rate for single people under age 24 rose from 47% in 1980 to almost 61% in 1997. The trend is similar for single persons aged 25 to 34. The incidence of poverty in this age bracket rose from 23% to 31%. Poverty also rose significantly for single people in the next age bracket, age 35 to 44, jumping from 20% to 27%.

The greatest burden of poverty falls on women, whether as single women, as women in families, or as single-parent women. Figure 5.11 compares the poverty rates for women to those of men. Lone-parent families, the majority of which are headed by women, continue to have extremely high rates of poverty. Over 56% of these families headed by women live in poverty.

Figure 5.11
Incidence of Poverty, Men and Women (1997)

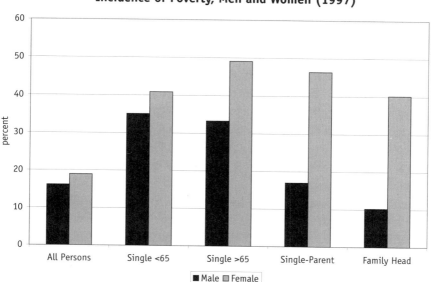

SOURCE: Statistics Canada, Income Distributions by Size in Canada, 1997.

In 1995, 44% of Aboriginal people lived in poverty compared to the national rate of 20%. About 60%, or three in five Aboriginal children under the age of six lived in poverty, compared to 20% of non-Aboriginal children. The incidence of poverty for Aboriginal children between the ages of six and 14 was 48%. (Statistics Canada does not document poverty on reserves, but there is much evidence that poverty on reserves is extremely high and, if counted, would raise the already shameful poverty rates of Aboriginal people captured in Statistics Canada data on Aboriginal people living in urban or rural centres).

People of colour experience higher rates of poverty than do other Canadians. Close to 36% of these Canadians lived in poverty in 1995, according to the last Census, compared to the 16% overall national poverty rate. The situation of their children is close to that of Aboriginal children. About 45% of children of colour under the age of six lived in poverty, compared to the national rate of 20% of children in poverty. Both rates are deplorable. The rate of elderly people of colour was higher than the national rate as well, at 32% compared to 19% in 1995. [Statistics Canada, *The Daily*, May 12, 1998]

As noted earlier, statistical data documenting the situation of people with disabilities is not readily available. This breakdown is not included in the yearly Statistics Canada catalogue which documents low income. We do know that poverty rates are higher for people with a disability. A study done in 1996 gives the poverty rates for such people in 1991. At that time, 21.9% had income below the poverty line, compared to 12.6% of Canadians without disabilities. And there was a gender differential: the poverty rate for men with a disability was 18.2%, compared to a poverty rate of 25% for women with a disability. [Gail, Fawcett, *Living with Disability in Canada: An Economic Portrait*, Human resources Development Canada, 1996, p130.] Given what we know about the significant increase in poverty since then, it would be reasonable to assume that poverty rates for Canadians with disabilities have outpaced the national growth in poverty.

Poverty rates also vary by province. As revealed in Table 5.9, poverty rates range from 9.3% in Prince Edward Island to nearly 18% in Newfoundland. Between 1989 and 1997, poverty rates have increased in all provinces except Saskatchewan and Alberta. Ontario recorded the largest percentage point increase over this period: from 8.2% to 12.6%.

The length of time people and families live in poverty is important, given what we know about its harmful impact in terms of health out-

Table 5.9
Provincial Poverty Rates, 1989 and 1997

	1989	1997
Newfoundland	13.5	17.7
PEI	8.9	9.3
Nova Scotia	11.4	14.9
New Brunswick	12.7	13.7
Quebec	12.8	16.4
Ontario	8.2	12.6
Manitoba	14.0	14.9
Saskatchewan	13.6	12.9
Alberta	13.3	12.7
British Columbia	12.1	13.8

Source: Statistics Canada, Income Distributions by Size, 1997.

comes, isolation from participation in mainstream society, and the diminishing of life potential. A recent Statistics Canada study shows that some Canadians experience long-term poverty. Overall, about 4% of Canadians lived in poverty for the full four years during the period of the study, (1993-1996), but the most vulnerable Canadians were at the highest risk of being in poverty for long periods of time. [Rene Morissette, *To what extent are Canadians exposed to low income?* Statistics Canada, March 1999.]

About 17% of Canadians who are people of colour lived in poverty for four consecutive years, between 1993 and 1996. The same was true for Canadians with a disability (17%), and 40% lived in poverty for at least one year. Immigrants who came to Canada after 1976 have a higher risk of living in poverty than do other Canadians. Close to 40% experienced at least one year of low income, more than double the 19% for people born in Canada. Fifteen percent of immigrants coming to Canada between 1977 and 1986 lived in poverty for the full for years, and 21% of those arriving after 1986 lived in poverty for the four consecutive years of the study. Almost 24% of lone-parent families lived in poverty continuously between 1993 and 1996.

Compounding the growing number of working class people and families living in poverty is the increase in the depth of poverty they experience—the 'poverty gap,' as it has been called. This gap represents the degree to which incomes of people in poverty are below the LICO set by Statistics Canada. Most people call this the poverty line. This line varies by family size and by rural and urban residence. For example, as shown in

Table 5.7 above, two-person families living in an urban city are below the LICO if their family income is $21,760 per year or under. The poverty gap measures how much below that line family incomes actually are. In 1997, it would have taken $19.8 billion to bring all persons living in poverty up to the low-income cutoff line.

On an annual basis, non-elderly families who are poor have incomes that are $9,700 on average below the poverty line. Two-parent families with children who are below the poverty line have incomes which, on average, fall almost $4,000 short of the poverty line. The incomes of single-parent mothers with children are $3,000 under the poverty line. The depth of poverty of families with children tended to fall in the 1980s and early 1990s, but has recently increased with deep cuts to UI and social assistance.

CONCLUSION

Over the 1989-1997 period, all families experienced a decline in market incomes because of labour market trends, but lower income groups were hardest hit. This led to sharp increases in market income disparities over the 1990s—increases that were, however, partly offset by government transfers. Indeed, because of the equalizing effects of transfers (and taxes) until social spending cuts began to bite, the after-tax income gap was only marginally higher in 1997 than in 1989. Overall statistical measures of after-tax income inequality in Canada, such as the *gini coefficient*, have shown little change. However, as noted, there has been a clear increase in inequality among the working-age population.

Against this backcloth, recent rounds of government cutbacks suggest that transfers will not be able to fully offset future increases in market inequality. Severe cuts to social assistance and unemployment insurance may also help explain why poverty rates remained stubbornly high throughout the decade, even as the economy recovered from the recession of the early 1990s.

The evidence suggests that governments need to play an active role in compensating for the growing inequality in the marketplace. As argued in the next chapter, the well-being of working-class Canadians is largely dependent upon whether in the years ahead governments rebuild the income support programs and public services which reduce poverty and inequality.

CHAPTER 6

The Shrinking Social Wage

While falling market incomes have been the most visible sign of the declining well-being of working Canadians, cuts in public programs and transfers, as suggested in the previous chapter, have also played a critical role.

The once universal Old Age Security program was income tested from 1990, while the Canada Pension Plan benefits were cut in 1998. Federal social housing programs have been drastically scaled back and administration devolved to the provinces and territories. After five rounds of cuts to unemployment insurance, the proportion of unemployed Canadians able to draw benefits has been cut in half. The universal Family Allowance Program has been eliminated, replaced with a means-tested Child Tax Benefit. Federal funding for health care, post-secondary education, and social assistance has been scaled back significantly.

What is alarming is that this weakening of the social safety net comes at a time when needs are greater than ever. In 1980, Canada had no food banks. Today, there are an estimated 2,000, and the number of Canadians visiting a food bank continues to grow despite the drop in unemployment. Homelessness, once considered a fringe phenomena, has become increasingly commonplace. The incidence of poverty—particularly among women, single-parent families, Aboriginal families, and persons with disabilities—remains stubbornly high even as the economy recovers from the severe recession of the early 1990s.

This chapter explores how government cuts to transfers and programs in the 1990s adversely affected the broader social well-being of working people by lowering the "social wage" they receive. By the social wage, we mean all government non-wage allowances, benefits and programs: everything from Unemployment Insurance and Old Age Security to health care and income assistance. Reductions in these programs have had a significant impact on the quality of life of working Canadians. Public sector cuts to health and education have shifted the burden of costs for these essential services onto families. Cuts to income support have seriously eroded the incomes of the most vulnerable at precisely the same time that market-based incomes have become more unequal.

ROLLING BACK THE WELFARE STATE

If the 1960s and 1970s were a period of social reform in Canada, the 1980s and 1990s can clearly be characterized as a time of impasse and retreat. Compared to the "Golden Age" of 30 years ago, Canada's social welfare system today has been radically redesigned and downsized.

 While the growth of the social welfare state appeared to stall by the late 1970s, the first serious signs of retrenchment were not really evident until the mid-1980s. In 1985, the newly elected government of Brian Mulroney de-indexed Family Allowances from the rate of inflation. Later, in 1989, the Conservative government "clawed back" benefits from higher income families. Similarly, Old Age Security benefits were gradually reduced for individuals earning over $51,000. In 1990, the Mulroney government initiated the first serious round of cutbacks under the Expenditure Control Plan, which limited federal cash transfers to the provinces to pay for health care, post-secondary education, and social assistance. Other cuts to social programs that followed included the elimination of the universal Family Allowance program in 1992; the termination of the federal government's direct role in financing social housing; and the reduction of benefits and tightened eligibility requirements for the Unemployment Insurance program.

 With the election of Jean Chrétien's Liberals in 1993, the pace of cutbacks accelerated. The newly-elected government's first budget in 1994 carried on the tradition of cuts to Unemployment Insurance, and the Liberal government's second budget in 1995 marked nothing less than a watershed in Canadian social policy. In presenting his budget that year, Finance Minister Paul Martin proudly proclaimed that his spending cuts were "unprecedented in modern Canadian history." [Paul Martin, *Budget Speech* (Ottawa: Public Works and Government Services, 1995), p. 25.]

 The centrepiece of the budget was the creation of the Canada Health and Social Transfer (CHST). The CHST was a new block funding arrangement that consolidated existing federal transfers to the provinces for post-secondary education and health care under Established Programs Financing (EPF) with the Canada Assistance Plan (CAP), a federal-provincial cost-sharing arrangement for social assistance and social services.

Implemented in 1996, this new "mother of all transfers" was projected to reduce federal cash contributions to these programs by about 40%, or $7 billion, and attached fewer conditions over how provinces spend the money.

Under the CHST, the federal government agrees to enforce the principles of Medicare: public administration, portability, comprehensiveness, accessibility, and universal coverage. Nevertheless, critics have pointed out that, as federal cash transfers for health care decline under the CHST, Ottawa will be left with less leverage to ensure that provinces adhere to these five principles. The federal government responded to these concerns after the 1997 election by raising the cash floor of the CHST from $11 billion to $12.5 billion and adding further increases specifically earmarked for Medicare in the 1999 budget. However, because the CHST is not indexed to inflation, the real value of the cash floor—and hence Ottawa's fiscal authority—will decline each year in the absence of future increases, putting further pressure on provincial governments to reduce their social spending.

With respect to social assistance, the CHST maintains only one of the five principles of the Canada Assistance Plan: that access to income assistance be provided without minimum residency requirements in a province. Standards requiring provinces to provide those in need with adequate levels of assistance, of not forcing recipients to work for benefits, of guaranteeing benefits to anyone demonstrating need, and of providing recipients with the right to appeal decisions regarding their case have been eliminated.

Figure 6.1
Federal Program Spending as % of GDP, 1961-2001

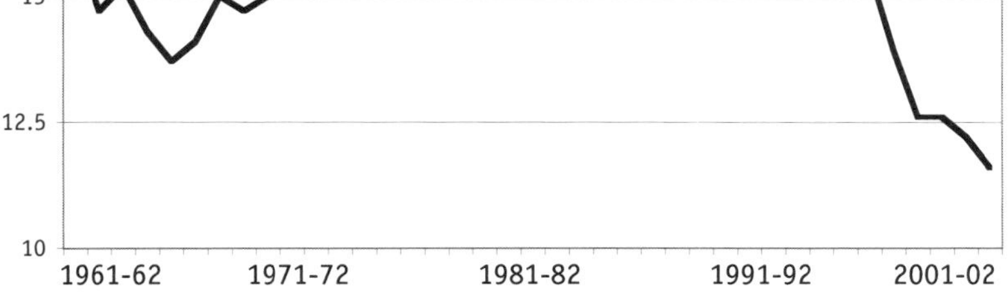

Source: Department of Finance, Fiscal Reference Tables; Budget Plan 2000.

The fallout from this retrenchment is graphically illustrated in Figure 6.1. Federal program spending, when measured as a share of the economy, has fallen dramatically in the 1990s to its lowest in more than four decades. Even with the deficit now eliminated, program spending is still set to decline as a share of GDP.

Table 6.1
Federal Program Spending
(% of GDP)

	Transfers to persons	Transfers to governments	Other program spending	Total Program spending
1989/90	4.6	3.6	7.6	15.8
1999/00	4.1	2.2	5.9	12.2
change	-0.5 pts	-1.4 pts	-1.7 pts	-3.6pts

SOURCE: Department of Finance, Fiscal Reference Tables; Budget Plan 1999.

Table 6.1 provides more detailed breakdown of the cuts in federal program spending during the 1990s. Transfers to persons—Old Age Security, Guaranteed Income Supplement, Spouse's Allowance and Unemployment Insurance—fell by about 0.5% of GDP. Federal cash transfers to the provinces to help pay for health care, post-secondary education and social assistance declined by about 1.4% of GDP. Overall, by the end of fiscal 1999, total program spending will have fallen by 3.6% of GDP. Put another way, *if program spending today was at the same level it was 10 years ago as a share of our national wealth, expenditures would be nearly $33 billion greater.*

Table 6.2 examines cuts to federal cash transfers for health care, post-secondary education, and social assistance. Prior to 1996, the federal government provided estimates of the share of federal cash transfers to the provinces devoted to these three program areas. With the introduction of the Canada Health and Social Transfer (CHST) in 1996, which combined existing transfers for these programs into one block fund, the Finance Department no longer provides these breakdowns. However, if we assume that CHST funds are apportioned according to their average pre-CHST shares, we can make a rough estimate of the impact of federal cuts on each program. Measured on a per capita and constant dollar basis, transfers for health are 16% lower in 1998/99 than they were in 1989/90. Education and social assistance transfers are down 40% and 25%, respectively.

Table 6.2
Federal Cash Transfers to Other Levels of Government,
1989/90 to 1998/99   ($1998 per capita)

	Health	Education	Social Assistance	Total
1989/90	$300	$99	$223	$622
1998/99	$251	$59	$168	$479
% change	-16.3%	-40.4%	-24.7%	-23.0%

SOURCE: Calculations based on Finance Department, Fiscal Reference Tables; Budget Plan 1999.

Looked at another way, in 1998 each Canadian received, on average, about 37 cents worth of government services for every $1 of cash income. (This does not include transfer payments or government debt payments. Some of these services are to businesses, but most of the business of governments is delivering services to citizens: everything from roads and highways to education, health care, social services and parks.) As shown in Table 6.3, real government spending on services per capita rose rapidly in the 1970s by 24.3%, and continued to increase in the 1980s. The high point was reached in 1991, and real per person spending then fell by 6% between 1991 and 1995. Importantly, this reduction was made in the context of an aging population, which added significantly to health care costs. Moreover, that figure covers only services and not transfers such as Unemployment Insurance, which were significantly cut.

Table 6.3
Growth of Real Government Current Expenditures on Goods and Services per Capita

1971-1981	24.3%
1981-1991	13.9%
1991-1995	-6.0%

SOURCE: Data from Centre for the Study of Living Standards.

The severe reduction in social spending has had the double effect of reducing transfers to persons and of shifting the costs of public programs privately onto families. Since what is not provided publicly has to be purchased in the private marketplace, government cuts to education and health have meant higher out-of-pocket expenses for Canadian families. As revealed in Table 6.4, average household spending on health care and education, while still representing a small share of total spending, have constituted the two fastest growing components of all major household

Table 6.4
Average Household Expenditures, Selected Items, 1986-1998
($1998)

	1986	1992	1998	% change 1986-98
Health Care	$901	$942	$1,190	32.1%
Education	$412	$467	$680	65.0%
Income taxes	$9,026	$9,852	$10,970	21.2%
Shelter[1]	--	--	$10,090	--
Clothing	$3,080	$2,413	$2,200	-28.6%
Food	$6,971	$6,175	$5,880	-15.7%
Transportation	$6,474	$6,125	$6,360	-1.8%
All expenditures	$48,917	$49,133	$51,360	5.0%

[1] 1992 figure not comparable to more recent periods due to changes introduced in the 1997 Survey of Household Spending.
SOURCE: Statistics Canada, Family Expenditure in Canada, 1992, cat. no. 62-555; The Daily, December 13, 1999.

expenditures since 1986. Between 1986 and 1998, household spending on health care jumped by over 32%, while expenditures on education ballooned by 65%. Expenditures on personal taxes also rose significantly (21.2%). By contrast, spending on clothing, transportation, and food all declined. (These changes also partly reflect the changing size and composition of households.)

HEALTH CARE

Canada's public health system has faced serious cutbacks in the 1990s as governments at all levels dealt with deficits. Particularly in the wake of the CHST, provincial governments have slashed health care budgets and de-insured services. Early discharge policies in the hospital sector have contributed to the rapid growth in the 1990s of non-hospital services such as home care and private nursing care, which are not covered by Medicare in most provinces.

As shown in Table 6.5, public sector spending on health care, when measured

Table 6.5
Growth of Real Public Spending on Health per Capita

1975 - 81	12.0%
1981 - 91	29.2%
1991 - 96	-3.1%

SOURCE: National Health Expenditure Data Base. Canadian Institute for Health Information. Table C.3.1.

Table 6.6
Private and Public Per Capita Health Expenditures, 1990-1998
($1992)

	Private Health Expenditures	Public Health Expenditures	Total
1990	$613	$1,930	$2,543
1995	$701	$1,720	$2,421
1998	$733	$1,680	$2,413
% change 1990-98	19.6%	-13.0%	-5.1%

SOURCE: Calculations based on Canadian Institute for Health Information, Private and Public Sector Health Expenditures. Expenditure at 1992 prices is calculated using Statistics Canada health and personal care price index.

on a per capita basis, has dropped off significantly in recent years. Real public expenditures grew 12% between 1975 and 1981, and by more than 29% in the next 10 years. Since 1991, however, public spending on health has contracted by more than 3%.

As governments have cut back services, the private sector has expanded its role in insuring and providing health care across the country. In turn, Canadians have been paying for more and more services privately. As shown in Table 6.6, private health expenditures grew by 20% between 1990 and 1998. Not all of this increase can be attributed to the expansion of private services and is related to the increase in total demand for health services, but it is also the case that during the same period the public health system contracted by 13%. In fact, over the past 20 years, private health care spending has risen from 23.7% of total health spending to over 30%.

Table 6.7 tracks changes in total private and public health care spending by major categories from 1975 until 1998. As illustrated, when measured in real per capita terms, expenditures for all categories, with the lone exception of capital spending, rose steadily from 1975 until 1990. Since 1990, however, expenditures on hospitals, physicians, and capital investments have declined. Of particular note is the dramatic decline in capital spending (spending on medical facilities and equipment), which is now at its lowest point in more than 20 years. This extremely low level of investment in medical infrastructure suggests that Canada may not be investing enough even to maintain its current capital stock in the sector. For anyone visiting a hospital recently and witnessing the sorry state of physical infrastructure, this observation may come as no surprise.

Table 6.7
Total Health Expenditure in Canada by Use of Funds, 1975-1998
($1992 per capita)

	Hospitals	Physicians	Other professionals*	Drugs	Capital
1975	687	229	136	134	67
1980	738	258	177	148	78
1985	864	319	174	200	87
1990	947	364	253	272	85
1995	845	346	276	324	75
1998	808	344	293	339	63
% change 90-98	-14.7%	-5.5%	15.8%	24.6%	-25.9%

Dental, vision care, chiropractic, home care, and other health professionals.
SOURCE: Calculations based on Canadian Institute of Health Information, *Total Health Expenditures by Use of Funds*. Expenditure at 1992 prices is calculated using Statistics Canada health and personal care price index.

As Table 6.7 also reveals, the two principal areas of rising health care costs are services offered by other professionals—such as dentists, optometrists, chiropractors, and home care providers—and drug costs. Expenditures on non-physician professional services have risen nearly 16% since 1990. Although this in part may reflect a broad social trend toward alternative health providers which operate outside of the provisions of Medicare, government cutbacks and the subsequent growth of private health providers to fill in the gaps of provincial health plans have no doubt also played role in this development.

Over the same period, the cost of prescription drugs exploded and are projected to have overtaken physician costs in 1999. Aggressive marketing and the over-prescribing of medication helps explain some of this increase, but federal legislation that provides extended patent protection for pharmaceutical companies has been the key contributor. In 1991, the Mulroney government passed a controversial new law, Bill C-91, which eliminated compulsory licensing—a provision that, until the new legislation, had permitted pharmaceutical firms other than the inventing company to copy brand-name drugs. Compulsory licensing helped keep drug prices low, with many generic drugs offered at 80% less than the brand name product. Bill C-91 completely eliminated compulsory licensing, effectively granting an inventing company 20 years protection from generic competition and thus keeping new drug prices high.

Cuts in Medicare and the trend toward greater private sector involvement in health care have raised concerns among many health advocates, who worry that access to services may be compromised, particularly for those Canadians with low incomes. Many families, after seeing little or no gain in incomes in the 1990s, are now facing escalating costs for drugs, privately-provided health services, and medical devices. Moreover, with Ottawa's share of public health care funding declining in the mid-1990s, the federal government was increasingly left with little clout to ensure that provinces adhere to the principles of the Canada Health Act which guarantee the accessibility, universality, portability, comprehensiveness, and public and not-for-profit administration of Medicare.

Public unease over these developments finally forced the federal government to increase health spending in its 1999 budget. CHST cash transfers were supplemented by $2 billion in each of the next two fiscal years, and by an additional $2.5 billion over the following three years, with the commitment from the provinces that the additional transfers would be earmarked solely for health care. Despite what appears to be generous extra funding, however, federal cash transfers for health care will still remain below their pre-CHST levels (see figure 6.2).

Figure 6.2
Estimated Federal Cash Transfers for Health, 1992-93 to 2000-01*

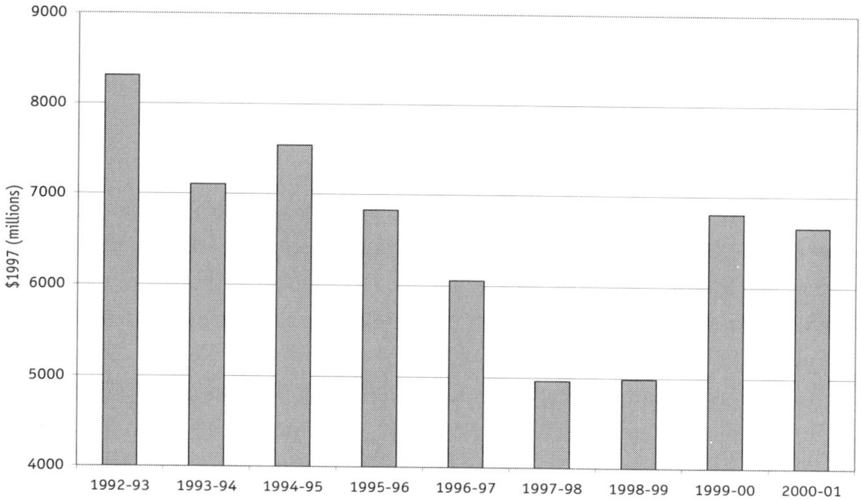

* Post-CHST health transfers calculated based on pre-CHST proportions. Estimates do not include measures taken in Budget 2000. Source: Calculations based on Department of Finance, Fiscal Reference Tables; Budget Plan, 1999.

POST-SECONDARY EDUCATION

As with health care, government funding for post-secondary education has dropped significantly in the 1990s. Among the provinces, the two exceptions to this trend, as illustrated in Table 6.8, are New Brunswick (which arguably began with a "poor" system in the first instance) and British Columbia, which increased real per capita funding by about 18% and 7%, respectively, between 1989/90 and 1997/98. In all other provinces, the picture is decidedly bleak. Funding was most drastically cut in Newfoundland (-30.8%) and Alberta (-30%), while Quebec (-9.3%), Manitoba (-8.6%), and Saskatchewan (-9.7%) experienced more moderate declines in relative terms.

Table 6.8
Public Expenditures on Post-Secondary Education by Province,
1989/90 to 1997/98 ($1997 per capita)

	1989/90	1997/98	% change
Canada	385	338	-12.2%
Newfoundland	429	297	-30.8%
PEI	347	261	-24.8%
Nova Scotia	380	325	-14.5%
New Brunswick	290	343	18.3%
Quebec	482	437	-9.3%
Ontario	321	272	-15.3%
Manitoba	301	275	-8.6%
Saskatchewan	351	317	-9.7%
Alberta	484	339	-30.0%
British Columbia	340	364	7.1%

SOURCE: Canadian Association of University Teachers, Education Review, Summer 1999.

Reduced public funding has precipitated a dramatic rise in tuition fees over the 1990s. Since 1990, tuition fees have ballooned, both in real terms and as a share of total university revenues. The result is that a university and college education is at risk of becoming far less accessible to working people and their children.

Average tuition fees for undergraduate arts students across Canada have increased by nearly 126% during the past nine years—from $1,496 in 1990 to $3,379 in 1999. As illustrated in Table 6.9, there has been considerable provincial variation in tuition fee increases—from an nine-year increase of 43% in British Columbia to 194% in Alberta.

Table 6.9
Average Undergraduate Arts Tuition Fees, 1990/91 to 1999/2000

	1990/91	1998/99	1999/2000	90/91 to 99/00	98/99 to 99/00
		$		% change	
Canada	1,496	3,156	3,379	125.9	7.1
Newfoundland	1,344	3,150	3,300	145.5	4.8
PEI	1,840	3,310	3,480	89.1	5.1
Nova Scotia	1,943	3,904	4,113	111.7	5.3
New Brunswick	1,989	3,194	3,329	75.4	4.2
Quebec[1]	902	2,278	2,387	164.6	4.8
Ontario	1,653	3,534	3,872	134.2	9.6
Manitoba	1,415	2,724	2,940	107.8	8.0
Saskatchewan	1,526	3,130	3,164	107.4	1.1
Alberta	1,244	3,452	3,658	194.1	6.0
British Columbia[2]	1,727	2,451	2,470	43.0	0.8

[1] Fees for both in- and out-of-province students are included in the weighted calculation.

[2] Fees for both public and private institutions are included in the weighted average calculation.

SOURCE: Statistics Canada

Higher tuition fees have translated into higher levels of debt for students and their families. The most recent figures available, presented in Table 6.10, show that the average debt of a student graduating with a bachelor's degree in 1995 was $13,300—a real increase of 37% since 1990 and 129% since 1982.

Table 6.10
Average Debt at Graduation, 1982-95 ($1995)

	Year of Graduation				
	1982	1986	1990	1995	% change 82-95
College	4,000	6,200	6,700	9,600	140%
Bachelor's	5,800	9,000	9,700	13,300	129%
First professional	9,500	13,700	14,600	21,100	122%
Master's	6,700	8,500	10,000	13,700	104%
Doctorate	5,400	6,900	9,500	12,900	139%

SOURCE: Statistics Canada, Perspectives on Labour and Income, vol. 11, no. 1 (Spring 1999), cat. no. 75- 001-XPE.

SOCIAL ASSISTANCE

Federal reductions to social assistance, first through CAP and then through the CHST, helped unleash a wave of provincial cutbacks in the 1990s. Since 1995, British Columbia, Alberta, Manitoba, Ontario, Quebec, Nova Scotia, Prince Edward Island, and Newfoundland have all reduced social assistance rates or tightened eligibility requirements. Only Saskatchewan and New Brunswick have not scaled back their rates, although New Brunswick's benefits have historically been very low compared to those in other provinces.

As Table 6.11 illustrates, between 1990 and 1996 welfare incomes, when measured as a percentage of the poverty line, have fallen in most provinces and remain grossly inadequate everywhere. The most extreme case is in Newfoundland where, after the government imposed severe cuts in 1996, a single employable person on assistance has an income equal to just 19% of the low-income cut-off line. Even in Ontario and Saskatchewan, which have the highest relative benefits, single employable individuals receive income assistance equivalent to just above 40% of the poverty line.

Sadly, the situation is not much better for disabled Canadians or families on social assistance. Benefit rates for disabled individuals range from 73% of the poverty line in Ontario to just 42% in Alberta. Single parents with one child receive income ranging from 68% of the poverty line in Newfoundland to 50% in Alberta. A couple with two children qualify for benefits that vary from just 48% of the poverty line in Newfoundland to 62% in Saskatchewan.

One immediately visible sign of the gross inadequacy of income support programs, and of the growing depth of poverty in Canada, is the increasing reliance of many families on food banks. An annual survey of emergency food programs, conducted by the Canadian Association of Food Banks, paints a grim portrait of the gaps in Canada's social safety net (see http://www.icomm.ca/cafb). According to the Association's 1999 HungerCount survey, the number of Canadians visiting a food bank jumped by nearly 11% over 1998. Since 1989 alone, food bank use more than doubled. Children, the study discovered, now account for more than 40% of food bank use.

The HungerCount survey also found that food bank use is on the rise even as the number of people on social assistance is declining. One culprit behind this phenomenon is the reduced real value of the minimum wage which has driven working poor Canadians deeper into poverty. As shown in Table 6.12, the real inflation-adjusted value of the minimum wage is well below levels of 20 years ago in all provinces. Between 1992 and 1999, there was some modest recovery in minimum wage rates in all provinces except Nova Scotia, Manitoba and Alberta. Even with these increases, however, the real value of the minimum wage remains anywhere between 11% and 37% below its 1976 level.

Table 6.11
Welfare Incomes as Percent of Poverty Line,* 1990-1996

	1990	1991	1992	1993	1994	1995	1996	% change 1990-1996
Newfoundland								
single employable	32	33	34	33	33	33	19	-40.6%
disabled person	63	63	64	63	63	62	61	-3.2%
single parent, 1 child	67	69	71	71	70	69	68	1.5%
couple, 2 children	56	56	56	55	55	54	53	-5.4%
Prince Edward Island								
single employable	60	62	62	62	56	43	40	-33.3%
disabled person	70	70	71	70	69	67	67	-4.3%
single parent, 1 child	69	71	71	71	70	67	64	-7.2%
couple, 2 children	58	58	57	56	56	55	58	nil
New Brunswick								
single employable	24	25	24	24	24	24	24	nil
disabled person	62	62	61	61	61	48	47	-24.2%
single parent, 1 child	55	55	55	55	57	59	59	7.3%
couple, 2 children	44	45	45	45	46	48	48	9.1%
Quebec								
single employable	48	41	41	41	40	39	39	-18.8%
disabled person	49	53	53	53	54	53	53	8.2%
single parent, 1 child	58	54	59	60	62	61	60	3.4%
couple, 2 children	59	52	52	53	52	51	51	-13.6%
Ontario								
single employable	52	54	55	55	55	51	42	-19.2%
disabled person	72	75	76	76	76	74	73	1.4%
single parent, 1 child	76	79	80	80	80	75	63	-9.2%
couple, 2 children	70	72	73	73	72	67	57	-18.6%
Manitoba								
single employable	46	46	47	47	44	42	39	-15.2%
disabled person	49	49	59	53	53	52	51	4.1%
single parent, 1child	54	55	60	54	54	53	52	-3.7%
couple, 2 children	65	67	68	63	64	62	56	-13.8%
Saskatchewan								
single employable	41	41	42	44	44	43	42	2.4%
disabled person	65	65	63	63	63	61	62	-4.6%
single parent, 1child	68	68	66	66	66	64	63	-7.4%
couple, 2 children	66	65	65	65	65	63	62	-6.1%
Alberta								
single employable	35	39	38	36	32	31	31	-11.4%
disabled person	43	60	45	44	44	43	42	-2.3%
single parent, 1 child	53	57	57	54	52	50	50	-5.7%
couple, 2 children	56	62	61	59	56	55	55	-1.8%
British Columbia								
single employable	42	40	43	43	44	43	39	-7.1%
disabled person	58	58	60	60	61	61	60	3.4%
single parent, 1 child	61	62	64	64	65	64	63	3.3%
couple, 2 children	54	54	56	57	57	57	56	3.7%

SOURCE: National Council of Welfare, Welfare Incomes 1996.

Table 6.12
Estimated Annual Salary* of Minimum Wage Workers
by Province, 1976, 1992 and 1999   ($1992)

	1976	1992	1999	Change 1992-99	Change 1976-99
Newfoundland	14,024	9,880	9,918	0.4%	-29.3%
PEI	13,463	9,880	10,516	6.4%	-21.9%
Nova Scotia	14,024	10,400	10,400	nil	-25.8%
New Brunswick	13,980	10,400	10,486	0.8%	-25.0%
Quebec	15,903	11,622	13,277	14.2%	-16.5%
Ontario	14,495	12,601	12,848	2.0%	-11.4%
Manitoba	15,415	10,400	9,750	-6.3%	-36.7%
Saskatchewan	15,706	10,461	10,986	5.0%	-30.1%
Alberta	15,210	10,140	9,914	-2.2%	-34.8%
British Columbia	16,828	11,353	13,338	17.5%	-20.7%

*Annual salary based on 40 hours a week of work.
SOURCE: Christopher Clark, "Work and Welfare: Looking at both sides of the equation," Perception, vol. 19, no.1, 1995; 1999 data calculated from information provided by the Saskatchewan Ministry of Labour.

UNEMPLOYMENT INSURANCE

The 1990s witnessed serious cuts to the Unemployment Insurance program, culminating with its replacement by the Employment Insurance (EI) system in 1996. Under the Mulroney Conservatives, UI was subjected to two major bouts of cutbacks at the same time as premiums were raised. Eligibility requirements were tightened, the maximum duration of benefits shortened, and the value of benefits scaled back in 1993 from 60% to 57% of insurable earnings.

The Liberal government of Jean Chrétien continued the assault on the UI program, including a $725 million cut in its first budget in 1994. Eventually, UI was completely restructured and replaced with the EI system. Under the latter program, every hour of work is now insurable, so that income benefits are based on hours rather than weeks worked. To qualify for benefits, workers need to accumulate over the course of a year anywhere from 420 to 700 hours—that is, between 12 and 20 weeks. The actual number of hours needed to qualify depends upon the unemployment rate of the region in which the claim is made. In most of the country, the minimum number of hours for those in the work force has risen from 240 hours to 560. For new entrants and re-entrants to the labour force, the number of hours required for eligibility has tripled, from 300 to 900 hours.

As well, the EI system further reduces benefits, from 57% to 55% of a claimant's insurable earnings. However, for lower income individuals, benefits were raised to 60%. The maximum duration of benefits was also reduced, from 50 weeks to 45 weeks.

Because of these cuts and tightened eligibility requirements, the number of unemployed people who actually receive benefits has dropped dramatically. As illustrated in figure 6.3, the percentage of unemployed Canadians receiving benefits fell from 74% in 1989 to just 36% in 1997. It has remained at this level in 1998 and 1999.

Cuts to unemployment insurance and changes in eligibility rules have spelled particular hardship for women. The most recent data avail-

Figure 6.3
Percentage of Unemployed Receiving UI Benefits, 1989-1997

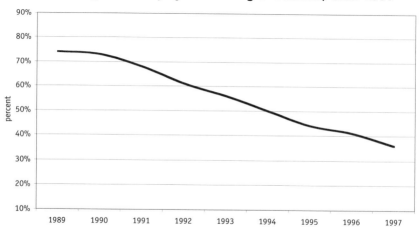

Source: Canadian Labour Congress, Left out in the Cold: The End of UI for Canadian Workers, 1998.

able show that 26,000 fewer women received regular benefits in 1998 than in 1997, a decline of nearly 11%. The hardest hit group, as shown in Table 6.13, is women under 35 years of age.

Women are losing unemployment insurance protection faster than men because more women work part-time and enter and re-enter the labour force more often for family reasons. Changes raising the minimum number of hours required to qualify mean that many women who work part-time and on a temporary basis cannot accumulate enough hours in a 12-month period to qualify. As well, women who leave their jobs for child care reasons are penalized when they re-enter the labour force by having to accumulate even more hours of work.

Table 6.13
Number of Regular UI Beneficiaries* by Age and Sex - monthly average

AGE	MEN Thousands	
	Change 1997 to 1998	Change 1996 to 1998
15 - 24	-1	-16
25 - 34	-8	-34
35 - 44	0	-14
45 - 54	0	-6
55 - 64	0	-4
Total	-9	-74
	WOMEN Thousands	
15 - 24	-4	-14
25 - 34	-11	-30
35 - 44	-7	-21
45 - 55	-3	-10
55 - 64	-1	-3
Total	-26	-78
	Both Thousands	
15 - 24	-6	-30
25 - 34	-18	-64
35 - 44	-7	-35
45 - 55	-3	-16
55 - 64	-1	-7
Total	-35	-152

SOURCE: Statistics Canada, unpublished data obtained from the Canadian Labour Congress.

Overall, the shrinking protection offered by today's EI system has been dramatic. Cuts to benefits and tightened eligibility requirements have not only eroded the support offered to unemployed Canadians, but have also intensified the anxieties of those working in insecure jobs or in the industries noted in Chapter 3.

HOUSING

Stagnant income growth and a weaker social safety net have translated into serious housing problems in many Canadian communities. Homelessness, once only associated with distant memories of the Great Depression, has once again surfaced as an increasingly common urban problem.

It is estimated that, between 1990 and 1996, the number of households in Canada paying more than 50% of their income on rent increased by 43% [Federation of Canadian Municipalities, *National Housing Policy Options Paper*, June 1999]. In large urban centres, there are nearly 100,000 households waiting for subsidized housing at the same time that the number of social housing completions is falling (see Table 6.14).

Table 6.14
Social Housing Completions, 1989-1998

	Total Housing Completions	Social Housing Completions	Social Housing as % of total completions
1989	217,371	9,828	4.4
1990	206,163	9,135	4.4
1991	160,014	9,273	5.8
1992	173,245	19,621	11.3
1993	161,794	15,718	9.7
1994	162,085	15,792	9.7
1995	119,501	5,271	4.4
1996	117,834	3,659	3.1
1997	143,386	1,997	1.4
1998	133,941	1,439	1.1
average 1989-93	183,717	12,675	6.9
average 1994-98	135,349	44,501	3.3
change from 89-93 to 94-98	-26.3%	-64.9%	

SOURCE: Canadian Federation of Muncipalities, National Housing Policy Options, June 1999.

Exacerbating the problem is the fact that many provinces have weakened or repealed rent regulations. In Ontario, for instance, the provincial government amended existing legislation so that landlords are no longer bound by rent controls when existing tenants move.

There is strong evidence that women are experiencing greater hardship than men as a result of the housing crisis. The Canada Mortgage and Housing Corporation recently documented the experience of women in Toronto who have suffered long-term homelessness. [Joyce Brown et. al., *Women on the Rough Edge: A Decade of Change for Long-Term Homelessness*, Ottawa: Canada Mortgage and Housing Corporation, April 1999. www.cmhc-schl.gc.ca] The report indicates that the proportion of women in Toronto who use emergency shelters increased from 24% to 37% between 1988 and 1998. The existing social service system and health system has fewer resources to assist homeless women and, as a result, women are remaining homeless for longer periods of time.

A high proportion of women who are long-term homeless have suffered extreme trauma and abuse, both sexual and emotional. Declining and insufficient resources for shelters has meant a rise in mixed-sex shelters, which pose a major threat to women who are more susceptible to victimization.

CHILD CARE

The lack of a national public day-care system has long been recognized as a major gap in Canada's social welfare system. Over the past two decades, both Conservative and Liberal governments have promised very modest child care proposals, yet none of these promises has been fulfilled. In fact, federal spending on child care services has declined in the 1990s, suffering a 33% cut between 1994 and 1998.

The lack of federal leadership in this area is made all the more significant, as a growing body of research suggests that early childhood programs and day-care improve young children's academic achievement and social adjustment. Perhaps most importantly, existing research also shows that early childhood education programs can narrow, although not completely eliminate, the gap in achievement between disadvantaged and advantaged children.

Recently released results from Statistics Canada's National Longitudinal Survey of Children and Youth reveal that children who are enrolled in early childhood programs and day-care centres appear to perform better when they enter kindergarten and Grade 1. The survey found that about 40% of children who were in an early childhood program at ages three and four were judged by their teachers as being near the top of their kindergarten class in communication skills, as opposed to just 25% who did not participate in such programs. The benefits of early childhood programs also carried over into Grade 1, with four- and five-year-old children who participated in such programs being 1.4 times more likely to be rated by their teachers as near the top of their class. The survey also found that higher proportions of children who attended early childhood programs were able to write a simple sentence, compare numbers, and understand simple concepts of time (see Statistics Canada, *The Daily*, October 14, 1999).

What is most intriguing about the survey is that the beneficial effects of participation in early childhood programs held true regardless of the education of the child's mother or the income of the child's household. This suggests that early childhood programs are critical in helping to partially overcome the disadvantages children from low- and modest-income households face. The trouble is that, without publicly accessible day care programs, the children who are most at risk are more likely to be left out because of the prohibitive costs of such programs and the shortage of subsidized spaces. As Table 6.15 reveals, children from households with in-

Table 6.15
Participation in Early Childhood Programs by Household Income

	Early Childhood Programs	At Home
Less than $20,000	17%	20%
$20,000-$29,999	22%	18%
$30,000-$39,999	25%	13%
$40,000 or more	28%	6%

SOURCE: Statistics Canada, *From Home to School – How Children Cope*, cat. no. 89F0117XIE.

comes above $40,000 are nearly twice as more likely to attend an early childhood program than children from families with household incomes of less than $20,000.

PENSIONS AND SENIORS' INCOME

As noted briefly in the previous chapter, government transfers are a particularly important income source for elderly Canadians. Despite recent measures that have reduced and clawed back benefits under the Canada and Quebec Pension Plan, Old Age Security, and the Guaranteed Income Supplement, these programs remain the single most important source of income for the vast majority of elderly households in Canada.

Table 6.16 provides 1996 data on the role played by different sources of income for different income deciles of elderly households. The data show the percentage of total income that comes from each source; the percentage of each decile that receives income from each source; and the average amount of income received by the recipients of each source of income in each decile.

The table illustrates the fact that OAS/GIS and C/QPP combined provide half or more of all income through the sixth decile, and come very close to doing so in the seventh. Two of the main sources of income provide increasingly large shares of total income as income rises—namely, employment income and investment income. Not only does the percentage of total income that comes from each source rise with income, but so does the percentage of the elderly that receive income from the source, and the average amount received per recipient. Even between the ninth and the tenth deciles, there are major differences in amounts received per recipient.

OAS/GIS represents close to a polar opposite to employment and investment income. The share of total income coming from this source declines steadily with rising income. In the first decile, it repre-

Table 6.16
1996 Source of Income of Elderly (Constant 1996 Dollars)

Persons 65+	Decile	Total Household Income	OAS/ GIS	CPP/ QPP	Net Investment Income	Total Government Tranfers	RPSA	Total Earnings
% of Total Income								
	1		81.5%	7.9%	1.7%	96.4%	0.6%	0.1%
	2		61.7%	25.5%	4.3%	92.2%	2.5%	0.5%
	3		44.2%	31.6%	7.7%	80.5%	9.0%	1.4%
	4		45.1%	24.2%	9.1%	75.4%	11.5%	1.8%
	5		45.3%	26.7%	9.3%	77.0%	10.6%	2.0%
	6		34.3%	27.6%	9.3%	66.6%	19.6%	3.3%
	7		25.4%	23.8%	11.5%	55.5%	25.0%	6.2%
	8		20.2%	20.0%	13.3%	44.3%	28.0%	12.6%
	9		15.6%	16.6%	12.4%	36.0%	31.0%	19.1%
	10		8.2%	9.1%	18.5%	19.6%	26.4%	33.6%
	Total		24.8%	17.8%	12.9%	46.7%	22.3%	16.5%
% that Drew from Source								
	1		95.6%	41.4%	18.4%	100.0%	--	--
	2		99.6%	87.3%	35.4%	100.0%	14.9%	--
	3		99.5%	88.9%	49.8%	100.0%	41.1%	--
	4		99.3%	83.2%	48.0%	100.0%	41.4%	--
	5		98.9%	92.7%	54.1%	100.0%	42.5%	--
	6		99.4%	94.8%	66.0%	100.0%	69.3%	12.4%
	7		99.3%	96.3%	65.3%	100.0%	75.4%	22.1%
	8		99.9%	94.7%	74.7%	99.9%	75.7%	29.6%
	9		99.1%	92.7%	78.1%	99.9%	80.0%	42.2%
	10		99.2%	92.3%	83.1%	100.0%	80.4%	61.0%
	Total		98.9%	86.5%	57.9%	100.0%	53.2%	20.3%
Average Income from Source								
for Seniors with Income from this Source *								
	1	$10,396	$8,857	$1,973	$948	$10,026	--	--
	2	$13,098	$8,114	$3,826	$1,606	$12,074	$2,170	--
	3	$14,939	$6,633	$5,300	$2,320	$12,019	$3,281	--
	4	$17,711	$8,131	$5,141	$3,361	$13,348	$4,910	--
	5	$21,154	$9,683	$6,089	$3,635	$16,293	$5,276	--
	6	$24,592	$8,479	$7,164	$3,461	$16,389	$6,937	$7,007
	7	$29,597	$7,580	$7,331	$5,325	$16,431	$9,795	$8,669
	8	$37,043	$7,483	$7,826	$6,648	$16,420	$13,677	$15,875
	9	$48,798	$7,701	$8,737	$7,770	$17,573	$18,941	$22,154
	10	$88,507	$7,293	$8,686	$19,905	$17,352	$29,026	$49,225
	Total	$31,834	$7,976	$6,563	$7,139	$14,861	$13,351	$26,199

NOTES: Cells marked by '--' denote unreliable estimates due to insufficient cell count.
* Mean averages exclude those respondents who reported values equal to or less than zero.
While all figures pertain to the household, age groups are based on the age of the head of the household.
SOURCE: Statistics Canada. Survey of Consumer Finances.

sents more than 80% of all income received but only 8% in the tenth decile. Even in the eighth decile, though, it accounts for more than 20% of all income received. In all deciles except the first, 98.9% or more of the elderly receive some OAS/GIS income. In the first, "only" 95.6% of households received OAS/GIS income. This likely reflects the impact of residence requirements on the receipt of OAS/GIS by adult immigrants to Canada.

Income from the C/QPP and pensions and annuities have been the most rapidly growing sources of income in recent years. They share in common the fact that they do not produce a consistent pattern of providing a growing or decreasing share of income as one moves up or down the income scale—although pensions and annuities come close to providing an increasing share as one moves up the scale. Pensions and annuities provide its greatest share of total income in the ninth decile, and there is a significant gap between the larger share of income it provides above the fifth decile and its contribution to lower levels of income.

On the other hand, the C/QPP provides its greatest share of total income in the third decile. It is a more significant source of income in deciles two through eight than it is below or above those levels. Overall, C/QPP income is now received by 86.5% of all elderly households. This is a huge increase from 28.4% in 1973, 61.7 per cent in 1981, and 76.7% in 1989.

The percentage of elderly households that receive pension and annuity income has also grown rapidly, but is far less widely received than C/QPP income. As of 1996, 57.9% of elderly households received some income from pensions and annuities, up from 27.9% in 1973, 35.1% in 1981, and 53.2% in 1989.

During the 1990s, both the OAS/GIS and C/QPP have been subject to attack. In the case of the OAS/GIS, the government raised the possibility that the universal OAS would be replaced by an income-tested Seniors Benefit.

In the case of the C/QPP benefits, cuts were made. The cuts fell most heavily on benefits for people with disabilities and widows. But retirement benefits were also subject to a relatively modest but important cut that took the form of a lengthening of the period over which wages would be averaged for purposes of upgrading C/QPP records of earnings.

Unfortunately, attacks on OAS/GIS and C/QPP will persist if only because the financial sector of the economy views these programs as being in competition with products of the private financial sector. However, the presence of OAS/GIS and C/QPP benefits is important to a very large portion of the elderly population. It is difficult to imagine how cuts to OAS/GIS or C/QPP benefits could be fully compensated for by income from other sources.

Current retirement income arrangements are not providing fully adequate incomes to older Canadians. Yet there are reasons to believe that the economic environment in which they have operated in recent years has allowed them to produce absolute and relative incomes that are greater than would have been the case under other circumstances. Among the factors in the economic environment that have had this effect are:

- low inflation which reduces the damage done to non-indexed workplace pensions;
- high returns on fixed income assets which have increased both investment income and pension and annuity income; and
- low rates of real economic growth which have slowed the income growth of the working age population and hence made the relative incomes of the elderly higher (even price-indexed benefits like OAS/GIS lose their relative value in the face of real economic growth).

The reversal of these conditions would reduce either or both of the real or relative incomes of the elderly. In addition, changes in the labour market are reducing the likelihood that the future elderly will retire with long years of service in workplace pension plans. Changes in this regard are: the increase in self-employment and term or contract employment; shifts in employment from large to small firms and establishments; and shifts in employment from sectors with high levels of workplace pension coverage (e.g., the public sector and manufacturing) to sectors with low levels of coverage (e.g., retail trade and personal services).

Thus, while existing retirement income arrangements have facilitated a substantial improvement in the incomes of older Canadians, economic and labour market circumstances of the recent past may have allowed these arrangements to produce much more for today's elderly than they will for tomorrow's.

SOCIAL WELL-BEING

While thus far our analysis has focused primarily on how the social wage affects the economic well-being of Canadian households, public programs like health care, education income, assistance and pensions also clearly provide non-monetary benefits, improving the social and even physical well-being of Canadians. To state the obvious, a universal health care program, for instance, generally contributes to a healthier population. Similarly, access to good housing, education and employment also promotes our social well-being and health. By contrast, poverty and unemployment, poor housing, and lack of education can all take their toll on our well-being. In short, public programs that address these social and economic conditions are crucial for improving the social well-being and health of Canadians.

Given the rollback of the welfare state, how has the health and social well-being of Canadians fared in recent years? By one common measure—life expectancy—Canada continues to make significant progress. As illustrated in Table 6.17, since 1961 life expectancy at birth has increased by more than seven years for both men and women.

Table 6.17
Life Expectancy at Birth, 1961-1996

	Male	Female
1961	68.4	74.2
1966	68.8	75.2
1971	69.3	76.4
1976	70.2	77.5
1981	71.9	79.0
1986	73.0	79.7
1991	74.6	80.9
1996	75.7	81.4

SOURCE: Statistics Canada, Compendium of Vital Statistics, cat. no. 84-214-XPE.

Nevertheless, the general increase in life expectancy hides more troubling trends. Much of this gain in life expectancy can be attributed to the declining rate of infant mortality over the last 25 years, which fell from about 15 deaths per 1,000 live births in 1974 to just 5.6 in 1996. Despite this progress, however, the improvement in Canada's infant mortality rate has lagged behind that of other countries. In 1990, Canada had the fifth lowest infant mortality rate among 17 OECD countries. In 1996, as shown in Figure 6.4, Canada had slipped to 12th place.

Figure 6.4
Infant Mortality Rates, Selected OECD Countries (1996)

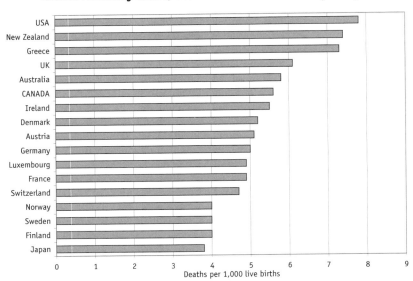

Source: Federal, Provincial and Territorial Advisory Committee on Population Health, Statistical Report on the Health of Canadians, 1999.

As well, compared with other countries, Canada has a significantly higher rate of youth suicides. Between 1991 and 1993, the suicide rate for male youth between 15 and 24 was exceeded only by Australia and the Russian Federation among the 10 leading industrialized nations. The female youth suicide rate was higher than in all other countries except Sweden and the Russian Federation. During the 1990s, there has also been a tragic increase in suicides among children age 10 to 14 [Federal, Provincial and Territorial Advisory Committee on Population Health, *Statistical Report on the Health of Canadians* (Ottawa: Health Canada, 1999)]

The general improvement in average life expectancy also masks inequities in population health between different segments of Canadian society. Life expectancy for Aboriginal people, for instance, is seven years less than the general Canadian population, and there are almost twice as many infant deaths. Suicide rates are estimated to be two and half times greater than the general population. High levels of unemployment, substandard housing, and poverty rates double that of the general population have all been identified as contributing to the poor health of First Nations people [see Monica Townson, Health and Wealth: How Social and Economic Factors Affect our Well-Being (Ottawa: Canadian Centre for Policy Alternatives, 1998)].

Overall, while Canada is ranked first according to the Human Development Index, Aboriginal Canadians, as shown in Table 6.18, would rank 48th on the same index. On-reserve Aboriginals are even more disadvantaged than those living off reserves, the former falling to 63rd place on the index.

Table 6.18
The Well-Being of Aboriginal Peoples

HDI Rank	Country	Real GDP per capita	Education Index	Life Expectancy	HDI
1	Canada	19320	0.93	77.2	0.932
2	Switzerland	21780	0.92	77.8	0.931
34	Russian Federation	6930	0.86	70	0.858
	Off-reserve Aboriginal	9905	0.82	72.2	0.857
35	Trinidad and Tobago	8380	0.83	70.9	0.855
47	Panama	4910	0.75	72.7	0.816
	Registered Aboriginal	8890	0.72	70.7	0.815
48	Poland	4500	0.84	71.5	0.815
61	Kazakhstan	4490	0.76	69	0.774
62	United Arab Emirates	17000	0.56	70.8	0.771
	On-Reserve Aboriginal	6542	0.62	67.6	0.761
63	Brazil	5240	0.64	65.8	0.756

SOURCE: Policy Research Initiative, Sustaining Growth, Human Development, and Social Cohesion in a Global World, February 1999: p.6.

INDEX OF SOCIAL HEALTH

Most attempts to measure social well-being to date have tended to aggregate individual social and economic indicators, such as life expectancy, infant mortality, literacy rates, poverty, income, and unemployment. The limitation with this approach is that it offers no overall summary of how all the indicators taken together determine social well-being. Other measures, such as the United Nations Human Development Index noted above, have been criticized for focusing only on a limited number of categories.

A recently developed Index of Social Health (ISH) is an attempt to provide a more comprehensive and detailed summary of social well-being by weighting 15 separate socio-economic indicators. The ISH provides researchers with a composite index that tracks a nation's social performance over time. It thus represents an attempt to present a more comprehensive portrait of the health of a society than traditional measures of well-being, such as Gross Domestic Product or the UN's HDI.

The ISH includes a set of socio-economic indicators covering 15 social issues dealing with health, morality, inequality, and access to services (see Table 6.19). They cover all stages of life and are closely linked to social institutions such as the family, school, the state, and the labour market.

Table 6.19
Components of the Index of Social Health

Children	Youth	Adults	Elderly	All Ages
infant mortality	teen suicides	unemployment	persons 65 and over in poverty	homicides
child abuse	drug abuse	average weekly earnings	out of pocket health costs for those 65 and over	alcohol-related fatalities
child poverty	high school drop-outs			number of social assistance beneficiaries
				access to affordable housing
				gap between rich and poor

SOURCE: Satya Brink and Allen Zeesman, "Measuring Social Well-Being: An Index of Social Health for Canada," (Hull: Applied Research Branch, Human Resources Development Canada, June 1997).

When calculated from 1971 to 1995, the ISH reveals some marked changes in the social well-being of Canadians. As revealed in Figure 6.5, from 1970 to 1980, the ISH grew impressively in Canada and mirrored the growth in GDP. However, since 1980 there has been a profound decline in the index, interrupted only by a modest and short-lived upturn in the late 1980s, despite the continuing growth in GDP. Even during the economic recovery of 1994 and 1995, the ISH remained low, largely because unemployment remained high, child poverty rose, and real wages declined.

Figure 6.5
Index of Social Health and GDP, 1970-95

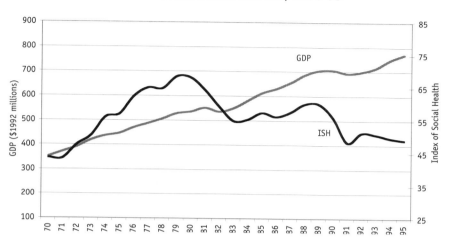

Source: Satya Brink and Allen Zeesman, *Measuring Social Well-Being: An Index of Social Health for Canada.* Hull: Applied Research Branch, Human Resources Development Canada, 1997.

CONCLUSION

Access to quality services provided to citizens partly or entirely on a non-market basis—such as education, health care and basic municipal services—would rank high for most of us on a list of contributors to our standard of living. Above and beyond cash income from the market and government transfers, people have a range of entitlements to public programs and services which can be collectively defined as *"the social wage."*

Most working people are the winners from the payment of taxes for public programs and services, for two key reasons. First, they get more than they pay for to the extent that the tax system as a whole is mildly progressive. This is true not just for low-income people, but also for most of the middle class who tend to be even heavier users of public services. Second, public services are provided more efficiently than their private equivalents. For example, the administrative overhead cost of private U.S.-style health care is huge compared to Canada's Medicare system, and the administrative cost of the Canada Pension Plan is trivial compared to that of private plans.

The great majority of working people are the losers when public services are cut back, because they are forced to buy the lost services on the market, often getting less at higher cost. The impact of the cuts of the 1990s are now starting to show up in household budgets as private spending on health care and education is rising dramatically. Moreover, low-income families may lose access to services completely when they are privatized.

Working people rightly feel that they have been paying more and more in taxes in the 1990s for less and less services. This is the result of mounting government debt costs, cuts to services, and, as discussed in the next chapter, rising and unfair taxes. But the fundamental point remains that cutting services to cut taxes is a losing proposition for all but the most affluent who want to stop paying for everybody else, leaving themselves "*free*" to enjoy the high-quality, private health care and education and recreational services that are available—at a price—on the market.

CHAPTER 7

The Tax System

In previous chapters, it was shown that the real pre-tax incomes of working families have fallen in the 1990s. In this chapter, we examine more closely what has happened to the after-tax or disposable incomes of Canadians. In particular, we ask what role the tax system plays in exacerbating or alleviating the growing gap in market incomes.

Three main conclusions arise from our analysis. First, despite some regressive changes in the 1980s, Canada's personal income tax system still remains relatively progressive and has played a modest role, along with the more critical impact of government transfers, in moderating the growing inequality in market incomes. In fact, without the redistributive effects of income taxes and transfers, the gap between the richest and poorest 10% of families would be more than 15 times greater than it is.

Secondly, the redistributive role of taxes has been somewhat offset in recent years as lower and modest income groups have been disproportionately hit with tax increases. These increases have been largely hidden, resulting from the government's decision to stop fully indexing the income tax system to inflation. Consequently, the tax burden on working families rose in the 1990s at the same time as the value of public services they received declined, thus setting the stage for the "tax revolt" of recent years.

Finally, when all sources of taxes, wealth and income are considered, the progressivity of the tax system is significantly reduced. The burden of sales, property, and so-called payroll taxes falls more heavily on low- and middle-income families, tending to flatten the overall tax rates of different income classes.

CANADIAN TAXES IN THE INTERNATIONAL CONTEXT

Virtually every economic ill suffered over the 1990s in Canada has been attributed in some form or another by conservative commentators to allegedly high rates of taxation. The claim that Canadians are "overtaxed" compared to other nations, and that high taxes are stifling growth and productivity gains, has been repeated with such frequency that it is often taken as simple fact.

In truth, the evidence clearly shows there is no discernable relationship between tax levels (when measured as a share of GDP) and growth rates. As shown in Figure 7.1, some of the nations with the highest tax levels, such as the Netherlands, Norway, and Denmark, enjoyed the highest growth rates between 1989 and 1996. By contrast, the United States, one of the low tax nations, experienced comparatively weak growth. In fact, Japan is the clear standout on the chart as the one country with below average tax revenues but above average growth. This is largely a function of Japan's somewhat unique economy, with many elements of social security provided not by the state, but by corporate employers.

Figure 7.1
Taxes and Growth

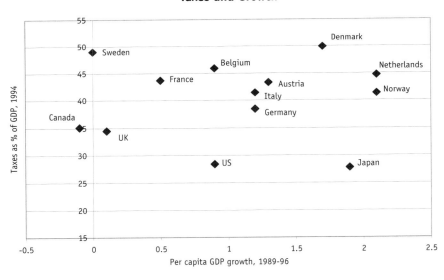

Source: OECD Statistical Working Party, Economic Growth in the OECD Area, 1999.

Similarly, as shown in Figure 7.2, productivity gains exhibit no discernable relationship to overall levels of taxation. In fact, if anything, the data show a small correlation between higher levels of taxation *and* greater productivity gains.

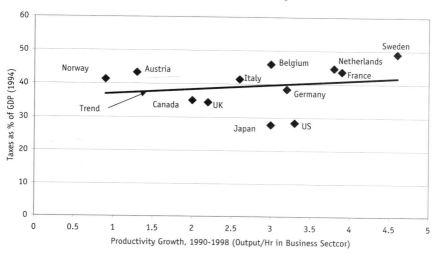

Figure 7.2
Taxes and Productivity

Source: OECD Statistical Working Party, Economic Growth in the OECD Area, 1999.

In comparison with other advanced industrialized countries, Canada's level of taxation is just below the average. Table 7.1 compares government revenues as a share of GDP with other OECD countries. In 1996, all levels of government in Canada collected taxes equal to about 37% of GDP. That is significantly more than collected in the United States (28.5%), but significantly less than the European Union (42.4%). More than other nations, Canada also tends to rely more heavily on the most progressive tax source, the personal income tax system, and less on more regressive social security or "payroll" taxes (e.g., CPP, Unemployment Insurance).

Table 7.1
Tax Revenue as a Percentage of GDP, 1996

	Personal Income Tax	Corporate Income Tax	Social Security	Taxes on Goods and Services	Other Taxes	Total Tax Revenue
Canada	13.9	3.3	5.9	9.1	4.6	36.8
United States	10.7	2.7	6.7	4.9	3.5	28.5
European Union	11.0	3.2	11.2	13.3	3.7	42.4
OECD average	10.1	3.1	8.4	12.3	3.8	37.7

SOURCE: OECD Revenue Statistics, 1965-1997 (Paris: OECD, 1998).

These figures must be read with caution, however. International tax comparisons raise numerous methodological problems. Some countries include in their revenues taxes paid by governments themselves, such as sales taxes on purchases. What is classified as a tax in one country might be categorized as a user fee in another. Most importantly, the cost of what is provided as a publicly-funded service in one nation may have to be borne privately in others.

For our analysis, a more interesting comparison is to consider what share of their gross income workers in different countries receive once taxes and social security premiums are paid. As Table 7.2 shows, when average production worker earnings are expressed in dollars with equal purchasing power, Canadian workers rank quite high in comparison with other nations. Of their gross earnings, Canadians pay on average about 22% in income tax and a further 6% in social security contributions, for a total of 28%. Interestingly, that is only slightly more than income taxes and social security contributions paid by American workers earning the average production wage (26%).

Table 7.2
Percentage of Average Gross Earnings Paid in Income Tax and Employees' Social Security Contributions, 1997

	Income Tax	Social Security Contributions	Total Payments	Average Gross Wage Earnings*
Australia	23%	2%	25%	$30,927
Canada	22	6	28	29,412
France	10	18	28	20,356
Germany	21	21	42	24,617
Italy	19	10	29	23,904
Japan	0	8	8	26,219
New Zealand	22	0	22	23,539
United Kingdom	17	8	25	25,864
United States	18	8	26	28,584

*Dollars with equal purchasing power.
SOURCE: OECD, The Tax/Benefit Position of Employees (OECD: Paris, 1998), p. 12.

This comparison still does not give us the complete picture because it leaves out the social benefits, such as family allowances and tax credits, that workers in different countries receive. When these government transfers and tax reliefs are added to the mix, Canadians slip below the OECD average, largely due to the more generous social benefits provided in most European countries. Table 7.3 shows that the average after-tax and after-

Table 7.3
Average After-Tax and After-Transfer Income,* 1989-97
(% of Gross Pay)

	1989	1991	1993	1995	1997
Australia	84.4	85.6	85.1	83.9	85.5
CANADA	88.2	86.0	84.5	83.4	81.8
France	89.1	88.8	86.9	86.2	84.7
Germany	77.5	77.6	78.5	75.0	77.9
Italy	84.2	84.5	84.1	80.4	83.0
Japan	91.1	90.6	90.2	91.4	90.4
New Zealand	82.0	79.2	77.8	77.6	83.8
UK	82.7	83.5	84.1	81.4	82.7
USA	81.0	81.0	81.1	81.4	81.7
OECD Average	84.8	85.0	85.7	85.1	85.0

*Employees' social security and personal income taxes less transfer payments as a share of gross earnings, one earner married couple earning the average production wage.
SOURCE: Calculations based on OECD, The Tax/Benefit Position of Employees (Paris: OECD, 1998), Table 12.

transfer income of Canadian workers is equal to about 82% of their gross pay, compared to the OECD average of 85%. Most surprising is that, despite shouldering a higher overall tax load than Americans, Canadian workers at the end of the day take home about the same share of their gross pay as their southern neighbours. Canadians are arguably even better off because they have already paid for the costs of medical care in taxes, costs which may have to be borne privately by American families if they are among the 43 million individuals without health care coverage.

One other observation arising from Table 7.3 is worth noting at this point. Since 1989, average Canadian workers have witnessed a steady and sizeable decline in their after-tax and after-transfer disposable income: from 88.2% to 81.8% of their gross earnings. This is largely explained by the combined effect of declining government transfers, and increased taxes and premiums.

PERSONAL INCOME TAXES

Concern about Canada's personal income tax rates has reached a new height in recent years, largely on the strength of a well-orchestrated anti-tax crusade led by the business lobby and a host of conservative political pundits. These groups were quick to leap on the news that by the late 1990s personal income taxes made up the largest share of average household spending. The Business Council on National Issues noted with condemnation that Canadians now "pay more to support governments than for roofs over the heads." [David Stewart-Patterson, "Tax Cut Delay Will Not Pay," Opinions, Ottawa: BCNI, February, 1999]. On the surface, this does seem to be the case. Statistics Canada notes that in 1998 the average Canadian family spent 21 cents of every dollar on personal income taxes, followed by 20 cents for shelter, 12 cents for transportation, and 11 cents for food.

However, there is a problem in using averages this way, which is easily seen by the following example. Suppose four families with $30,000 incomes each pay $4,500 in income tax, or 15% of their incomes. Now, add in a wealthy family with $250,000 income that pays $92,500, or 37%. Using an approach based on averages, one would conclude that these five families pay an average 30% of their income on taxes (total tax payments of $110,500 divided by total income of $370,000 equals 30%). The trouble is that the 30% figure is completely misleading. The majority of people (the four middle-income families) pay just 15% of their income in income tax, not 30%.

Based on *averages*, then, Canadian families appear to spend more on personal income taxes than any other expenditure, but the truth is that most families do not. Table 7.4 illustrates the percentage of household budgets spent on food, shelter, transportation, and personal income taxes. Rather than using averages, however, the data is broken down into five equal-sized income groups or quintiles, ranging from the 20% of households with the lowest income to the 20% with the highest income. Using this approach, we find that, for the 40% of Canadian households that earn less than $35,111, income taxes represent the *smallest* share of major ex-

Table 7.4
Percentage of Household Budget Spent on Four Major Categories, 1998

	Lowest quintile	2nd quintile	3rd quintile	4th quintile	Highest quintile
Food	18	16	13	11	9
Shelter	32	24	21	20	16
Transportation	11	14	13	13	12
Personal income taxes	3	10	17	21	30

The upper bounds for the lowest to the fourth quintiles are $20,530, $35,111, $52,976, and $77,000.
SOURCE: Statistics Canada,The Daily, December 13, 1999.

penditures. For the 3rd or middle quintile earning between $35,111 and $52,976, shelter remains the largest expenditure. In fact, it is only for the top two income groups that taxes are the major household expenditure. In short, when critics use averages to describe taxes paid by Canadians, it produces skewed results which ascribe tax rates to the average person that only taxpayers at considerably higher income levels actually pay.

This is not to dismiss concerns about the overall level of taxation or tax fairness that animates much of the debate and discussion about Canada's personal income tax system. Do wealthy individuals pay their fair share or they "overtaxed?" Are middle- and low-income Canadians carrying too much of the tax load?

These questions were highlighted throughout the 1980s and into the early 1990s in the wake of two major rounds of tax changes in Canada. In the first phase of these reforms in 1985 and 1986, corporate rates were reduced, a $500,000 lifetime capital gains exemption was introduced (this has since been eliminated), and the tax system was partially de-indexed from the rate of inflation (full indexation was restored in the 2000 Federal budget). This was followed in 1988 by the Mulroney government's introduction of a broad tax reform package that included personal and corporate rate reductions, bracket consolidation, the conversion of most personal exemptions into credits, and the announcement of the government's intention to replace the Manufacturers' Sales Tax with a general Goods and Services Tax (GST) by 1991.

In a comprehensive study assessing the fallout of the first phase of changes, it was found that the tax burden had been shifted from wealthy onto middle-income Canadians. Between 1984 and 1988, there was an average overall decline of 2.7% in disposable—i.e., after-tax—income. The top 1% of income earners, however, saw only a 1.3% decrease, largely due to the generous capital gains exemption introduced in 1985. The bottom two deciles experienced a modest increase in disposable income, but middle-income Canadians—those earning about $30,000 a year—saw their disposable income fall by 3.6% [Allan Maslove, *Tax Reform in Canada: The Process and Impact*. Ottawa: Institute for Research on Public Policy, 1989].

The sweeping tax reforms which took effect in 1988 offered up more mixed results. These reforms were marked by the consolidation of the existing ten tax brackets, which reached a top rate of 34%, into three brackets: 17%, 26%, and 29%. The reduction of the top rate was supposed to be at least partially offset by the conversion of basic deductions into non-refundable credits. Unlike deductions, which reduce the taxable income assessed, credits reduce the amount of tax payable. The credits are "non-refundable" because they can be used to reduce or eliminate federal tax payable, but any unused portion is not returned to the taxpayer. Because the non-refundable tax credits are calculated by multiplying eligible exemptions by 17%—the same as the lowest marginal tax rate—the change made no difference to low-income taxpayers. On the other hand, it did have the effect of raising taxes for most of those in the middle and high income tax bracket.

Overall, the effect of the 1988 reforms was to reduce the effective federal tax rate paid by most income groups, but much more so for the top. Table 7.5 compares taxes paid as a share of income in 1987, before the reforms were introduced, with the effective rates of the post-reform period. Taxpayers with less than $10,000 in assessed income actually saw a small increase in their effective rate of federal tax. Those with incomes between $10,000 and $40,000 experienced a moderate drop. Between $50,000 and $90,000, the effective rates were virtually unchanged. By contrast, higher income groups saw a significant reduction, with the top income group experiencing a drop of about 4 percentage points between 1987 and 1988.

In spite of these regressive changes, Canada's taxes on income still remain relatively progressive. Figure 7.3 illustrates the effective com-

Table 7.5
Average Effective Federal Tax Rate* by Income Class, 1987, 1988 and 1989 (%)

Assessed Income	1987	1988	1989
$1-10,000	3.0	3.4	3.4
$10,000-20,000	8.0	7.6	7.6
$20,000-30,000	11.4	10.3	10.4
$30,000-40,000	13.5	12.7	12.8
$40,000-50,000	15.0	14.8	15.0
$50,000-60,000	16.2	16.0	16.2
$60,000-70,000	16.9	16.7	17.1
$70,000-80,000	17.1	17.1	17.7
$80,000-90,000	17.9	17.2	18.0
$90,000-100,000	18.5	17.7	17.7
$100,000-150,000	20.1	18.8	19.0
$150,000-250,000	22.7	19.7	20.6
over $250,000	26.4	22.1	23.4

*Net federal tax payable as a share of assessed income.
SOURCE: Calculations based on Revenue Canada, Individual Income Tax Statistics, 1987, 1988, and 1989 tax years.

Figure 7.3
Average Effective Income Tax Rate* by Income Class, 1996

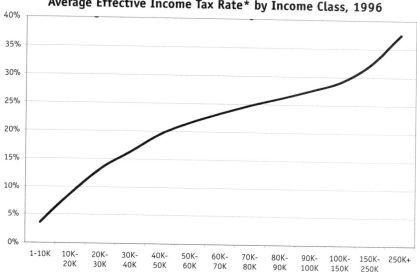

* Income tax payable as a % of taxable income.
SOURCE: Calculations based on Revenue Canada, Individual Tax Statistics, 1996 Tax Year

bined federal and provincial income tax rate—i.e., actual taxes paid as a share of assessed income—for 1996 (the most recent year for which detailed data is available). The effective income tax rate rises steadily from about 4% for those with incomes between $10,000 and $20,000 to over 37% for tax filers reporting income greater than $250,000.

Table 7.6 further explores the progressivity of the personal income tax system by examining the distribution of income taxes paid by different income groups. As shown, while most taxpayers are concentrated at low- and middle-income levels, a greater proportionate share of

Table 7.6
Personal Income Tax Distribution, 1996

Taxable Income	% of all taxpayers	% of all taxable income	% of all federal tax	% of all provincial tax
under $30,000	53.7	33.0	16.2	14.0
$30,000-60,000	35.6	38.6	40.2	38.5
$60,000-100,000	8.3	15.7	21.1	21.6
$100,000-150,000	1.4	4.4	6.7	7.4
over $150,000	1.0	8.3	15.2	18.5

SOURCE: Canadian Tax Highlights, vol. 7, no. 6, 1998.

taxes are paid by upper income earners. More than half of all taxpayers reported less than $30,000 in taxable income in 1996. While this group accounted for one-third of all income, it paid only about 16% of all federal personal income tax. A further 35.6% of taxpayers had incomes between $30,000 and $60,000, while contributing about 40% of the total federal income tax bill in 1996. Only 10.7% of taxpayers reported taxable income above $60,000, but they accounted for 28% of all income and paid 43% and 47.5% of all federal and provincial income taxes, respectively. The top 1% of taxpayers—those with incomes above $150,000—held more than 8% of all income and paid more than 15% of all federal income tax.

THE PERSONAL INCOME TAX SYSTEM AND WELL-BEING

One often overlooked dimension of the personal income tax system is the role it plays in promoting equity and providing much-needed assistance to modest income households. One way these goals are met is through the refundable tax credits, such as the child tax benefit and the GST credit. Unlike non-refundable credits, refundable tax credits are awarded even if an individual has no taxable income. As shown in Table 7.7, these credits largely benefit lower income households, although they are arguably clawed back at relatively low thresholds. The GST credit is sharply reduced when household income rises above $25,000 and all but disappears for those earning over $40,000. Similarly, the child tax benefit is significantly lowered for households reporting income over $25,000, and is quickly phased out when income rises above $50,000.

Combined with direct government transfers, refundable tax credits and the progressivity of the income tax system have performed a re-

Table 7.7
Percentage Distribution of Benefits by Income Levels, 1996 Tax Year

Income	Child tax benefit	GST credit
under $25,000	59.4	85.0
$25,000-30,000	7.0	11.4
$30,000-40,000	14.2	3.4
$40,000-50,000	10.0	0.2
$50,000-60,000	5.9	0.0
$60,000-70,000	2.3	0.0
over $70,000	1.3	0.0

SOURCE: Canadian Tax Highlights, vol. 7, no. 1, 1999.

Table 7.8
Income Gap Among Canadian Families with Children, 1989-1997
(Income ratio of highest to lowest decile)

	Market income	Income after transfers	Income after transfers and tax
1989	38.7	9.4	7.0
1990	56.6	9.7	7.0
1991	87.6	9.3	6.7
1992	130.3	9.0	6.5
1993	257.2	8.5	6.2
1994	184.9	8.7	6.3
1995	112.5	9.0	6.5
1996	198.4	10.0	7.1
1997	108.7	10.0	7.2

SOURCE: Statistics Canada, Survey of Consumer Finances, unpublished data obtained from the Centre for Social Justice.

markable job in keeping rising market income inequality in check. Table 7.8 provides a dramatic illustration of this. In 1997, the share of pre-transfer and pre-tax income going to the top 10% of families with the highest income was more than 100 times greater than that earned by the lowest 10%. After transfers, that gap dramatically narrows to about 10 times, and then falls more modestly but not insignificantly to a ratio of 7 after taxes are taken into account. Remarkably, given the widening gap in market incomes, the after-transfer and after-tax income gap between the top and bottom deciles has held steady since 1989.

While government transfers and taxes have to date been very effective in countering the widening gap in market incomes, there are signs that this impact may be weakening. Table 7.9 illustrates changes in in-

Table 7.9
Gini Coefficient, 1989-97 (Families)

	Market income	Income after transfers	Income after transfers and tax
1989	0.397	0.330	0.294
1990	0.404	0.331	0.292
1991	0.420	0.331	0.298
1992	0.427	0.338	0.297
1993	0.429	0.339	0.298
1994	0.425	0.334	0.293
1995	0.428	0.341	0.298
1996	0.431	0.347	0.303
1997	0.425	0.343	0.302

SOURCE: Statistics Canada, Income After Tax, Distributions by Size in Canada, 1997, cat. no. 13-210- XPB.

come inequality from 1989 to 1997, using a statistical tool known as the "Gini coefficient." This is a measure of inequality where 0 represents a state of perfect equality (everyone has the same income) and 1 represents a state of total inequality (where one person has all the income). The closer the Gini is to zero, the greater the level of income equality.

As revealed in the table, there has been a general ratcheting up of the Gini coefficient for pre-transfer and pre-tax market incomes since 1989. However, government transfers and taxes have helped to offset this trend. By 1994, despite a significant increase in market inequality, when transfers and taxes are taken into account the level of income inequality was about the same as in 1989. Between 1994 and 1996, however, after-transfer and tax income inequality has shown an upward trend as transfers and taxes have not been able to fully counter a rise in market inequality. The Gini fell slightly in 1997, but this was due entirely to a modest decrease in market inequality. Indeed, what is surprising is that the inequality in income after transfers and taxes did not narrow more.

REGRESSIVE TAXATION

There is, of course, a flip side to Canada's tax system. While the rate of taxation levied on income appears relatively progressive, the bigger picture is less rosy. Many wealthy Canadians, for instance, have income from sources not taxed, such as inheritances and gifts. Canada eliminated its inheritance tax in 1970 and remains virtually alone in the industrialized world by not taxing wealth. When these other sources of income and wealth are considered, the progressivity of the tax system weakens considerably. Figure 7.4 presents the findings of a comprehensive study measuring effective tax rates as a broad-based share of all sources of income. By this measure, Canadians with income over $300,000 paid just 14.4% of that amount in personal income tax. That is only slightly more than what people earning $50,000 paid. (Unfortunately, a more recent study of this kind is not available.)

Moreover, when other taxes are included—such as property, sales and EI and CPP premiums—the total tax burden as a share of income is far less progressive. To illustrate this, consider the case of three families of four living in British Columbia. All three families have two income earners. One family earns $30,000, the second $55,000, and the third $90,000. The two- income family with $30,000 has both spouses earning $15,000; the family with $55,000 is assumed to have one spouse earning $35,000

Figure 7.4
Effective Personal Income Tax Rates as % of Broad-based Income, 1988

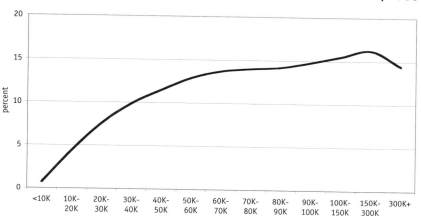

Source: F. Vermaeten, W.I. Gillespie, and A. Vermaeten, "Tax Incidence in Canada," Canadian Tax Journal (vol. 42, no.2), 1994.

and the other $20,000; and the family with $90,000 is assumed to have one spouse earning $50,000 and the other $40,000.

To calculate the taxes paid by each family, we assume they pay CPP and EI premiums, as well as federal and provincial income taxes, based on basic personal credits, applicable provincial credits, and typical major deductions at each income level. Each family owns a home and pays taxes assessed on the basis of the Canada Mortgage and Housing

Table 7.10
Taxes Paid by Three Families, British Columbia, 1998

	$30,000 income	$55,000 income	$90,000 income
Federal income tax	2,347	6,191	13,176
Prov'l income tax	1,162	3,065	6,522
Child Benefits	(766)	0	0
Net property tax	1,168	1,168	1,168
Prov'l sales tax	480	724	969
Fuel tax	165	165	165
Net GST	266	1,086	1,454
Health premiums	691	864	864
CPP	736	1,536	2,138
EI	885	1,623	2,106
Total above taxes	**7,134**	**16,422**	**28,562**

SOURCE: Calculations based upon Revenue Canada, Individual Income Tax Statistics, 1996, and Government of British Columbia, Budget Reports 1999.

Corporation's review of property taxes buyers are likely to pay in major cities in each province. Sales and fuel tax estimates (including sales tax on meals, liquor and accommodation) are calculated based on expenditure patterns from Statistics Canada 1996 Survey of Family Expenditures. GST estimates are reduced by the GST credit, where applicable. The total tax bill for each family is shown in Table 7.10.

Table 7.11 extends the analysis by presenting the taxes paid by the three families as a share of their total income. As illustrated, the personal income tax system is quite progressive: the effective rates at which tax is applied rises from about 9% for the family earning $30,000 to 22% for the family with $90,000 in income. On the other hand, sales and fuel taxes as a share of total income remain relatively constant among all three families, while property taxes and social insurance premiums are clearly regressive.

Table 7.11
Taxes as Share of Family Income, British Columbia, 1998

	$30,000	$55,000	$90,000
Net income taxes	9.1	16.8	21.9
Sales and fuel taxes	3.0	4.0	2.9
Property taxes	3.9	2.1	1.3
Social Security and Health Premiums	7.7	7.3	5.7
Total above taxes	23.8	29.9	31.7

SOURCE: As in Table 7.10.

Consequently, when all taxes and premiums are added up, the overall progressivity of the personal income tax system is significantly reduced.

This situation may in fact get worse if certain political forces have their way. The idea that different income tax brackets need to be eliminated is gaining some support in Canada. The conservative government of Alberta has announced its intention to phase in a flat tax system in the year 2002. Flat taxes are a central plank in the political platform of the federal Reform/Alliance Party. In short, if the drive for flat income taxes gathers momentum, Canada's overall tax system is in danger of becoming even more regressive than it is currently.

WHO BEARS THE BURDEN?

Many of the arguments advanced by those in favour of flat taxes centre on the perceived need to reduce marginal tax rates for upper income earners. The assumption is that the very rich are "overtaxed," a situation that threatens to either discourage them from investing and working harder or drive them to re-locate to lower tax jurisdictions (and hence threaten our future economic prosperity). Economist John Kenneth Galbraith once noted that, when coupled with calls for cuts in income support programs for the unemployed and poor to coerce them back into the labour market, this line of reasoning exposes a certain paradox in neo-conservative economics: that the rich are not working because they have too little income, while the poor are not working because they have too much.

But, as we have seen above, when all taxes and all sources of income are considered, it is difficult to make the case that wealthy Canadians are shouldering an unfair burden. Even in the personal income tax system, the highest income earners receive a number of generous breaks. As Table 7.12 shows, the top 1% of taxpayers accounted for more than 55% of all capital gains income and 40% of dividend income. This is significant since capital gains is taxed at a lower rate than income from employment. Dividend income paid to shareholders also receives preferential treatment through a system of credits. Taxpayers are also allowed to deduct "carrying charges"—interest payments, brokerage fees, and other expenses—related to investments.

As indicated in Table 7.12, these tax subsidies are highly concentrated among the top 1% of high-income earners. In 1996, more than 60% of the total value of capital gains exemptions were claimed by this élite

Table 7.12
Income Sources and Tax Subsidies for High Income Taxpayers, 1996

	$150,000-250,000	over $250,000	Total
% of all taxpayers	0.6	0.4	1.0
% of all employment income	2.2	3.8	6.0
% of all taxable capital gains income	14.2	41.6	55.8
% of all dividend income	10.3	29.8	40.1
% of dividend tax credit amount	9.7	28.0	37.7
% of capital gains exemption amount	24.9	38.5	63.4
% of carrying charges deduction amount	10.3	22.7	33.0

SOURCE: Revenue Canada, Individual Income Tax Statistics, 1996 Taxation Year.

group. They also claimed a third of the total value of deductions for carrying charges and nearly 40% of the value of the dividend tax credit.

The very wealthy are also more likely to take advantage of tax deductions for Registered Retirement Savings Plan (RRSP) contributions. Canadians earning less than $30,000 a year, while making up nearly 70% of all tax filers, made just 18% of all RRSP contributions in 1996. Only about 14% of people in this group even made a contribution, which averaged a little over $2,000.

By contrast, just the top 1.6% of tax filers—those earning over $100,000—accounted for more than 12% of all RRSP contributions. More than 70% of those in this income class made a contribution in 1996 and on average put aside more than $12,000, or six times the amount of those with incomes under $30,000. In total, the top 12% of tax filers—individuals earning over $50,000—made more than half of the RRSP contributions in 1996.

These favourable tax credits and the absence of any tax on wealth make it difficult to swallow the claim that Canada's rich are overtaxed. On the contrary, in an extensive survey assessing tax rates on high-income earners in Canada and the United States, one researcher concluded that: "The absence of estate and gift taxes, the evidence that many rich Canadian families are largely able to avoid PIT [personal income tax], and the lengthening of the extreme upper tail of the Canadian income distribution...all powerfully suggest that an extremely favourable tax environment has been created in Canada for the genuinely wealthy." [James B. Davies, "Tax Incidence: Annual and Lifetime Perspectives in the United States and Canada." In J.B. Shoven and J. Whalley (eds.) *Canada-U.S. Tax Comparisons*. Chicago: University of Chicago Press, 1992, p. 168].

Table 7.13
RRSP Contributions by Income Class, 1996

Income Class	Under $30,000	$30,000-50,000	$50,000-100,000	Over $100,000
Share of Tax Filers	68.3	19.5	10.6	1.6
% claiming RRSP deduction	13.8	52.7	69.6	71.1
Average RRSP contribution	$2,178	$3,526	$5,889	$12,250
Share of total contributions	18.0	29.3	37.9	12.3

SOURCE: Calculations based on Revenue Canada, Individual Income Tax Statistics, 1996 Taxation Year.

Table 7.14
Average Family Income Tax Rates by Quintiles, 1979-1997

	Lowest	Second	Third	Fourth	Highest	Ratio of top quintile to bottom
1979	1.9	9.1	13.6	16.0	19.7	10.4
1981	2.5	9.7	13.8	16.4	19.7	7.9
1983	2.0	8.8	13.9	16.8	20.9	10.5
1985	2.3	9.4	14.3	17.4	21.4	9.3
1987	3.2	11.7	16.5	19.7	23.5	7.3
1989	3.6	12.2	17.0	20.0	24.8	6.9
1991	3.3	11.6	17.3	20.6	25.6	7.8
1993	2.6	10.6	16.6	20.0	25.1	9.7
1995	2.7	11.0	16.7	20.7	26.1	9.7
1997	3.1	11.4	17.5	21.1	26.0	8.4
% change 79-97	63.1	25.3	28.7	31.9	32.0	-19.2

SOURCE: Statistics Canada, Income After Tax, Distributions by Size in Canada, various years, cat. No. 13-210-XPB.

On the other hand, while the income of low- and middle-income families has fallen in recent years, they are also paying a larger share of tax. Table 7.14 presents the effective income tax rate by income quintile from 1979 to 1997. Between 1979 and 1981, average income tax rates increased for all quintiles except the highest. Then, after falling somewhat for modest and lower income groups as a consequence of reduced income shares during the recession of the early 1980s, average rates climbed for all groups during the subsequent economic recovery until 1989. During this period, the largest proportionate increase was for the lowest quintile: a jump of 89%, from 1.9% to 3.6%. As a result, the overall progressivity of Canada's income tax system, when measured as the ratio of the effective rate payable by the top quintile to that payable by the bottom quintile, declined over the same period.

Interestingly, between 1989 and 1997 the effective rate of taxation for the bottom two quintiles fell. Unfortunately for these families, this was almost entirely due to the dramatic deterioration in their income. As shown in Table 7.15 , for the bottom quintile, real average market income fell by 20%; the 2nd quintile experienced a decline of more than 16%. In fact, what is surprising is that the fall in income before transfers for the two lowest quintiles was greater than the decline in effective tax rates. Similarly, for the middle and two upper quintiles, effective tax rates actually rose while market income fell. In the 1990s, then, income taxes for most Canadians were rising proportionately faster than incomes.

Table 7.15
Percentage Change in Average Real Market Income
and Effective Tax Rates by Quintile, 1989-97

	Real Income	Effective Tax Rate	Difference
Lowest	-19.8	-13.9	5.9 pts
Second	-16.2	-6.6	9.6 pts
Third	-7.4	0.6	10.4 pts
Fourth	-4	5.5	9.5 pts
Highest	-2.7	4.8	7.5 pts

SOURCE: Calculations based on Statistics Canada, Income after tax, distributions by size in Canada, 1997, cat. no. 13-210-XPB.

What primarily explains the rise in personal income taxes over the 1990s, despite the fall in incomes, is the fact that tax brackets and credits were not fully adjusted for inflation over this period. Between 1972 and 1985, Canada's personal income tax system was fully indexed to the rate of inflation. That is, as the cost of living rose, so too did the value of personal exemptions and tax brackets. In 1986, however, the Mulroney government in-dexed the tax system only to the rate of inflation exceeding 3%. That meant that, if inflation was 4%, personal exemptions, credits and tax brack-ets would be adjusted by just 1%. The effect of this partial de-indexation has been enormous, as adjustments in exemptions and brackets have failed to match the full rate of inflation. Between 1986 and 1998, the tax system was adjusted by only 7.6%. If it had been fully indexed, it would have been adjusted 32.9% [Ken Battle, *No Taxation Without Indexation*, Ottawa: Caledon Institute for Social Policy, 1998].

One immediate effect of the partial de-indexation of the tax system is that many low and modest income Canadians are now paying more tax despite little or no growth in their incomes. Because income tax brack-ets do not rise with the rate of inflation, taxpayers may find themselves falling into higher tax brackets even if their real income remains flat. This is the phenomenon known as "bracket creep."

Table 7.16 provides a simplified example of how bracket creep works. It is assumed that a tax filer had an income of $25,000 in 1988 and the same inflation-adjusted income in 1998. For the sake of keeping the example simple, only the basic personal credit is included in our calcula-tions.

In 1988, our tax filer was able to claim a basic personal amount of $6,000, which translated into a personal credit of $1,020 applied against

---

Table 7.16
Federal Income Tax Payable, 1988 and 1998
(in constant $1988)

	1988	1998
Income	25,000	25,000
Basic Personal Amount	6,000	4,856
Basic Personal Credit	1,020	826
Tax Brackets and Marginal	1 - 27,500 (17%)	1-22,256 (17%)
Tax Rates	27,501 - 55,000 (26%)	22,257 - 44,514 (26%)
	55,001 + (29%)	44,515 + (29%)
Marginal Federal Tax Rate	17%	26%
Federal Income tax	3,230	3,671
Effective tax rate	12.9	14.7
Income after tax	21,770	21,329

SOURCE: Ken Battle, No Taxation Without Indexation (Ottawa: Caledon Institute for Social Policy, 1998).

---

gross federal income tax payable. With $25,000 in income, our tax filer fell into the 17% tax bracket and was charged $4,250 minus the credit of $1,020, for a total tax bill of $3,230. The effective rate of tax paid—i.e., the net tax bill as a percentage of taxable income—was 12.9%.

Jumping ahead 10 years, we can see how the effects of inflation have increased the total tax payable, despite the fact that our tax filer had no real increase in income. Measured in constant dollars, the real value of basic personal exemption fell about 19% to $4,856. The non-refundable personal credit is now worth just $826. As well, inflation has eroded the threshold level at which the three tax brackets take effect. While in 1988 the second tax bracket of 26% applied only to income above $27,500, by 1998 it affected income above $22,256 measured in constant terms. Consequently, our tax filer now pays 17% of $22,256 *and* 26% of the remaining income ($2,744) for a pre-credit tax bill of about $4,497. Subtracting the $826 non-refundable credit produces a final tax bill of 3,671, about 14% higher than in 1988. Because of bracket creep and the erosion in the basic personal credit, the effective tax rate is now 14.7%.

One of the more objectionable aspects of the partial de-indexation of the income tax system is that it has pushed many low-income Canadians onto the tax roll by lowering the threshold at which federal tax is payable. Figure 7.5 tracks the federal income tax threshold, in constant dollars, from 1980 to 2003 for single tax filers. In 1980, individuals earning less than $10,505 were not subject to any tax. By 1997, however, the threshold had fallen to just $6,924.

Figure 7.5
Federal Income Tax Threshold, 1980-2003 ($1998)

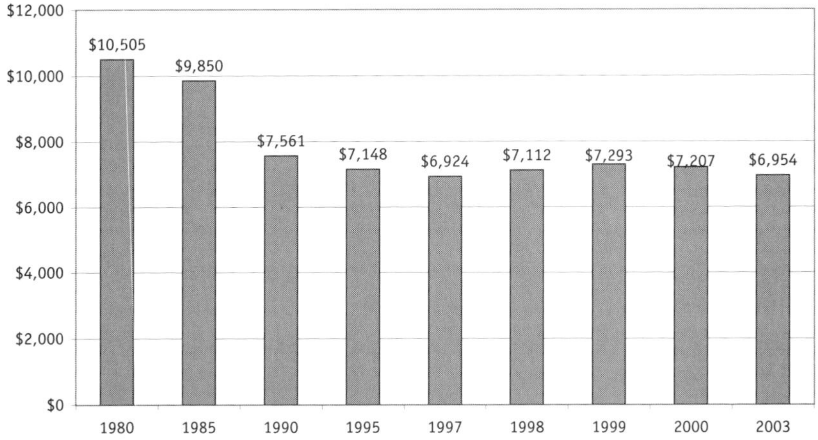

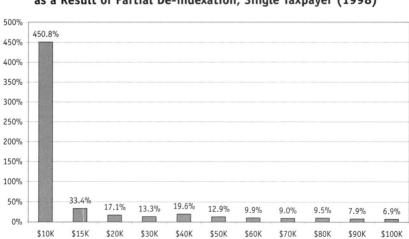

Source: Ken Battle, No Taxation without Indexation, Caleton Institute for Social Policy, 1998

When measured in constant 1998 dollars, the threshold rose to an estimated $7,112 in 1998 and $7,293 in 1999 due to modest tax relief measures. The 1998 federal budget increased the basic personal amount and spousal and equivalent-to-married amounts by $500 for low-income tax

Figure 7.6
Percentage Increase in Income Taxes by Income Class
as a Result of Partial De-indexation, Single Taxpayer (1998)

Source: as in figure 7.5

filers. The 3% general surtax was also eliminated for those earning under $50,000 and reduced for those earning up to $65,000. The 1999 budget followed on these changes by increasing the basic personal amount another $175—to $7,131— and extending it to all taxpayers. Similarly, the 3% surtax was eliminated for all taxpayers. Nevertheless, even with these changes, the threshold at which single Canadians start to pay federal tax remains at a very low level of income. For the year 2000, the threshold will be an estimated $6,448 below the average minimum wage and $10,614 below Statistics Canada's low income cut-off line for a metropolitan centre. [Ken Battle, *Credit Corrosion: Bracket Creep's Evil Twin* (Ottawa: Caldeon Institute of Social Policy, December 1999).]

While taxpayers at all income levels are now paying more tax because of partial de-indexation, lower-income Canadians have been hit the hardest. Figure 7.6 illustrates the increase in federal and provincial taxes for single people in different income groups. Individuals earning $10,000 a year have seen an astounding 450% increase in their tax bill as a result of the declining value of credits and brackets. By contrast, those earning $100,000 a year have experienced just a 7% increase in taxes as a result of partial de-indexation.

A similar trend can be found when looking at the taxes paid by families with children. As Figure 7.7 reveals, the increase in income taxes

Figure 7.7
Percentage Increase in Income Taxes by Income Class as a Result of Partial De-indexation, Two Earner Couple with Two Children, 1998

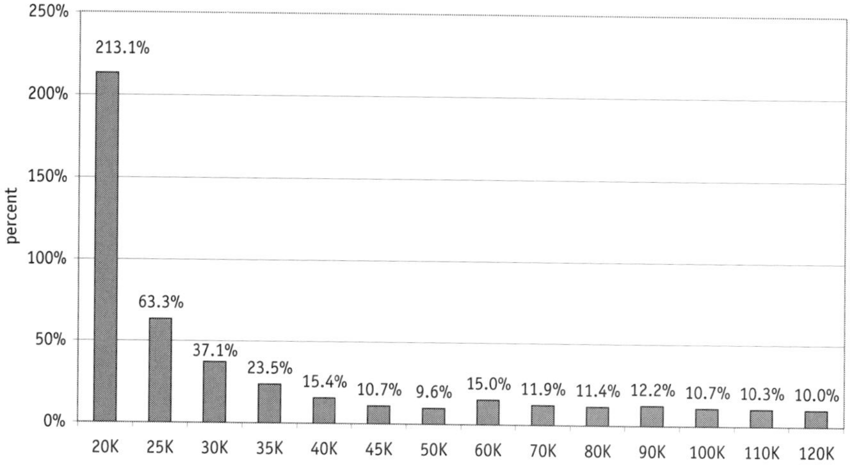

Source: as in figure 7.5

resulting from partial de-indexation has disproportionately hit low- and modest-income families with children the hardest. Families earning just $20,000 a year have seen their tax bills soar over 213%. For the wealthiest families, the increase has been just 7.5%.

The data presented in figures 7.6 and 7.7 do not reflect actions taken in the 1999 Federal budget. The $500 increase in the basic personal amount for low-income earners, introduced in 1998, was raised by $175 and extended to all taxpayers. As shown in Table 7.17, for someone earning $20,000, the combined effect of extending the $500 basic supplement and raising it by $175 is a tax saving of $101. For someone earning $100,000, the total saving arising from these two measures is $248.

The biggest gain for upper-income earners, however, came with the elimination of the 3% federal surtax. The 1998 budget eliminated the surtax for those earning under $50,000 and the 1999 budget extended this to all taxpayers. For those with an income of $60,000, the tax saving will amount to $179, compared to $658 for those earning $100,000.

Table 7.17
1999 Budget Tax Reduction Measures, Single Taxpayers

Total Income	Extending the $500 supplement	$175 basic amount increase	Surtax Elimination	Total 1999 tax reductions
13,500	0	0	0	0
20,000	41	60	0	101
30,000	109	60	0	169
40,000	170	60	0	230
50,000	170	60	0	230
60,000	185	65	179	429
75,000	184	64	440	688
100,000	184	64	658	906

SOURCE: Department of Finance, Budget Plan 1999.

Overall, the income tax cuts announced deliver more in dollar terms to higher-income groups, although they are mildly progressive in percentage terms. As well, lower-income families with children will benefit through modest increases to the Child Tax Benefit.

CORPORATE TAXATION

Business lobbyists routinely complain that corporate taxes in Canada are uncompetitive and are to blame for their shrinking profit margins. Yet, as

Table 7.18
Statutory Corporate Income Tax Rates for G-7 Countries (%)

	1983	1990	1997
Canada[a]	44.9 - 52.9	35.3 - 45.8	38.1 - 46.1
United States[a]	48.7 - 51.4	34.0 - 41.9	35.0 - 42.5
France	50	37	41.6
Germany	56	50	57.4
Italy	38.8	46.4	53.2
Japan	53	52	51.6
United Kingdom	52	35	31
Cdn. manufacturing rate*	38.8 - 46.8	32.8 - 43.3	24.6 - 39.1

[a] Rates vary by province or state.
SOURCE: Report of the Technical Committee on Business Taxation (Ottawa: Department of Finance), 1998.

Table 7.19
Corporate Taxes as a Share of GDP, 1996 (%)

	Corporate income tax	Employers' social security contributions	Total
Australia	4.7	–	4.7
Canada	3.3	3.9	7.2
France	1.7	12.2	13.9
Germany	1.4	7.8	9.2
Japan	4.7	5.3	10.0
United Kingdom	3.8	3.5	7.3
United States	2.7	3.7	6.4
EU Average	3.2	6.9	10.1
OECD Average	3.1	5.5	8.6

SOURCE: OECD Revenue Statistics, 1965-1997 (Paris: OECD, 1998).

illustrated in Tables 7.18 and 7.19, figures show that the corporate tax bill compares quite favourably with other nations, including the United States. Moreover, the effective rate of corporate taxation, when measured as a share of before-tax profits, has actually declined since 1950 and has remained relatively stable since 1970.

The fact that effective corporate income tax rates have remained flat since the 1970s is at first glance somewhat surprising, since corporate taxes make up a much smaller share of total government revenues than in the past. Figure 7.8 plots changes in the tax mix since 1961. In the early 1960s, corporate income taxes made up about 14% of all federal, provincial and local government revenues, compared with 19% for personal in-

Figure 7.8
The Tax Mix, 1961-1998

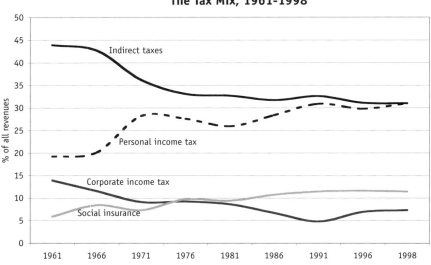

Source: Calculations based on Canadian Economic Observer, Historical Statistical Supplement, cat. no. 11-210-XPB, 1998/99.

come tax. By the 1970s, however, corporate income taxes dipped below 10% while personal income taxes rose to about 28%. In the early 1990s, corporate income taxes as a share of all revenues fell below 5%.

This decline in the corporate share of total revenues was not due, as is commonly assumed, to reduced rates and tax "giveaways," but rather to the steady drop in corporate profits over this period. As a share of GDP, corporate profits averaged more than 10% in the 1960s, but just over 7% in the 1990s.

Despite grumblings from business leaders, when all taxes paid by corporations are factored into the picture, the overall corporate tax load has remained surprisingly constant over the past two decades. As shown in figure 7.9, the major taxes paid by corporations have hovered between 8% and 9% of GDP since 1975. What has changed, however, is the overall mix of taxes paid by corporations. In 1950, corporate income tax made up the biggest share of the tax mix, at just over 5% of GDP. By 1995, corporate income taxes amounted to just above 2% of GDP, less than payroll taxes which climbed from about 0.6% in 1950 to 2.8% in 1995. This is significant, since most research shows that the cost of payroll taxes paid by employers is eventually passed on to workers in the form of lower wages.

Figure 7.9
The Corporate Tax Mix as % of GDP, 1950-1995

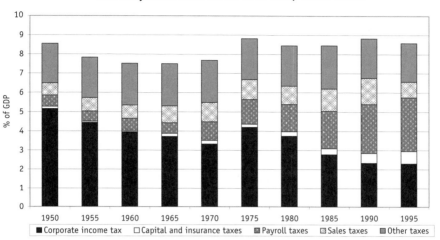

Source: Calculations based on Sargent et. al., "The Evolution of Business Taxes in Canada: Data and Estimates," Working Paper 97-17, Technical Committee on Business Taxation, Ottawa: Department of Finance, 1998.

Figure 7.9 also reveals that corporate capital taxes have increased sharply since 1975. Capital taxes are those assessed on corporations based on their paid-up capital. Business groups have long objected to capital taxes on the grounds that they are "profit-insensitive." That is, they are paid even if a corporation has not made a profit.

Nevertheless, a modest case can be made for applying capital taxes on large corporations. Capital taxes act as a proxy for a benefits tax. Whether a corporation is profitable or not, it nevertheless benefits from publicly-provided goods and services. Businesses also impose real costs on the country, whether they are profitable or not. Noise, congestion, and problems of waste disposal and environmental damage are the inevitable costs of economic activity. Corporate capital taxes may also be important in ensuring fairness in the tax system. Many corporations are able to avoid paying income taxes by adopting creative accounting procedures, such as transfer pricing which permits them to shift taxable profits outside of Canada. Capital taxes are far more difficult to evade.

Finally, in assessing the corporate tax system in Canada, it is worth noting that corporations are able to take advantage of a number of tax subsidies and preferences. Most of these are quite legitimate and are designed to help stimulate investment and economic development. Others are of more questionable value. Based on 1999 tax expenditure estimates, for example, it is projected that the 20% deduction corporations may claim for meals and entertainment purposes will cost the federal treasury about $200 million. Similarly, corporations may deduct the cost of lobbying, granting them in effect a subsidy for what is clearly self-interested activity.

CONCLUSION

The rapid growth of pre-tax and pre-transfer income inequality during the 1990s has to a remarkable extent been offset by the tax and transfer system. The fact that Canada's personal income tax system remains mildly progressive, despite changes introduced in the 1980s, has helped to hold market inequality in check.

However, other elements of the tax system tend to offset this progressivity. Many wealthy individuals enjoy income from sources not taxed, such as inheritances. Very wealthy individuals may also take advantage of generous credits and deductions in the income tax system that can significantly reduce their tax bills. Sales, property and so-called payroll taxes, when expressed as a share of household income, tend to fall much more heavily on low- and middle-income Canadians. In fact, when all taxes and all sources of income are considered, Canada's overall tax system is relatively flat.

As well, the decision to partially de-index the tax system from the rate of inflation has disproportionately hurt low- and middle-income families. As the effects of inflation erode the value of tax credits and push modest-income earners into higher income tax brackets, the progressivity of the personal income tax system will be further eroded.

To redress these inequities, a number of basic reforms would be required. First, indexing the personal income tax system and the value of tax credits to the rate of inflation as was done in the 2000 federal budget will ensure that lower- and modest-income families are not burdened with hidden tax increases.

Within the personal income tax system, a serious rethinking of the preferential tax treatment of retirement savings is also required. RRSP deductions are the single most significant tax expenditure in the personal income tax system, costing the government an estimated $8.5 billion in foregone revenue in 1999 alone. Yet the distribution of this tax subsidy is skewed toward the wealthiest tax filers. The maximum eligible contributions are higher than most working people can afford, so the full benefit of this program is delivered to the wealthiest.

Another striking gap in Canada's tax system is the absence of any tax on wealth. In fact, Canada is virtually alone in the industrialized world in not levying a wealth tax of any kind; only Australia and New Zealand share this dubious distinction. Given the fact that, when all sources of wealth and income are considered, Canada's overall tax system is regressive, a tax on wealth transfers at death would go a long way toward ensuring that Canada's wealthiest individuals pay a fair share. To ensure that such a tax is truly progressive, it would exempt the first $1 million from taxation and transfers between spouses.

Overall, a truly progressive income tax system, while not completely reversing the tide, is nevertheless a modestly important tool for redressing market inequality. Against this backcloth, attempts to further reduce the progressivity of the personal income tax system must be viewed with alarm by those concerned about the growing income divide in Canada.

CHAPTER 8

Conclusion:

The State of Working Canada in the New Millennium

Entering the new millennium, Canadians could hope that the economic disaster of the 1990s—surpassed in severity only by the Great Depression of the 1930s—was behind them. And indeed, after a decade of falling behind, Canadians did see some positive signs that the worst was finally over.

The growth of the Canadian economy has more or less recovered to a "normal" level of 3-4% since 1996. And by the turn of the century, the national jobless rate was lower than at the peak of the expansion of the late 1980s, and indeed had dropped to its lowest level in more than 20 years. In contrast to the 1990s as a whole, when most employment growth came in the form of precarious jobs, almost all of the jobs created in 1999 were full-time. The number of part-time jobs actually fell by about 3%, and self-employment declined marginally, further sign of a strengthening labour market. The number of Canadians who were working rose by 3% over the year, with most of the increase coming in the manufacturing, trade, transportation, educational services, and construction sectors.

As employment expanded, the number of jobless Canadians fell by 191,000 over the year, a drop of almost 15%. That pushed the unemployment rate down from 8.1% in January to 6.8% in December— the lowest rate since April 1976. As shown in Figure 8.1, the fall in the unemployment rate between December 1998 and December 1999 was most pronounced in Newfoundland, Prince Edward Island, and New Brunswick. Despite these gains, however, east of Quebec the unemployment rate still remained in double-digit territory.

While the drop in the official unemployment rate is certainly an encouraging sign, there still remains a high level of hidden unemployment. The labour force grew by just 1.2% over 1999, which was in line with the growth in the working age population. The participation rate of young people is still well below past levels, and significantly lower than

Figure 8.1
Unemployment Rate by Province, December 1998 to December 1999

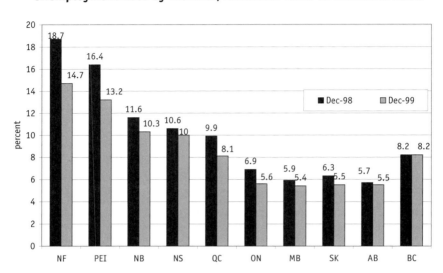

Source: Statistics Canada, Labour Force Survey.

that in the United States. If more young people and other discouraged workers are enticed back into the labour force on the strength of an improving job market, then this may limit further drops in the unemployment rate.

Further, despite some recent decline, the rate of self-employment is, at 17% of all workers, still very high. A significant number of these would likely prefer to take permanent, paid jobs if they were available.

SLOW GROWTH IN WAGES CONTINUES

Overall, the major imbalance and potential problem in the Canadian economy is that strong economic growth has not yet fully spilled over to working people in the form of income and wage gains. Pre-tax corporate profits staged a robust recovery in 1999 over the previous year, reaching a decade high 10.6% of GDP. By way of contrast, the broadest measure of wages showed no increase at all in real terms. Average hourly earnings rose just 1.2% between September 1998 and September 1999, and average weekly earnings grew by just 1.5% over the same period. This was well below the 2.6% increase in the consumer price index. (Total labour income did rise 4.4% in the third quarter of 1999, compared to a year earlier, but this was driven more by an increase in hours worked than by increases in wages).

Unionized workers, as expected, have fared somewhat better. In the third quarter of 1999, wage settlements averaged 2.2%. Across the labour force as a whole, however, workers have been sharing very little of the productivity gains, and real wages for many have been flat or falling. Real income per person has finally shown signs of improvement, on the strength of new hiring in the labour force, but these gains have been extremely modest.

THE VULNERABILITY OF WORKING HOUSEHOLDS

The growth in consumer spending at the end of the 1990s was financed largely by rising consumer debt. Household debt levels have risen from about 89% of GDP in 1989 to nearly 100% in 1999.

Some economists like to argue that rising debt has been more than balanced by the increase in the value of household financial assets, notably shares, but it can hardly be assumed that the stock market boom has made everyone richer. We lack data on the current distribution of wealth in Canada, but evidence suggests that only the top 5% or so of households have significant financial assets outside of pension plans, with much of that wealth being concentrated in the hands of the super-rich. (Fortunately, Statistics Canada is currently conducting a survey on the distribution of wealth in Canada, for the first time since 1984.)

While high levels of personal debt and low savings rates in part reflect stronger consumer confidence as the job market rebounds, it also seems likely that many low- and modest-income households are taking on more debt to stretch their stagnant pay cheques. If this is the case, it leaves many households extremely vulnerable to fluctuations in interest rates. If the Bank of Canada shows less tolerance for inflation than it has in recent months and fears that the relatively robust rate of job growth is leading to inflationary pressures, it will inevitably move to jack up interest rates (as it began to do in February 2000). This, in turn, will increase the costs to households of servicing their high debt loads, putting a further squeeze on already tight family budgets.

Moreover, government cuts to income support programs mean that working people will be much more vulnerable to the next downturn in the economy than to the last, when it comes (as it undoubtedly will some day). In the past, UI and social assistance worked as "automatic stabiliz-ers," putting money into households as the unemployment rate rose. To some degree, income support programs offset the downturn in the busi-ness cycle by partially stabilizing household income. The fact that more and more working Canadians no longer qualify for UI because of tighter rules means the next recession could be far more severe. As unemploy-ment rises, more people will be forced onto the welfare rolls as they quickly exhaust limited financial and other assets, while dual-income working fami-lies will be forced to endure a steep drop in their standard of living with the loss of one wage.

Many will fall through the cracks of provincial income assistance plans. This, coupled with the drop in tax revenues associated with a fall in employment, will put tremendous strain on government budgets. The prov-inces will be particularly hard hit since, in the wake of the Canada Health and Social Transfer, the federal government no longer shares the cost of social assistance. If governments respond to rising deficits, as they did in the 1990s, by further cutting programs and transfers to persons, the down-turn will be far more severe on working people.

WILL THE EXPANSION CONTINUE?

As this book went to press, most Canadian economists expected strong growth to continue through 2000 and for the next few years, tailing behind the seemingly unstoppable momentum of the buoyant U.S. economy. It is worth noting that strong growth in the U.S. over the past three years has, at long last, begun to raise real wages and incomes for even the least well-off U.S. workers and households, without the feared increase in inflation. The idea that high unemployment had to be deliberately maintained to keep inflation low and stable has, to a considerable extent, been under-mined by the recent ability of the U.S. to combine low unemployment and low inflation. Right-wingers, of course, stress the importance of the "flex-ible" U.S. labour market created by relatively weak unions and employ-ment standards, and by weak or non-existent income support programs for unemployed workers. But there is a different story to be told, even in the U.S. (Note also that the combination of low unemployment and low infla-tion has also been achieved in a number of European countries which are far distant from the U.S. labour market model.)

The U.S. expansion has been recently marked by quite strong productivity growth (output per hour worked), partly reflecting high rates of investment in new technology, but also indicating the positive impacts of moving closer to full employment. Many previously marginalized U.S. workers—particularly minority workers—have been hired and trained by employers facing shortages of skilled workers, and this has allowed other workers to move into better jobs and to similarly upgrade skills and work experience. In the dry language of economists, close to full employment has been good news, not just in terms of the well-being of workers themselves, but also in terms of the growth of "human capital." Productivity growth achieved as a result has allowed real wages to grow—somewhat faster than in Canada—while keeping inflation stable.

The lesson for the Bank of Canada from this experience is that it should attempt to keep the Canadian expansion growing, and not "slam on the brakes" prematurely due to an unfounded fear of hitting an imagined "non-accelerating inflation rate of unemployment," or "NAIRU." Canadian wages can and should rise in line with growing productivity, and the Bank of Canada should see this as good news. If working people do not benefit from the economic expansion, then it will not continue for long.

Unfortunately, there are real questions as to whether U.S. growth will continue to be strong, given the speculative frenzy going on in the stock market. The Federal Reserve is hiking interest rates partly to bring Wall Street back to earth, and a U.S. or even global stock market crash could yet take place and derail the expansion. As Jim Stanford has argued in the recent CCPA book *Paper Boom*, the financial economy must be controlled to maintain growth of the real economy. Continued expansion at the global level will similarly require reining in the dangerous excesses of footloose financial capital (see Brian McLean, ed., *Out of Control,* Ottawa: Canadian Centre for Policy Alternatives, 1999).

Moreover—and taking us even further afield from events in Canada—the governments of the world will have to work together to build a new international economic order capable of promoting sustainable and fairly shared growth. International co-ordination of macro-economic policy, deep reform of the World Trade Organization, the IMF, the World Bank and other institutions, debt relief for developing countries, and genuine global action to move decisively towards environmental sustainability are all crucially important if the expansion is to continue. Working Canadians will not prosper if the dangerously unstable and grossly unequal global economic system is not challenged and fundamentally reformed. That is, of course, a topic for many other books.

WHAT ABOUT TAX CUTS?

As noted above, there are strong indications that more job creation is still required to offset the damage done to wages and incomes in the grim decade of the 1990s. An easing of fiscal policy at the federal and provincial level—and in particular an increase in social spending and spending on public services and public investment, as called for in the *2000 Alternative Federal Budget* of the CCPA and CHO!CES—would certainly help secure continuation of the current recovery and provide a much needed boost to the living standards of all Canadians. Government spending increased only modestly in 1999. However, with governments at all levels now running a cumulative surplus likely to reach $25 billion in 1999, there is plenty of room available for reinvestment in programs and services, and the introduction of badly needed new programs such as a national not-for-profit child care program, elder care, and initiatives to deal with climate change and the deterioration of core public infrastructure.

The debate that has been raging, of course, is whether the government should primarily focus on repairing the damage done to Canada's social programs, or devote the bulk of the surplus to reductions in income taxes and corporate taxes. Against the backdrop of what has been happening to the incomes of poorer Canadians and growing income inequality and exclusion, the moral case for social spending is unassailable. That is why the BCNI and other corporate lobby groups like to dress up tax cuts for themselves as policies that will "grow the pie," as BCNI president Tom d'Aquino put it to the House of Commons Finance Committee. But, while broad across-the-board income tax cuts would increase disposable income and provide some stimulative boost to the economy (as long as they are not offset by expenditure reductions), their impact pales in comparison to renewed government spending.

The economic model developed by the economic forecasting firm Informetrica shows that tax cuts provide less bang for the buck in terms of job creation and GDP growth. In the first year, a $1 billion across-the-board cut in corporate income tax would raise GDP by just 0.07% and generate 9,000 jobs. Direct government spending on health and education, by contrast, would boost GDP by 0.14% and create between 24,000 and 25,000 jobs. An across-the- board personal income tax cut would have about half the immediate growth and jobs impact of such a spending increase.

The major downside of across-the-board tax cuts is they will erode the fiscal capacity of the federal government and delay the badly needed restoration of social programs and public services that were cut in the name of deficit reduction. As we noted in Chapter 6, the impacts of these cuts have been felt hardest by low- and middle-income Canadians. For most families, tax cuts announced in the 2000 Federal Budget will be cold comfort if it means continuing problems in the health care system, high tuition fees for post-secondary education, a hollowed-out UI system, and reduced income security programs.

Because social spending, combined with a progressive income tax system, has, until very recently, offset the increasingly unequal distribution of market income, the great majority of working people would be losers under tax cuts proposed by the business lobby. Proposals (several of which were adopted in the 2000 federal budget) such as further reducing the proportion of capital gains liable to income tax, raising the RRSP contribution limit, eliminating the high income surtax, and lowering the top marginal rate would deliver the greatest proportionate benefits to the top 10% of Canadians with the highest incomes. To follow this path at a time when Canada's social infrastructure continues to deteriorate and when poverty and inequality remain serious social problems is surely morally indefensible.

Moreover, the claims that such an unfair package will boost economic growth are vastly overblown. The evidence shows that the social choice of paying relatively high taxes in order to pay for good social programs and public services does not come at the price of lower incomes. For the OECD countries as a whole, as we noted in Chapter 7, there was no statistically significant correlation between the tax "burden" and GDP per-person growth rates or growth of productivity in the 1990s. In fact, a number of relatively high tax/high social standard jurisdictions—such as Denmark, Norway, and the Netherlands—have grown just as fast as the low-tax but very unequal United States in the 1990s, and today enjoy similarly low unemployment rates.

The lack of a clear linkage between the tax "burden" and economic growth and efficiency is due to two major reasons. First, a lot of public investment financed by taxes—such as spending on infrastructure, education, training, research programs, health care, and so on—contributes directly and indirectly to higher productivity in the private sector.

For business itself, the tax "burden" finances significant benefits.

Second, there is little strong evidence that progressive tax systems and relatively high taxes negatively impact on business investment. Taxes are a small part of the cost of doing business, and Canadian business tax rates (particularly in manufacturing) are not out of line with those in the U.S. Moreover, businesses invest because of growing markets for what they produce, not because of a small difference in costs.

Of course, there can and should be a lot of discussion over what kind of spending and tax policies should be pursued, now that the federal government has begun to run large budget surpluses. The Alternative Federal Budget has put forward one set of proposals, which includes some important tax changes such as reindexing the tax system fully to inflation, and giving a big boost to child tax benefits. The key point is that, if the expansion continues, the "fiscal dividend" will allow us to make major re-investments in programs and services, and to overhaul the tax system as well.

THE LOST DECADES

Our analysis has shown that, for the vast majority of Canadian households, the 1990s were little short of a disaster. It is no coincidence that the erosion in wages and incomes, deteriorating job quality, eroding social programs and public services, and greater economic insecurity that characterized the 1990s and indeed the past 20 odd years were accompanied by a profound shift in the thrust of public policy. Since the 1970s, economic policy has generally moved toward creating a more deregulated, laissez-faire, and "business-friendly" environment. Over this period, government influence over the economy have been steadily weakened, taxes on corporations and high-income individuals have been reduced, monetary policy has been re-focused narrowly on fighting inflation at the expense of job creation, social programs have been cut back, unions have been under attack, and free trade agreements giving more power to corporations and financial markets have been negotiated.

All of this was done with the repeated promise that the pay-off from the short-term pain of this restructuring would be long-term gain— in the form of rising standards of living and income for all Canadians. Was there an overall improvement in the well-being of Canadians to justify this pain? Our review has shown that this has not been the case. And that surely begs the question: is it not time to fundamentally shift direction?